ACCENTS ON SHAKESPEARE

General editor: TERENCE HAWKES

Shakespeare in Psychoanalysis

The link between psychoanalysis as a mode of interpretation and Shakespeare's works is well known. But rather than merely putting Shakespeare on the couch, Philip Armstrong focuses on the complex, fascinating and fruitful mutual relationship between Shakespeare's texts and psychoanalytic theory. He shows how the theories of Freud, Rank, Jones, Lacan, Erikson and others are themselves in large part the product of reading Shakespeare; and that, in turn, their theories shape our interactions with literary texts in ways we may not recognise.

Armstrong provides an introductory cultural history of the relationship between psychoanalytic concepts and Shakespearean texts. This is played out in a variety of expected and unexpected contexts, including:

- the early modern stage
- *Hamlet, The Tempest,* and *Romeo and Juliet*
- Freud's analytic session
- the Parisian intellectual scene
- the contact zone of pre-apartheid South Africa
- the virtual spaces of TV, PC, and cinema.

Philip Armstrong teaches at the University of Canterbury in Christchurch, New Zealand. He is the author of *Shakespeare's Visual Regime: Tragedy, Psychoanalysis and the Gaze,* and has also published articles on New Zealand literature.

ACCENTS ON SHAKESPEARE
General editor: TERENCE HAWKES

It is more than twenty years since the New Accents series helped to establish 'theory' as a fundamental and continuing feature of the study of literature at the undergraduate level. Since then, the need for short, powerful 'cutting edge' accounts of and comments on new developments has increased sharply. In the case of Shakespeare, books with this sort of focus have not been readily available. **Accents on Shakespeare** aims to supply them.

Accents on Shakespeare volumes will either 'apply' theory, or broaden and adapt it in order to connect with concrete teaching concerns. In the process, they will also reflect and engage with the major developments in Shakespeare studies of the last ten years.

The series will lead as well as follow. In pursuit of this goal it will be a two-tiered series. In addition to affordable, 'adoptable' titles aimed at modular undergraduate courses, it will include a number of research-based books. Spirited and committed, these second-tier volumes advocate radical change rather than stolidly reinforcing the status quo.

IN THE SAME SERIES

Shakespeare and Appropriation
Edited by Christy Desmet and Robert Sawyer

Shakespeare without Women
Dympna Callaghan

Philosophical Shakespeares
Edited by John J. Joughin

Shakespeare and Modernity: Early Modern to Millennium
Edited by Hugh Grady

Marxist Shakespeares
Edited by Jean E. Howard and Scott Cutler Shershow

Shakespeare in Psychoanalysis
Philip Armstrong

Shakespeare and Modern Theatre: The Performance of Modernity
Edited by Michael Bristol, Kathleen McLuskie and Christopher Holmes

Shakespeare and Feminist Performance: Ideology on Stage
Sarah Werner

Shakespeare in Psychoanalysis

PHILIP ARMSTRONG

London and New York

First published 2001
by Routledge
11 New Fetter Lane,
London EC4P 4EE

Simultaneously published in
the USA and Canada
by Routledge
29 West 35th Street,
New York, NY 10001

Routledge is an imprint of the
Taylor & Francis Group

© 2001 Philip Armstrong

Typeset in Baskerville by Keystroke,
Jacaranda Lodge, Wolverhampton
Printed and bound in Great Britain
by TJ International, Padstow,
Cornwall

British Library Cataloguing in Publication Data

A catalogue record for this book is
available from the British Library

Library of Congress Cataloging in Publication Data

Armstrong, Philip, 1967–
Shakespeare in psychoanalysis /
Philip Armstrong.
p. cm. — (Accents on Shakespeare)
Includes bibliographical references
and index.
1. Shakespeare, William, 1564–1616
—Knowledge—Psychology.
2. Psychoanalysis and literature—
England—History—16th century.
3. Psychoanalysis and literature
—England—History—17th century.
4. Drama—Psychological aspects.
5. Psychology in literature. I. Title.
II. Series.

PR3065 .A76 2001
822.3'3–dc21   00–065310

ISBN 0–415–20722–3 (pbk)
ISBN 0–415–20721–5 (hbk)

'Were *you* born Hamlet? *Or did you not rather create the type in yourself?*'
(Deleuze and Guattari 1977: 112–13)

Contents

General editor's preface

In our time, the field of literary studies has rarely been a settled, tranquil place. Indeed, for over two decades, the clash of opposed theories, prejudices and points of view has made it more of a battlefield. Echoing across its most beleaguered terrain, the student's weary complaint 'Why can't I just pick up Shakespeare's plays and read them?' seems to demand a sympathetic response.

Nevertheless, we know that modern spectacles will always impose their own particular characteristics on the vision of those who unthinkingly don them. This must mean, at the very least, that an apparently simple confrontation with, or pious contemplation of, the text of a 400-year-old play can scarcely supply the grounding for an adequate response to its complex demands. For this reason, a transfer of emphasis from 'text' towards 'context' has increasingly been the concern of critics and scholars since the Second World War: a tendency that has perhaps reached its climax in more recent movements such as new historicism or cultural materialism.

A consideration of the conditions – social, political or economic – within which the play came to exist, from which it derives, and to which it speaks will certainly make legitimate demands on the attention of any well-prepared student nowadays. Of course, the serious pursuit of those interests will also inevitably start to undermine ancient and inherited prejudices, such as the supposed distinction between 'foreground' and 'background' in literary studies. And even the slightest awareness of the pressures of gender or of race, or the most cursory glance at the role played by that strange creature 'Shakespeare' in our cultural politics, will reinforce a similar turn towards questions that sometimes appear scandalously 'non-literary'. It seems clear that very different and unsettling notions of the ways in which literature might be addressed can hardly be avoided. The worrying truth is that nobody can just pick up Shakespeare's plays and read them. Perhaps – even more worrying – they never could.

The aim of *Accents on Shakespeare* is to encourage students and teachers to explore the implications of this situation by means of an engagement with the major developments in Shakespeare studies over recent years. It will offer a continuing and challenging reflection on those ideas through a series of multi- and single-author books which will also supply the basis for adapting or augmenting them in the light of changing concerns.

Accents on Shakespeare also intends to lead as well as follow. In pursuit of this goal, the series will operate on more than one level. In addition to titles aimed at modular undergraduate courses, it will include a number of books embodying polemical, strongly argued cases aimed at expanding the horizons of a specific aspect of the subject and at challenging the preconceptions on which it is based. These volumes will not be learned 'monographs' in any traditional sense. They will, it is hoped, offer a platform for the work of the liveliest younger scholars and teachers at their most outspoken and provocative. Committed and contentious, they will be reporting from the forefront of current critical activity and will have something new to say. The fact that each book in the series promises a Shakespeare inflected in terms of a specific urgency should ensure that, in the present as in the recent past, the accent will be on change.

Terence Hawkes

Acknowledgements

A few of my debts of gratitude for support in the writing of this book are institutional, some are academic, and most are personal.

First, I must yet again thank Terence Hawkes for his support: this volume is another of the many critical works published over the last two decades that could not have come into existence without Terry's interest, encouragement and intellectual drive. I am also grateful to the Department of English at the University of Canterbury, for a research grant to help me complete this volume on time. In particular, I owe thanks to Sarah Mayo for her attentive reading of a late draft; any errors that remain I must have contributed after she finished. I am indebted to Michael Neill for his advice on aspects of selected extracts, and for giving me the opportunity to deliver a version of Chapter 3 as a paper at the Australian and New Zealand Shakespeare Association Conference in July 2000. I also thank Janet Adelman for the reservations she voiced about certain aspects of that paper, as well as about the project as a whole; my response to her concerns has made this a better book, but I apologise to her in advance that not all will have been answered to her satisfaction. I also appreciate the interest shown in my work by Gail Paster.

A number of friendships have been crucial to me during the writing of this book: I am immensely grateful to Sarah Beaven, Claudia Marquis, John Newton and Denis Walker, each of whom has provided a perfect balance of support and challenge at both the personal and the intellectual level; to Sarah and John also for lending me what seemed like hundreds of volumes of their Penguin Freuds; to Howard McNaughton, who also lent me an endless stream of texts; to Diana Harris, for her clarifying thoughts on film, delivered through a cloud of smoke; to John O'Connor, for a relationship durably founded on a triviality that comes right from the heart; to Fiona Carswell, whose return to Aotearoa provided me with some much-needed hilarity; and to Faith Potts, for her company, help and humour over the years I have been working on the project.

As always, I owe an immeasurable debt to my family – my parents Ian and Doff, my sister Susan and my brother David – for their unfailing interest in and support for my work. I also want to acknowledge with gratitude the sometimes overwhelming input of my non-human companions – especially that of G.T., who died while I was completing the final revisions.

Finally, I owe my greatest debt of gratitude to Lola and to Annie Potts, to whom this book is dedicated. Near the start of *Anti-Oedipus*, Deleuze and Guattari suggest that taking a stroll is more therapeutic than hours spent lying on the psychoanalyst's couch: 'A breath of fresh air, a relationship with the outside world' (1977: 2). Like all dogs, Lola knows this very well, and reminded me of it whenever I had been immersed for too long in reading or writing. As for my other best friend: for a decade now Annie has brought a fresh breath of irreverence, and a relationship to the world not enclosed by academic analysis. I owe and dedicate to her whatever evidence there may be in this volume of a resistance to the merely conventional, or of an attentiveness to political concerns outside of the literary text and the analytic session.

A note on references

All references to Shakespeare's plays are to the Arden editions unless otherwise stated.

All references to the works of Sigmund Freud, unless otherwise stated, are to *The Penguin Freud Library*: parentheses after references and quotations indicate the relevant volume and the appropriate pages: for example (*PFL* 14: 303) refers to page 303 of *The Penguin Freud Library 14: Art and Literature.*

All other references follow the Harvard author–date system, corresponding to entries in the final bibliography.

Introducing . . .

. . . Shakespeare and Freud. Is it just me, or do these two look pretty much alike these days? I'm thinking, of course, of the current state of both Shakespeare criticism and psychoanalytic theory, each of which owes more to the other than is generally admitted; the working out of these debts will provide one major focus of this volume. But I also have in mind the most recent popular embodiments of Shakespeare's status as a hero of global culture, and in particular of *Shakespeare in Love*, the film that in 1998 celebrated the enduring cultural authority of both terms in my title, as well as attempting the difficult feat of crossover between arthouse movie and blockbuster flick, between critical praise and acclaim by the Academy (which it certainly achieved, winning a few Oscars, including Best Picture, in the final awards of the millennium).

Joseph Fiennes, who starred as the title character, didn't win Best Actor, but he did bring off a striking simultaneous impersonation of Shakespeare and Freud – both of course younger than we are accustomed to seeing them, with a full head of hair and a beard still youthfully scanty, a kind of goatee, a look suturing together the turn of three centuries: seventeenth, twentieth and twenty-first. For my money, then, the film might just as well have been entitled *Freud in Love*, or indeed, *Shakespeare in Psychoanalysis*.

The film's first shot of the eponymous lover shows us a moody young playwright, practising writing his name; hounded by Henslowe, the manager-owner of the Rose Theatre, for the play that he needs to keep his creditors at bay, Will Shakespeare strides through London streets full of antitheatrical Puritans and emptying chamber pots. 'Where are you going?' asks Henslowe breathlessly; 'My weekly confession' is the reply. No Catholic, of course, Will uses the term in another sense, as becomes apparent when we read the nameplates outside the door he enters: 'Dr Moth: Seer, Apothecary, Alchemist, Astrologer'. By the time we glimpse two more signs, 'Interpreter of Dreams' and 'Priest of Psyche', and see Will lounging on a couch while a bearded and earnest Antony Sher takes notes, we recognise the allusion to Shakespeare's therapeutic analysis by an early modern Freud. Lest we miss it, the psychoanalytic humour remains pretty blatant throughout this scene:

> *Will*: It's as if my quill is broken . . . as if the organ of my imagination is dried up . . . as if the proud tower of my genius has collapsed . . . Nothing comes . . . it's like trying to pick a lock with a wet herring.
> *Dr Moth*: Tell me, are you lately humbled in the act of love? How long has it been?
> *Will*: A goodly length in times past, but lately –

It is Freud's legacy that enables Dr Moth, along with *Shakespeare in Love*'s audience, to diagnose an association between sexual libido and artistic creation. As Freud puts it, 'As soon as writing, which entails making a liquid flow out of a tube on to a piece of white paper, assumes the significance of copulation', it becomes impossible, because it 'represent[s] the performance of a forbidden sexual act' (*PFL* 10: 240). Here, the association between writing and sex results in a creative block due to underlying sexual repression; elsewhere, in 'Civilisation and Its Discontents', for example, Freud develops more fully the notion of artistic endeavour deriving its energy from the redirection or 'sublimation' of the libido (*PFL* 12: 255–340).

Perhaps it needs no Freud to come from the grave (or rather from the future) to tell Dr Moth this, but *Shakespeare in Love* goes on to proffer an even more psychoanalytic narrative: the fundamental cause of Will's loss of 'will' (the playwright's nickname entails, as critics never tire of pointing out, a series of Elizabethan phallic puns) actually anticipates the inaugural psychoanalytic reading of Shakespeare as both a son and a father with a double dose of Oedipal guilt requiring therapeutic working out.

Dr Moth: You have a wife and children?
Will: Ay . . . I was a lad of eighteen, Anne Hathaway was a woman half as old again . . .
Dr Moth: And . . . your marriage bed?
Will: Four years and a hundred miles away in Stratford. A cold bed too since the twins were born. Banishment was a blessing.
Dr Moth: So now you are free to love.
Will: Yet cannot love, nor write it.

'A lad of eighteen' marries 'a woman half as old again', only to find his marriage bed cold after the birth of their twins: half a mother and half a wife, no longer a wife since a mother two times over, Anne Hathaway (never seen in the film) provides the figure whose simultaneous union with and distance from her husband/ son embodies a version of that Oedipal drama diagnosed in Shakespeare, and identified as the source and theme of all his work, by Sigmund Freud, Otto Rank and Ernest Jones. The plays and poems, for these analysts, constitute not just opportunities for psychoanalytic reading; they are, in this sense, acts of psycho- analysis themselves. So, too, in *Shakespeare in Love*. Will needs to fall in love, to complete his Oedipal separation from this shadowy maternal figure and start writing again.

There is much more to be said about the psychoanalytic debts of the new Shakespeare cinema, and Chapter 5 of this volume will attempt some of it. For now, I invoke *Shakespeare in Love* to demonstrate the curious ease with which a modern globalising Anglo-American popular cultural form can associate the plays of a sixteenth-century Warwickshire playwright with some of the wilder hypotheses of a nineteenth-century Viennese physician. The association is produced, of course, because both figures are, in various important ways, part authors of that globalising culture.

On 31 December 1999, *Time* magazine's special turn-of-the- millennium edition conducted a century-by-century account of the great and influential figures of the last thousand years. Needless to say, Shakespeare made 'Bard of the Century' for 1600–1700. The accompanying note is worth citing in full, because it sums up a still-powerful and widespread attitude:

In an age that haughtily made man the measure of all things, Shakespeare betrayed the essential fragility of the species, defining humanity with stories that continue to be our parables,

> both existentialist and romantic. His words are still the vessels
> of our dreams and thoughts . . . For generations after him,
> Shakespeare would be . . . a seer into what Coleridge called
> 'the interior nature' of human existence. We know little of
> Shakespeare's interior life, and some even question his identity.
> But there is no need for pyramids or monuments. As John
> Milton wrote, 'Dear son of memory, great heir of fame, /What
> need'st thou such weak witness of thy name?' His monument is
> his name. Shakespeare is now the global word for culture.
>
> (*Time*, 31 December 1999: 123)

This compressed and ideologically transparent summary of his enduring (and supposedly worldwide) cultural pre-eminence finds in Shakespeare an anticipation of and reflection upon every stage in the life-history of a way of thinking about the 'individual self' that remains the default setting of global culture, at least to its Western proponents: the precocious infancy of the humanist self in the Renaissance, its Romantic youth, its existentialist midlife crisis, and its cultured, confident (and in some accounts, corrupt) capitalist maturity (or dotage).

Of course, whether Shakespeare or his contemporaries would have recognised this humanist individual remains in doubt, to say the least. The formulation offered by the *Time* journalist relies on the kind of historical hindsight unavailable to Shakespeare, taking in as it does four centuries of fine tuning of that putative sensibility. And of course our own recognition of the end product depends, at least in part, on psychoanalysis as well, to which we owe that emphasis on the 'fragility' of the humanist individual's 'interior life', as accessed through its 'dreams and thoughts'.

With an ethnocentric arrogance both breathtaking and characteristic, *Time* concludes that the name Shakespeare has become 'the global code word for culture'. It is this attribution to Shakespeare of a combination of acute psychological acumen with a cultural capital of global proportions that provides the impetus for this study, and that, as I will argue, represents the prodigious offspring of the union between Shakespeare and psychoanalysis.

By the term 'cultural capital' I mean the various possible privileges and investments that attach to judgements of taste. The term derives from the work of Pierre Bourdieu, for whom the values associated with taste are in no way inherent in their objects, but are instead produced by an acquired capacity to make distinctions, for example, between elite cultural products versus popular ones, high versus low, good versus bad. Acquisition of taste is thus at once the product and the expression of one's socio-cultural, economic, educational and class positioning (Bourdieu 1984).[1] Linda Charnes has described the particular brand of cultural capital associated with Shakespeare in terms of his 'notorious identity': '"Shakespeare" has come to function as a commodity fetish whose name provides instant authoritative cachet. It is precisely Shakespeare's prior high-cultural "history" that is . . . dragged along underfoot, effaced but never forgotten, in his transformation into the transcendental cultural signifier' (1993: 157).

Returning to the relationship between the two terms, Shakespeare and psychoanalysis, I want to identify how their rather different versions of '"the interior nature" of human existence' have come to seem so compatible. In short, I think this is because Shakespeare has been in *psychoanalysis* for as long as psychoanalysis itself has been around, and in two senses: that is, Shakespeare has been both subject *to* psychoanalysis and a constitutive presence *in* psychoanalysis at least since Freud's inaugural formulation of the Oedipus complex, which depended, as I am far from the first to point out, upon *Hamlet* as much as on the Sophocles play that gave the theory its name.[2] A substantial proportion of this volume will therefore be concerned not only to demonstrate how psychoanalytic theories and categories may inform our reading of Shakespeare, but also to examine the many moments at which the reading of Shakespeare has contributed to the formation of psychoanalytic theory itself and the development of its categories.

In this way, the chapters that follow will seek to explore the various locations in which the collaboration between psychoanalysis and Shakespeare has been played out. The first half of the volume deals with the role played by 'Shakespeare in Psychoanalysis', the results of psychoanalysing Shakespeare, by examining the ways in which the reading and rereading of *Hamlet* contribute to the establishment of the psychoanalytic enterprise, from Freud's Vienna to Ernest Jones's London in Chapter 1, to Lacan's Paris in Chapter 2, to Johannesburg in Chapter 3. Along the way, this first half of the volume aims to introduce the reader new to psychoanalytic theory to some of its fundamental principles, and show them at work on Shakespearean texts.

The rest of the book addresses aspects of the cultural history of the development of 'Psychoanalysis out of Shakespeare', by which I mean the ways in which psychoanalytic theory can be shown to have developed, in various key aspects, out of early modern culture as mediated through Shakespeare: Chapter 4 focuses on memory and the unconscious; Chapter 5 on gender and sexuality. In both cases these studies are also concerned to demonstrate the impact upon psychoanalytic Shakespeares of some of the most influential recent developments in criticism: feminism, cultural materialism and new historicism, queer theory, postcolonial critique and cultural studies.

In the service of clarity and depth, I have avoided attempting to survey the field of psychoanalytic Shakespeare criticism, which is immense. The reader disappointed by the range of reference to psychoanalytic readings included here will be better satisfied by reading Norman Holland's *Psychoanalysis and Shakespeare* (1964), which comprehensively surveys the field prior to the 1960s, followed by the first few footnotes of each chapter of Janet Adelman's *Suffocating Mothers* (1992), which provides such a comprehensive range of references to psychoanalytic criticism up to the 1990s that there seemed little point attempting to repeat it.

I also thought it best to limit my discussion to a very few plays: a couple of tragedies, a comedy (or romance), bits and pieces of Roman plays and histories. The psychoanalysis of *Hamlet* could easily fill several volumes; I have given it half of this one in some attempt at thoroughness, and with the intention of using it as an exemplary text by which to introduce basic psychoanalytic concepts. A consideration of *Romeo and Juliet* concludes the volume because, as I will argue, this became the crucial text in the popular dissemination of a psychoanalysed Shakespeare at the end of the twentieth century. In between, in the context of my consideration of memory I devote some space to *The Tempest*, which remains for obvious reasons the most productive play for postcolonial Shakespeares.

In fact, it will be seen that a concern for the politics of colonisation and globalisation underlies much of what follows. If this seems unexpected in a volume on Shakespeare and psychoanalysis, I can only say that from where I stand it seems imperative. As a Pakeha – that is, a New Zealander of mainly British descent – I belong to a society that has sometimes thought of itself, whether with anxiety or with pride, as more or less devoid of a history peculiarly our own. In some ways, we have only begun quite recently to remember how we came to be where we are, and to address a few of the debts we owe. My sense of the urgency of this process fundamentally shapes the approach I have taken in this book. It is for this reason that what follows often aims less to introduce the practice of psychoanalytic criticism than to introduce its histories in particular textual, institutional and epistemological locations: because in locations like Aotearoa New Zealand, it has become apparent that any system of knowledge that does not know its place, or cannot remember its genealogy, may not know very much, or very well.

Part I
Shakespeare in psychoanalysis

1
In Vienna

Introduction

At one time the literary critic was like a social climber at a highbrow party, whose aim is to become familiar with the most important person available, who can then be introduced to everyone else as an intimate. And for many critics, for a long time, Shakespeare was the guest of honour. By posing as a go-between for Shakespeare's relation to the wider populace, the critic gained a vicarious cultural capital that paid dividends in various fields: social, economic, political and epistemological.

However, the necessity of introducing others to Shakespeare – or of demonstrating an intimacy with that infinite sensibility – created a problem of authority. How was the authenticity of the critic's 'Shakespeare' to be established? The difficulty compounded as literary criticism grew into an institutional academic discipline, and inevitably diversified, because each brand offered a different version of the authentic Shakespeare. Historicists and antiquarians looked for the historical figure, the actor–writer–businessman who was born in 1564 and died in 1616 in Stratford-upon-Avon, England; textual critics sifted competing quartos and folios to find the original text; new critics found the true Shakespeare embodied in an immaculate sense of 'organic form'; meanwhile, as it had for centuries, British nationalism and imperialism kept churning out as an exportable commodity the icon of Shakespeare the cult figure, the greatest literary genius the world has ever seen.[1] All these enterprises shared one thing, however: the quest to breathe in the miasma of genius that emanates from the name 'Shakespeare'. This special feeling – of privileged access to the man *behind* Hamlet, Macbeth, Falstaff or the Sonnets – remains one of the most vivid available instances of that effect of uniqueness, originality and authenticity which Walter Benjamin designated as 'aura'.[2]

Meanwhile, alongside as well as within literary criticism, another powerful mode of interpretation was evolving, which would claim greater access than any other analytical method to the Shakespearean aura. For one of the founding promises of psychoanalysis was that of a thoroughgoing penetration of any given personality; another was that no individual could better sustain this scrutiny, and offer greater credibility in return, than Shakespeare. As a kind of inaugural showcase – or case history perhaps – demonstrating what it could do, psychoanalysis promised what no literary critic had: insight into those thoughts and desires of which even the historical man from Stratford himself may not have been conscious. In this way, of course, psychoanalysis also smuggled in its own version of what constitutes human personality; in fact, the privileged position of psychoanalytic theory in twentieth-century Western thought no doubt has everything to do with its contribution to the establishment of precisely this definition of the 'real' self as a deeply interiorised and thus largely impenetrable authentic core. On those terms – because they are so much his own – only the methods pioneered by Freud possess the key to unlock the innermost recesses of the plays, and the means to find hidden there the deepest intimacies of the Shakespearean psyche.

Moreover, if Shakespeare's tragedies were to provide, in the phrase used by Freud to describe dreams, the royal road to the unconscious, then it's easy to guess which was likely to prove most royal. For Freud, Jones, Rank, Lacan and most other psychoanalytically inclined readers, *Hamlet* provides the key to Shakespeare's psychic closet. In certain ways, this only continues a valorisation of that play well established before the nineteenth century; but certainly, by the time Freud and his colleagues had finished, the play's protagonist was thoroughly established as the apotheosis of something called 'the human condition'.[3] It is in Hamlet – the play, but even more so the character – that the psychoanalyst finds the mind and soul of Shakespeare himself. Hamlet is Shakespeare, at his most thinly disguised. Nor, of course, did psychoanalysis invent this notion.

Bradley: Hamlet writing Shakespeare

Around the time Freud began contemplating *Hamlet*, A. C. Bradley – the pre-eminent if not the only begetter of 'Eng. Lit. Crit.' as an academic discipline, and of Shakespearean criticism as a profession – was mapping out, in pre-psychoanalytic terms, the path to be followed by those wishing to encounter the presiding genius of English culture face to face. For Bradley, too, Hamlet provides the privileged point of entry, since he is 'the only character in Shakespeare who could possibly have composed his plays' (Bradley 1955: 355). More than anything else, the identification between this character and his author depends upon their mutual skill with words: what speaks to us in Hamlet is his creator's own tongue, his 'turns of phrase', the language that makes Shakespeare, pre-eminently and tautologically, Shakespeare. This explains

> why Hamlet is the most fascinating character, and the most inexhaustible, in all imaginative literature. What else should he be, if the world's greatest poet . . . put his own soul straight into this creation, and when he wrote Hamlet's speeches wrote down his own heart?
>
> (Bradley 1955: 357)

Something reads oddly here nowadays, perhaps because postmodernism has taught us to consider verbal skill incommensurable with directness of access to the soul and heart, to suspect that language tends to give us the lie, that it is two(-or-more)-faced, that it misrepresents as often as it represents, and that meaning can slip out from under us. This suspicion itself foreshadows psychoanalysis, or more correctly constitutes one of its major legacies, one of the ways in which the Freudian slips between Bradley's psychology (and his Shakespeare) and ours.

In contrast, assuming that 'art seeks necessarily for unity and for a resolution of differences' (Brown, in Bradley 1992: xxvi), Bradley dedicated his critical practice to the service of an overall meaning (a ruling 'vision' or 'idea') that would not only organise all aspects of the play, but also allow the reader's psychology to meet that of the playwright, celebrating a marriage of true minds between critical interpretation and authorial intention. Thus, in the infamous 'Notes' that follow his lectures, Bradley works apparent contradictions or imperfections in the plays into a coherent and therefore credible representation of some authentic aspect of human experience. To this end, he has to envisage a life for each main cast member prior to the action: so he speculates on the timing of 'Events before the opening of the action in *Hamlet*', and asks, 'Where was Hamlet at the time of his father's death?' (Bradley 1992: 355–62). Realism demands that the characters have a documented biography that precedes, and exceeds, what is actually represented on stage. Elsewhere Bradley confronts 'puzzles' that, although they arise during the action, would be most unlikely to strike an audience watching a performance, as even he admits (134). For example, why does Hamlet choose to transcribe in such an indirect form the Ghost's repeated injunction to 'Remember me'?; as Bradley points out, what he actually writes in his 'tables' – the observation that 'one may smile, and smile, and be a villain' (1.5.91–108) – is only tangentially related to the paternal dictate itself. The reason must be that

> tables are stealable, [but] if the appearance of the Ghost should be reported, a mere observation on the smiling of villains could not betray anything of his communication with the Ghost. What follows shows that the instinct of secrecy is strong in him.
>
> (Bradley 1992: 368)

Such questions, along with their solutions, are produced by a vision that insists the action is part of a wider reality encompassing all sorts of events, life-histories and hidden thoughts not included in the play-as-performance.

Specifically dramaturgical dimensions prove most difficult to subsume within this vision because they threaten to pull the play towards a theatricality that detracts from its supposed realism. In such cases, Bradley suggests that it is not the critical perspective that falls short, but Shakespeare himself – because he allows inconsistencies to occur, or because he writes in an over-indulgent style (Bradley 1992: 370–81). Bradleyan criticism thus implies a distinction between a fallible Shakespeare and an ideal 'Shakespeare', the latter authorising both a 'reality' beyond the actual plays, and a 'human nature' beyond particular characters – a 'Shakespeareality' *so real* that even the text and its historical author will sometimes fall short of it.

This faith in an essentialised realism serves Bradley well, insofar as it reinforces simultaneously the institutional roles of both Shakespeare and the professional literary critic. Both are assigned the privileged task of representing 'the human condition', and each guarantees the status of the other: criticism cements Shakespeare into place as the foremost recorder of the human drama; Shakespeare's immense cultural authority – that of the presiding genius of British national and imperial identity – strengthens the claim on the contemporary intellectual field that is being advanced by both his mediator and the developing institution of Eng. Lit. Crit.

As Terry Eagleton has argued, for critics from Matthew Arnold to I. A. Richards, the ideological justification for literary studies resided in its moral mission, so that by the early 1930s, English had positioned itself midway between science and culture, in that powerful location left vacant by religion: to study literature was to enter

> an arena in which the most fundamental questions of human existence – what it meant to be a person, to engage in significant relationship with others, to live from the vital centre of the most essential values – were thrown into vivid relief and made the object of the most intensive scrutiny.
>
> (Eagleton 1983: 31)

If we accept that this capacity to delineate most accurately something called 'human nature' would come to be recognised as literary criticism's best claim to academic credibility, it will not be surprising that Bradley's full-length lectures on the tragedies concentrate more than anything else on the question of character, and the associated issue of motivation. 'Why does X act as he or she does?' is the Bradleyan enquiry *par excellence*. And it is in pursuit of this question, of course, that the psychologism of an emergent literary studies moves like a ghost towards its meeting with an incipient psychoanalysis.

Hence Bradley focuses on precisely the 'problem' that will

provide Freud with his entry into Shakespeare: why, after his encounter with the Ghost, does Hamlet delay his revenge against Claudius for so long?[4] Prior to the nineteenth century, as Bradley points out, critics were not particularly interested in this question; it is only 'when the slowly rising sun of Romance began to flush the sky that the wonder, beauty and pathos of this most marvellous of Shakespeare's creations began to be visible!' (Bradley 1992: 75). The obsessive interiority of the Romantic notion of self produces an account of character as that which must be read *in depth*, thus introducing the question of psychological motivation, scripting a *Hamlet* – and a Hamlet – that will come to be read precisely for that which is most difficult to read: the indecision of the protagonist.

'It is sometimes said that Hamlet's character is not only intricate but unintelligible,' writes Bradley, and he offers three possible explanations for this: first, our historical and cultural distance from the play ('there may be questions which we cannot answer with certainty now . . . but which never arose for the spectators who saw *Hamlet* acted in Shakespeare's day'); second, the fallibility of its author ('from carelessness or because he was engaged on this play for several years, Shakespeare left inconsistencies'); third, the illustration by the playwright of 'certain strange facts of human nature, which he had noticed but of which we are ignorant' (Bradley 1992: 76–7). Many a modern critic would opt for the first or the second option – neither of which, for the institutional reasons mentioned already, Bradley can afford to admit. His favoured explanation is the one he puts in lucky last place: the ultimate illegibility of human nature, which is the best investment for those wanting to perpetuate the authority of a caste of professional or professorial readers – and which once again, of course, uncannily prefigures Freud.

Ultimately, Bradley's explanation of Hamlet's delay seems both like and unlike the Freudian account. The Prince's hesitancy derives from the melancholic despair which results not so much from his father's death, nor his suspicions about his uncle, nor the loss of the crown, but rather from

> the moral shock of the sudden ghastly disclosure of his mother's true nature . . . All his life he had believed in her, we may be sure, as such a son would. He has seen her not merely devoted to his father, but hanging on him like a newly-wedded bride

. . . And then within a month . . . she married again and married Hamlet's uncle, a man utterly contemptible and loathsome in his eyes; married him in what to Hamlet was incestuous wedlock.
(Bradley 1992: 98–9)

Melancholia, the maternal and marital incest: Bradley concludes his reading of the play at the very point at which psychoanalysis will take it up.[5]

Before leaving Bradley, it is worth reiterating those aspects of his reading of the play that produced, from a nineteenth-century humanist psychologism, the epistemological niche that early psychoanalysis would identify and occupy. In the first place, for Bradley Hamlet's delay becomes a *necessary problem*, insofar as it proves Shakespeare's pre-eminence in the representation of character as an internal store of secrets to be discovered, a hidden account to be made legible. It is this fixation on the psyche as an interior space of exploration to which psychoanalysis will also address itself – although its answer to the question of character will prove ultimately disruptive to the humanist discourse that poses it.

But I also want to suggest that Bradley foreshadows aspects of this disturbance. For if its significance depends upon an act of reading by another – by the critic, by the audience – then 'character' (a word which Shakespeare could use to mean writing, either as a verb or a noun) seems to exist only as a kind of cipher, which can be appropriated and made to signify differently by different readers. The emblem of this process, in Bradley, is the suggestion that because his 'tables' are 'stealable', Hamlet's most intimate self-expression – the transcription of his father's Ghost's injunction to 'remember', that which comprises the motivating force of his 'character' – occurs in disguise, as an act performed for imagined hostile eyes: he does not write his father's actual words, but employs a stand-in, a code, for whatever it is that he *really means*. And that message in turn suggests that language – even body-language – can be deceptive: 'one may smile, and smile, and be a villain'. As well as guaranteeing the tenure of the professional critic over her or his material, this alleged duplicity of the text could hardly fail to appeal to psychoanalysis. The liability of letters to be purloined, moreover, will be crucial to a later psychoanalytic rereading of the play by Lacan, as I will discuss in the next chapter.

Freud: Hamlet rewriting Oedipus

It has been noted that many of the key concepts of *The Interpretation of Dreams*, Freud's most important and sustained early treatise, are foreshadowed in the letters he wrote to his colleague, Wilhelm Fliess, during the 1890s.[6] Thus the first extant reference to Freud's most important 'discovery' occurs in the letter dated 15 October 1897. He writes that, as a result of a long period of experimental 'self-analysis', 'A single idea of general value dawned on me. I have found, in my own case too, [the phenomenon of] being in love with my mother and jealous of my father, and I now consider it a universal event in early childhood' (Freud 1985: 272). This idea is offered as an explanation for the high proportion of incest accounts among his 'neurotic' clients – which Freud previously had taken to be factual. Examining his own childhood memories, Freud 'finds' that such scenes are fantasies, produced by the child's desire for one parent and its corresponding jealousy towards the other. Thus the material presented to the analyst by the client – the very stuff of psychoanalysis – whether in the form of memories, fantasies or dreams, will henceforth be read as *fiction*.

Moreover, the route that Freud's discussion now takes makes it clear that this 'discovery' itself maintains a crucial relationship with other items within that category: he goes on, in the same letter, to explicate this hypothesis by means of reference to two literary works. In the first, *Oedipus Rex* by Greek tragedian Sophocles, the eponymous protagonist accidentally kills his father and marries his mother (Freud 1985: 272). But why, at this point, should Freud turn to literature for verification?

Freud's ambition to invent and patent psychoanalysis as a scientific discipline remains haunted by an anxiety regarding the necessity of – and the difficulties of providing – empirical evidence for its conclusions. Because he wishes to claim a universal provenance for his delineation of the operation of dreams, and of the unconscious mind generally, his own personal memories cannot bear the whole burden of proof – especially insofar as they, too, must be considered subject to those very processes of repression and distortion which psychoanalysis would consider characteristic of every psychology.[7] Therefore, to underwrite his authority at key points such as this, Freud invests in a kind of cultural capital different from that offered by science – namely, that of art, and in particular of tragic drama. And so the other crucial reference point for Freud's development of the Oedipal theory will hardly surprise us:

> Fleetingly the thought passed through my head that the same thing might be at the bottom of *Hamlet* as well. I am not thinking of Shakespeare's conscious intention, but believe, rather, that a real event stimulated the poet to his representation, in that his unconscious understood the unconscious of his hero.
>
> (Freud 1985: 272)

Freud repeats but refines this argument for public scrutiny in *The Interpretation of Dreams* (1900):

> In my experience, which is already extensive, the chief part in the mental lives of all children who later become psycho-neurotics is played by their parents. Being in love with the one parent and hating the other are among the essential constituents of the stock of psychical impulses which is formed at that time and which is of such importance in determining the symptoms of the later neurosis.
>
> (*PFL* 4: 362)

Freud immediately recuperates the false modesty of that initial phrase – 'In my experience' – by means of the qualifying assertion that this is 'already extensive'. Furthermore, it is clear in the overall context of *The Interpretation of Dreams* – which claims to offer 'a scientific enquiry into the phenomena of dreams' (*PFL* 4: 63) – that this experience should in no way be considered merely subjective; on the contrary, it is both theoretically informed and clinically derived, and therefore partakes of the legitimacy proper to science.

This legitimacy, however, remains tenuous; for just a few sentences later, the authorising power of clinical observation itself becomes dubious:

> It is not my belief, however, that psychoneurotics differ sharply in this respect from other human beings who remain normal . . . It is far more probable – and this is confirmed by occasional observations on normal children – that they are only distinguished by exhibiting on a magnified scale feelings of love

and hatred to their parents which occur less obviously and less intensely in the minds of most children.

(*PFL* 4: 362)

Here the possibility arises that even clinical observation might prove inadequate, offering only a 'probability', confirmed only by '*occasional* observations on normal children'. Such moments betray another anxiety, recurrent among the first generation of psychoanalytic theorists, that their emergent discipline could be dismissed by science insofar as it relied upon the observation of the 'abnormal' psychologies of neurotics, hysterics and psychotics, and could therefore claim little authority in regard to 'the human condition' in general.[8]

Once again, then, in order to forestall this possible dismissal of psychoanalysis as a 'science' of the merely marginal, another form of authorisation must be deployed, which moves Freudian theory to a higher ground beyond the reach of empiricism. This strategy elevates a 'probability' to the status of a 'discovery', which, Freud goes on to assert,

is confirmed by a legend that has come down to us from classical antiquity . . . whose profound and universal power to move can only be understood if the hypothesis I have put forward in regard to the psychology of children has an equally universal validity. What I have in mind is the legend of King Oedipus and Sophocles' drama which bears his name.

(*PFL* 4: 362–3)

The privileges of high culture – the universality and profundity of the original legend, and the antiquity of its artistic manifestation in classical drama – are thus brought into a mutually reinforcing relationship with the hypothesis derived from both personal experience and clinical observation. In fact, by means of a curious chiasmus (which will prove to be typical of Freudian logic) the passage above binds the validity of high culture and psychoanalytic theory together inseparably, inasmuch as the profundity and universality of both legend and art 'can only be understood' if the Freudian hypothesis 'has an equally universal validity'. Freud's syntax thus crosses the 'confirmation' of the psychoanalytic 'hypothesis' by the Oedipus story with the validation of the meaning and status of both legend and play themselves by psychoanalysis.

In other words, in the space of a sentence, the Freudian 'discovery' graduates from a hypothesis requiring verification by art to a universally validating principle in its own right; henceforth, to deny the truth of the psychoanalytic interpretation will be to deny the significance of art and legend alike.

Nowhere is this chiasmatic bond tighter than in Freud's attachment to *Hamlet*. He seasons many of his works liberally with citations from the play, and returns to it often when seeking an illustration, or a comparison, of the effectiveness of the psychoanalytic method. In 1914, writing about 'The Moses of Michelangelo', he wants to argue that the proper comprehension of 'great works of art . . . would never be possible without the application of psychoanalysis':

> Let us consider Shakespeare's masterpiece, *Hamlet*, a play now over three centuries old. I have followed the literature of psychoanalysis closely, and I accept its claim that it was not until the material of the tragedy had been traced back by psychoanalysis to the Oedipus theme that the mystery of its effect was at last explained. But before this was done, what a mass of differing and contradictory interpretive attempts, what a variety of opinions about the hero's character and the dramatist's intentions!
>
> (*PFL* 14: 254–5)

Once more, a double-bind logic sutures the credibility of psychoanalysis into its reading of literature. A decade and a half after producing his analysis of the play, Freud achieves a retroactive institutionalisation of the procedures of psychoanalysis: he sounds as if he is conducting a disinterested survey and assessment of psychoanalytic material – as if he were not the author of the interpretation which he describes as explaining the mystery of *Hamlet*'s effect. Again, then, the validating function that dramatic and literary texts fulfil for an emergent discipline, by lending their supposed universality and profundity to psychoanalysis, is reversed by a sleight-of-hand which installs, in a position prior to the texts themselves, those Freudian precepts upon which literature can now be said to depend, both in its production by writers and its (proper) reception by audiences.

The same, of course, goes for Shakespeare, who could not have written *Hamlet* without his Oedipal complex:

> Shakespeare's *Hamlet* . . . has its roots in the same soil as *Oedipus Rex*. But the changed treatment of the same material reveals the whole difference in the mental life of these two widely separated epochs of civilization: the secular advance of repression in the emotional life of mankind. In the *Oedipus* the child's wishful phantasy that underlies it is brought into the open and realized as it would be in a dream. In *Hamlet* it remains repressed; and – just as in the case of a neurosis – we only learn of its existence from its inhibiting consequences. Strangely enough, the overwhelming effect produced by the more modern tragedy has turned out to be compatible with the fact that people have remained completely in the dark as to the hero's character.
>
> (*PFL* 4: 366–7)

This passage demonstrates several of the characteristics that will typify the psychoanalytic reading of literary texts.

The first is the assumed consistency between the structure and function of the literary work and that of the unconscious. In this sense, the function of psychoanalysis simply repeats that of literature, the only distinction being that the creative writer fulfils, in a single person, the roles of both analyst and analysand. In his essay on 'Delusions and Dreams in Jensen's *Gradiva*', Freud suggests that, while his own procedure 'consists in the conscious observation of abnormal mental processes in other people so as to be able to elicit and announce their laws', the creative writer

> directs his attention to the unconscious in his own mind, he listens to its possible developments and lends them artistic expression instead of suppressing them by conscious criticism . . . the conclusion seems inescapable that either both of us, the writer and the doctor, have misunderstood the unconscious in the same way, or we have both understood it correctly.
>
> (*PFL* 14: 115)

It is, then, the similarity in the inner mechanism of neurotic symptoms, dreams and literary works that authorises the psychoanalytic method, insofar as it can thereby claim to tie together several necessary dualities: art and science, writing and reading, creation and analysis, literature and psychopathology.[9]

The literary work will therefore be organised according to the same structures of concealment and revelation that structure the dialogue between psychoanalyst and analysand during the therapeutic session. More specifically, for Freud as for Bradley, the literary hero's character constitutes that necessary mystery which offers psychoanalysis its privileged point of entry. It is this obscurity, resulting from repression, upon which only Freud can shed light – 'the fact that people have remained completely in the dark as to the hero's character' – that gives Shakespeare's tragedy an even more 'overwhelming' Oedipal effect than that of *Oedipus Rex* itself.

The presence of this kind of central obscurity, around which the meanings of the text are organised, can be compared with what Freud refers to as 'the dream's navel, the spot where it reaches down into the unknown':

> The dream-thoughts to which we are led by interpretation cannot, from the nature of things, have any definite endings; they are bound to branch out in every direction into the intricate network of our world of thought. It is at some point where this meshwork is particularly close that the dream-wish grows up, like a mushroom out of its mycelium.
>
> (*PFL* 4: 671–2)

Given that creative writing operates in the same way as the dreamwork, it follows that *Hamlet* will also have a mysterious navel around which its meanings are configured. And, of course, only psychoanalysis can locate and penetrate this central organising lacuna: 'The play is built up on Hamlet's hesitations over fulfilling the task of revenge that is assigned to him; but its text offers no reasons or motives for these hesitations and an immense variety of attempts at interpreting them have failed to produce a result' (*PFL* 4: 367). *Hamlet*, then, is characterised by layer after layer of repression, a structure that 'both resists and enables Oedipal reading as such' (Lupton and Reinhard 1993: 15), making it a more suitable occasion for psychoanalytic praxis than *Oedipus Rex*, which does its own psychoanalytic work by bringing 'into the open' the child's fantasy of patricide and maternal incest that underlies it (363).

For Freud, then, the advantage of *Hamlet* is that it typifies what he calls 'the secular advance of repression in the emotional life of mankind' (*PFL* 4: 366). This comment also demonstrates the most radical divergence of the psychoanalytic project from that of Bradleyan criticism. Where Bradley's puzzles and solutions were in service of an all-encompassing celebration of the human condition, an aspect of the dominant nineteenth-century vision of European civilisation as a ceaseless progress towards universal enlightenment, Freud suggests a view of history as a succession of repressions or forgettings. This anti-humanist or anti-Enlightenment aspect of psychoanalysis will be abandoned by some of his followers (notably Carl Jung, and, in literary criticism, Alex Aronson and Northrop Frye), but adopted and radically extended by others (especially, but not exclusively, by Jacques Lacan and his followers).

Another disparity emerges between the psychology of Bradley and the psychoanalysis of Freud in relation to the attitude of each towards the author. For Bradley, as noted earlier, the reading of *Hamlet* (and in particular the analysis of Hamlet) brings the reader as close as possible to Shakespeare – not in historical terms, but rather as a real, living personality: the 'real' Shakespeare, presiding genius of English culture, template for and true transcriber of the human condition. In contrast, a psychoanalysis of the play, even as it aims to read the mind of its author, has the peculiar effect of displacing 'Shakespeare' – both the historical man and his idealised counterpart.

Initially, Freud appears to make an untroubled progress through analysis of the work to the mind of the character, and thence into the mind of the author:

> Hamlet is able to do anything – except take vengeance on the man who did away with his father and took that father's place with his mother, the man who shows him the repressed wishes of his own childhood realized . . . Here I have translated into conscious terms what was bound to remain unconscious in Hamlet's mind . . . The distaste for sexuality expressed by Hamlet in his conversation with Ophelia . . . was destined to take possession of the poet's mind more and more during the years that followed, and which reached its extreme expression in *Timon of Athens*. For it can of course only be the poet's own mind which confronts us in Hamlet . . . *Hamlet* was written immediately after the death of Shakespeare's father (in 1601), that is, under the immediate impact of his bereavement and, as we may well assume, while his childhood feelings about his father

had been freshly revived. It is known, too, that Shakespeare's own son who died at an early age bore that name of 'Hamnet', which is identical with 'Hamlet'.

(*PFL* 4: 367–8)

From the text to the unconscious of the protagonist, and thence to the psychobiography of the poet: in two easy moves, Freud discovers the holy grail of nineteenth-century Shakespearean criticism – the contents of the 'deepest layer of impulses in the mind of the creative writer' (*PFL* 4: 368).

Characteristically, though, Freud in 1930 adds to this passage a footnote which seems to represent a radical form of 'secondary revision', demonstrating a quite different kind of psychoanalytic relation to the author: 'Incidentally, I have in the meantime ceased to believe that the author of Shakespeare's works was the man from Stratford' (*PFL* 4: 368, n. 1). Given the dependence of his argument on this man's autobiography, such a change in attitude can hardly be considered incidental; moreover, Freud returns to the subject repeatedly in his later works. In 'An Outline of Psycho-Analysis' (1938), he writes (again in a footnote) that

The name 'William Shakespeare' is very probably a pseudonym behind which a great unknown lies concealed. Edward de Vere, Earl of Oxford, a man who has been thought to be identifiable with the author of Shakespeare's works, lost a beloved and admired father while he was still a boy and completely repudiated his mother, who contracted a new marriage very soon after her husband's death.

(Freud 1966, vol. XXIII: 192, n. 1)

In at least three other places in his extant writings Freud returns to the same argument.[10] Why does he now wish to repudiate the Stratford man, whose mind he had so convincingly penetrated in 1900? One possible answer is clear enough: the proffered biography of Edward de Vere fits more closely with the Freudian Hamlet than do the scanty details from the life of the Stratford candidate. So, just as Bradley located his reading of *Hamlet* in the mind of an ideal 'Shakespeare' beyond the limits of the mortal playwright or his actual play, Freud's psychoanalytic solution to the play authorises or even requires him to kill off an author (a father?) and to search for a better one.[11]

An alternative hypothesis emerges if greater emphasis is placed on the initial sentence of the footnote – the suggestion that the name William Shakespeare 'is very probably a pseudonym behind which a great unknown lies concealed'. Such an assertion might hint at a tendency within Freud's mode of reading – which at this point remains implicit, and is still recuperated by the claim that follows it – to move away from a psychoanalytic criticism that reads the text as the author's symptomology. Later in the century, as psychoanalysis encounters structuralism and the 'death of the author', it sheds the guise of a more penetrating form of authorial biography, and instead seeks the 'unconscious' in locations outside of the author's head: in the mind of the reader, or in the text itself, or in the cultures, histories, literary traditions and languages that produce text, reader and author alike.[12] Thus Freud's search for unconscious meaning in the text inaugurates a critical move – which he himself cannot complete – away from an understanding of meaning as originating in the mind of an individual author, and towards the notion of meaning produced elsewhere and otherwise.

Rank and Jones: Hamlet underwrites Freud

The early dissemination of the Freudian *Hamlet* is best represented by two works: *Hamlet and Oedipus* by Ernest Jones, and Otto Rank's study of the play in his volume on *The Incest Theme in Literature and Legend*.

The expansion of Jones's argument from an essay first published in 1910 to book length in 1949 reveals a desire to stake a strong claim for psychoanalysis as a valid field alongside literary criticism, which by the middle of the century had become, in Britain and the United States, a powerful discourse in its own right. Between the New Critics on one hand, and the Leavises and I. A. Richards on the other, Eng. Lit. Crit. was able to make strong claims for credibility and disciplinary rigour in its scrutiny of both textual forms and, by extension, the psychological states and social formations represented therein; Jones, it would seem, aims to gain for psychoanalysis a slice of this action.

He begins his book-length study of *Hamlet* as a response to his version of the New Criticism: 'It has . . . been rather fashionable of late to assert that every work should be judged "purely on its merits" independently of any knowledge of its author' (Jones 1949: 11). Jones considers, however, that psychoanalytic reading provides that royal road to the mind of the author which is the proper function of criticism, thus reinstalling one aspect of the project of Bradley – whose assessment of the play, as the ultimate expression of the world's greatest poet, he quotes with approval (20–1). Such a judgement remains consistent with the grandiose claims of psychoanalysis itself, which Jones appears to preserve intact, commenting that the play's 'universal appeal shows that its inmost theme must contain something to which the heart of mankind in general reverberates' (21).

Yet Jones's discussion also makes more explicit the extent to which psychoanalytic reading – for all its apparent complicity with Bradley's – constitutes a sustained and radical attack on humanism:

> Man's belief that he is a self-conscious animal, alive to the desires that impel or inhibit his actions, is the last stronghold of that anthropomorphic and anthropocentric outlook on life which has so long dominated his philosophy, his theology, and above all, his psychology.
>
> (Jones 1949: 51)

In this account *Hamlet* demonstrates not the omnipotence of the rational mind celebrated by Enlightenment humanism, but rather the enslavement of human agency to forces which remain obscure and illegible – in short, to the unconscious. Hamlet's overt motives for delay – cowardice, doubt about the truthfulness of the ghost, bad timing – constitute merely plausible alibis for his real (that is, his unconscious) motivation: 'When a man gives at different times a different reason for his conduct it is safe to infer that, whether consciously or not, he is concealing the true reason' (Jones 1949: 54). Jones concludes that Hamlet's delay arises 'not from physical or moral cowardice, but from that intellectual cowardice, that reluctance to dare the exploration of his inmost soul, which Hamlet shares with the rest of the human race. "Thus conscience does make cowards of us all"' (91). Hamlet thus provides an allegory of a failure in human agency generally, a failure in the will to *read* – more particularly, to read his own interior 'character'. Jones cites Hamlet's comment to Ophelia – 'I could accuse me of such things that it were better my mother had not borne me' (3.1.123–4) – as an indicator of his repressed incestuous desires; in this he demonstrates, once more, the psychoanalytic construction of character as a hollow space, signifier of an immeasurable depth: 'there are thoughts and wishes that no one dares to express even to himself. We plumb here the darkest depths' (Jones 1949: 100).

Paradoxically, the anti-humanism of the psychoanalytic 'discovery' therefore arises from another aspect of its universalism. Jones refutes the notion that Hamlet suffers from a specific clinical disorder, suggesting instead that Shakespeare's insight portrays, three centuries in advance, what psychoanalysis calls 'psycho-neurosis', that 'intermediate plight, in the toils of which perhaps the greater part of mankind struggles and suffers . . . where the person is unduly, and often painfully, driven or thwarted by the "unconscious" part of his mind' (Jones 1949: 69). The universality of the unconscious – which is wayward, unpredictable and inco-herent – is what challenges the humanist emphasis on rationality, and also distinguishes the psychoanalytic mode of reading from Bradley's (which locates meaning in the intention of the author), and from New Criticism (which finds it in the text).

Both Jones and Otto Rank therefore follow Freud in suggest-ing that the work of the creative writer combines that of analyst and analysand in one. Rank refers to playwrights as 'those most profound of unconscious psychologists' (Rank 1992: 45), while Jones similarly portrays Shakespeare as a kind proto-psychoanalyst whose rewriting of the original Amleth legend from which his play derives brings the unconscious thoughts of the protagonist near to the surface, revealing the various processes of repression that have hitherto obscured the narrative. Rank adds to this view the suggestion that psychoanalytic significance does not reside only in modifications or additions by the playwright to his sources: 'The playwright's omissions from the sources have deep psycho-logical motivation as well . . . [They] arise from a tendency to inhibit the expression of painful, repressed emotions' (168). Literary revision thus parallels the process of 'secondary revision', the operation of ego-drive repression that censors the primary processes of the unconscious.

In particular, surveying Shakespeare's modifications to the Hamlet story, Jones focuses on the author's 'intention of trans-forming the play from an external struggle into an internal tragedy' (Jones 1949: 153). This is why Shakespeare adopts Kyd's intro-duction of the Ghost; in the earlier versions the murder is public knowledge. Shakespeare's sensitivity to his own unconscious 'revealed to his feeling, though not to his conscious intelligence, the fundamental meaning of the story. His own Oedipus complex was too strong for him to be able to repudiate it as easily as Amleth and Laertes had done, and he could only create a hero who was unable to escape from its toils' (155). Thus, as Rank points out, the advance in psychoanalytic sophistication represented by Shakespeare's version accompanies – or is necessitated by – the increasingly psychoneurotic nature of the human mind itself, 'the advancing process of repression in society' (Rank 1992: 44). The psychotherapeutic value of artistic creation thus resides in its simultaneous revelation and repression, disclosure and closure, of unconscious desires and fears, which allow

> not only the author himself, but also most normal persons, to gratify in a psychically hygienic and therefore socially approved and highly valuable manner those repressed emotions that the dreamer sometimes lives out in his inner life and that the paranoiac, assisted by his delusion, can only partially master.
>
> (Rank 1992: 50)

This constitutes the psychoanalytic updating of the Aristotelian notion of catharsis: as a culture becomes more complex, its fears and anxieties are more powerfully repressed, and its artistic modes of managing these become more sophisticated. This model of historical development plainly parallels the psychoanalytic view of the maturation of the individual, who in later life retains in unconscious form traces of those traumas which had most impact in childhood; and so, too, tragedy's social value parallels the individual need for psychoanalysis: both offer a form of psychic hygiene in which the repressed can be gratified safely and without threat to either the social order or the individual ego. This account of the cultural function of drama will re-emerge, unexpectedly, in the new historicist readings of early modern culture produced during the 1980s and 1990s, which, influenced also by Mikhail Bakhtin's notions of carnival and Marxist concepts of ideology, tend to suggest that drama allows the dominant order to keep the populace in its place by allowing them a contained space in which to express in a 'socially hygienic form' their fantasies of subversion.[13]

Dream machineries

As well as developing the above notions about the psychological and social function of artistic creation, both Jones and Rank spell out more clearly than Freud the various kinds of fictional machinery that the Shakespearean text shares with the operation of the unconscious. Closer attention to their accounts of the play, therefore, will serve to introduce some of the fundamental concepts of psychoanalytic reading.

Projection

Insofar as literary, and particularly dramatic, creation can be viewed as comparable to either dreamwork or the process of psycho-analysis, the characters in a play can be read as personifications, or 'projections', to use the psychoanalytic term, of various aspects of the author's unconscious. In this regard, as Rank points out, psychoanalytic reading breaks with realist (and, I would add, with Bradleyan) critical practice:

> In the past, in the critical analysis of dramatic works and their creators . . . the principal mistake has been to regard the characters as real and to evaluate their behaviour according to the standards of real life. If one stops to consider that the dramatis personae are to be regarded as psychic reflections of certain emotions in the playwright, however . . . the behavior of a dramatic character [that] may appear incomprehensible or even impossible from the perspective of real life yet may be completely comprehensible and justified from a psycho-logical perspective . . . certain emotions of the playwright are projected outward and are embodied as dramatic characters that serve the protagonist as external driving or inhibiting forces.
> (Rank 1992: 42)

This mode of reading has various implications. For one thing, characters whose behaviour makes no sense according to the conventional standards of 'real life', can be analysed as aspects of (a) the unconscious of the protagonist or (b) of the author, or even (c) of the text itself or (d) of the culture that produces it – although these latter two options will not be taken up until a later generation of psychoanalytic critics emerges. Thus, for example, the 'motiveless malignity' of Iago, which baffled critics from Coleridge onwards, can be read, according to each of the afore-mentioned options, as an incarnation or projection of (a) the jealousy of Othello, (b) the machiavellian manipulative aspect of the playwright's mind, (c) the repeated deferral of ultimate or transcendental meaning required for dramatic tension and narrative extension, or (d) cultural fears and desires circulating in the discourses on race, gender and sexuality in early seventeenth-century London.[14] In the case of *Hamlet*, of course, Freud, Rank and Jones stop short of the third and fourth possibilities, and continue to read the main male characters as projections of the 'father complex' (in the first place) of the play's protagonist, and (in the second place) of its author.

Displacement, condensation, decomposition

Projection is one form of that broader category of transferred affect which Freud refers to as 'displacement', a 'psychological process by which . . . indifferent experiences take the place of psychically significant ones'. Displacement can also entail the transference of affect on to objects, images and words. Freud once again offers a specifically Shakespearean example: 'when, in *Othello*, a lost handkerchief precipitates an outburst of rage' (*PFL* 4: 263). Jones describes two other modes of displacement, 'decomposition' and 'condensation', which he defines as opposites:

> Whereas in the latter process attributes of several individuals are fused together in the creation of one figure, much as in the production of a composite photograph, in the former process various attributes of a given individual are disunited, and several other individuals are invented, each endowed with one group of the original attributes.
>
> (Jones 1949: 131)

Freud himself gives a Shakespearean instance of decomposition in his paper on 'Some Character-types Met with in Psychoanalytic Work' – the greater part of which, despite the explicit claim of the title, he devotes to a discussion of literary characters. In analys-ing Macbeth and Lady Macbeth as examples of 'Those Wrecked by Success', Freud introduces the theory that 'Shakespeare often splits a character up into two personages, which, taken separately, are not completely understandable and do not become so until they are brought together once more into a unity.' He goes on to enumerate the various ways in which Lady Macbeth manifests the signs of anxiety and guilt that Macbeth himself represses: her lack of sleep, her obsession with blood, her mental disorder. 'Together they exhaust the possibilities of reaction to the crime, like two disunited parts of a single psychical individuality, and it may be that they are both copied from a single prototype' (*PFL* 14: 307–8). Presumably the 'single psychical individuality' who provides the 'prototype' for both of the parricide Macbeths – 'Had he not resembled / My father as he slept, I had done't' (2.2.11–12) – is the same author whose father-complex produced *Hamlet*.

For all three first-generation psychoanalytic readers of the play, the most important example of decomposition in *Hamlet* itself is provided by that 'splitting' or 'duplication' which produces for the protagonist not a single 'real' father but rather two projected or fantasised ones:

> In Hamlet the two contrasting elements of the normal ambivalent attitude towards the father were expressed towards two sets of people; the pious respect and love towards the memory of his father, and the hatred, contempt, and rebellion towards the father-substitutes, Claudius and Polonius. In other words, the original father has been transformed into two fathers, one good, the other bad, corresponding with the division in the son's feelings.
>
> (Jones 1949: 122)

Later, Jones adds that 'Hamlet's contrast of the two pictures in the bedroom scene is a perfect delineation of the "good father" and "bad father" as melodramatically imagined by the infant' (Jones 1949: 124, n. 2).

So, for Rank and Jones – as for Freud – plays such as *Julius Caesar* and *Hamlet* represent Shakespeare's working out of his own 'family romance'. As rebellious sons, Brutus and Hamlet become interchangeable, just as Polonius, one of Hamlet's 'bad fathers', can be associated with Caesar – whose part in a dramatic performance, as Rank reminds us, Polonius claims to have played in his youth (3.2.100–5). Moreover, just as in *Hamlet* the role of the son splits into two (Hamlet and Laertes), in *Julius Caesar* three different aspects of the filial relation are represented by different characters: 'Brutus represents the son's rebelliousness, Cassius his remorsefulness, and Antony his natural piety' (Jones 1949: 123). Rank recites the legend that Shakespeare originally played the Ghost of Hamlet's father at the Globe as further proof that the play represents the simultaneous psychodramatic 'working out' of his mourning for both his father and his son (the conveniently named Hamnet Shakespeare), both of whom, as Freud also reminds us, died prior to the composition of the play (*PFL* 4: 368).

> While he played the ghost of the father, the ghost of his own father (his painful thoughts of him) could not plague him . . . As a playwright he had resisted his feelings of hate, but as an actor he once again adopted them by identifying with the ghost of his father, which plagued him, in order to turn to plague as a 'ghost' his own son (represented by Hamlet) and to admonish him for his reprehensible thoughts and actions. In the 'ghost', however, Shakespeare also identified with the son . . . in order to justify his own feelings as a son. Thus he played the role to escape anxiety associated with his fateful and repentant thoughts of his dead father and in connection with the similar feelings he believed he had to fear as a father himself. He played the role to prevent an attack of anxiety . . . one would almost say, to cure himself . . . Freud is responsible for the insight 'that the symptom is constructed to prevent the outbreak of anxiety'.
> (Rank 1992: 187–8; citing *PFL* 4: 738)

Because Shakespeare's own performance represents a 'compromise formation' between his feelings as a father and his feeling as a son, Rank finds in the Ghost's pronouncements the projection of quite contradictory feelings: on one hand, the Ghost expresses filial hatred for and envy of the 'bad father' (Claudius); but on the other hand,

> as a father and a husband, he adds (for his son):
>
> > But howso[m]ever thou pursuest this act,
> > Taint not thy mind[,] nor let thy soul contrive
> > Against thy mother aught (1.5.84–6).

In the father's fantasy of the mother's (the queen's) incest with the son lies also the fulfilment of the son's wishes. In the 'ghost of Hamlet's father', then, a whole series of powerful unconscious emotions of the playwright coincide and are expressed in compromise: his infantile hatred of his father and his erotic affection for his mother, but also the reactively revalued incest complex that respects the father while despising the mother; and finally also the punishment for those rejected feelings: that is, the fear of similar retribution by his own son.

(Rank 1992: 185–6)

The father–son relation in *Hamlet* is not merely complex, it is *a* complex, in the strongest Freudian sense of the word, most traumatically embodied in the appearance on stage of the Ghost of the murdered father.

Introjection and superego

As Rank and Jones point out, a ghostly murdered father-figure also appears in *Julius Caesar*– which, conveniently for the psychoanalytic argument, appears to have been written around the same time as *Hamlet*. In both plays, moreover, this manifestation of filial guilt is accompanied by that process which, in psychoanalytic terms, often accompanies and reverses 'projection', that is, 'introjection'. The former term refers to the displacement of psychic feelings or attributes outwards, on to others; the latter, to the assimilation of attributes or feelings perceived in others into the self. Thus, as Hamlet and Brutus externalise (or project) their guilt towards the slain father, they simultaneously internalise (or introject) that set of imperatives and judgements which the Ghost delivers.

In the case of Brutus, the two poles of this dialectic function quite explicitly. As he sits reading before the battle against Octavius and Antony, Brutus receives a visit from the ghost of Caesar, the 'father' he has slain in the first half of the play.

> *Brutus:*   Ha! Who comes here?
> I think it is the weakness of mine eyes
> That shapes this monstrous apparition.
> It comes upon me. Art thou any thing?
> Art thou some god, some angel, or some devil,
> That mak'st my blood cold, and my hair to stare?
> Speak to me what thou art.
>
> (4.3.273–9)

The same doubts attach to Hamlet's apparition as well: is it a projection of the viewer's own mind (or in Brutus's case, a product of his bad eyesight), or some external agent whose dictates require introjection?

This process, for which Hamlet's Ghost provides the model, will be described in Freud's later work as the formation of the 'superego', that largely unconscious body of guilt complexes which the individual takes in from the external world in the place of the prohibitions and commandments enforced during childhood by the father. Jacques Lacan, as I discuss in the next chapter, renames this aspect of the psyche the *nom-du-père*, the 'name- [or law] of-the-father' with a pun in French on *non-du-père*, the 'no- [or prohibition] of-the-father'. Hamlet's introjection of this superegoic or paternal law is perfectly emblematised by the acting out on stage of his obedience to the Ghost's final injunction to 'Remember me':

> Yea, from the table of my memory
> I'll wipe away all trivial fond records,
> All saws of books, all forms, all pressures past
> That youth and observation copied there,
> And thy commandment all alone shall live
> Within the book and volume of my brain,
> Unmix'd with baser matter.
>
> (1.5.98–104)

As I will also argue in the next chapter, the metaphor of writing – emphasised by Hamlet's actual inscription on his 'tables' a few lines on (and of course by the scene of *reading* that immediately precedes the appearance to Brutus of *his* ghost, *his* paternal apparition) – fits the psychoanalytic notion of introjection as a kind of imprint upon the psychic mould, and, in particular, Lacan's emphasis on the *nom/non-du-père* as a function of the symbolic order, the realm of language.

Another scene of superegoic projection and introjection mirrors this one, however, when Hamlet finds himself – where else? – in his mother's bedchamber. He describes to Gertrude his intention: 'You go not till I set you up a glass / Where you may see the inmost part of you' (3.4.18–19). He then goes on to show her two pictures, one of old Hamlet, and one of Claudius, the good father and the bad. Gertrude is thus invited to introject that doubled paternal image which Hamlet himself holds. In the process, Hamlet comes too close to transgressing both of the Ghost's injunctions: failing to remember him, and failing to keep an appropriate distance from his mother. True, he does in this scene manage to dispatch one bad father (Polonius), but not the right one: 'Is it the King?' (3.4.26). And then, at the moment at which, according to the psychoanalytic reading, he comes closest to the fantasy of incest which motivates his every thought and action – that is, as he verbally paints a picture of Claudius and Gertrude 'In the rank sweat of an enseamed bed, / Stew'd in corruption, honeying and making love / Over the nasty sty!' (3.4.92–4) – the Ghost reappears, to set him back on the straight and narrow: 'Do not forget. This visitation / Is but to whet thy almost blunted purpose' (3.4.110–11). For Rank, 'Just as the ghostly apparition reminds one of the dream image of the father's death, the son's visit to the mother's bedchamber can be seen as a dampened act of incest impeded by the appearance of the father' (Rank 1992: 50).

Doubling and identification

In addition to the proliferation of father-figures, both Rank and Jones focus on the duplication of the son, so that Laertes becomes a rival to Hamlet. In fact, both Laertes and Fortinbras are seen as 'doubles' of the young hero who seeks revenge for a wrong done to the dead father (Jones 1949: 142). Taken together, the dual processes of projection and introjection, when focused upon such a rival, brother, or other 'ego ideal', constitute what psychoanalytic theory calls an 'identification', the process whereby the individual tries to match up to, and assimilate, the attributes of an image perceived as a 'better self' (Laplanche and Pontalis 1988: 205).

Reading Freud's Will

The extended application of the Freudian approach to *Hamlet* by Jones and Rank, as well as offering a series of exemplary applications of psychoanalytic terminology to dramatic elements, anticipates a number of later developments in the psychoanalysis of Shakespearean texts.

In the first place, Jones's account of the identification between Hamlet and Laertes gestures towards a mode of psychoanalytic reading that does not necessarily locate the unconscious mechanisms which it takes as its object of study (displacement, condensation, decomposition, and so on) in the protagonist alone. For Jones, it appears, Hamlet himself features at times as a projection of Laertes's Oedipal complex:

> Hamlet's relation to Laertes is, mythologically speaking, a double one, a fusion of two primary Oedipus schemes, one being the reverse of the other. On the one hand Laertes, being identified with the old Polonius in his attitude towards Ophelia and Hamlet, represents the tyrant father, Hamlet being the young hero; Hamlet not only keenly resents Laertes' open expression of his devoted affection for Ophelia – in the grave scene – but at the end of the play kills him, as he had killed Polonius, in an accurate consummation of the mythological motive. On the other hand, however, as was remarked earlier, from another point of view we can regard Hamlet and Polonius as two figures resulting from 'decomposition' of Laertes' father, just as we did with the elder Hamlet and Claudius in relation to Hamlet. For in the relationship of the three men Hamlet kills the father Polonius, just as the tyrant father kills the good father . . . and Laertes, who is from this point of view the young hero, avenges this murder by ultimately slaying Hamlet.
>
> (Jones 1949: 139)

In this reading of the play from different perspectives – choosing the position of characters other than the obvious protagonist as a focal point – Jones anticipates later styles of reading that will seek to reconstruct those perspectives or narratives which are marginalised or repressed by the dominant ones. Thus feminists might read *Hamlet* from the perspective of Ophelia (Showalter 1985), or *King Lear* from the perspective of the 'absent mother' (Kahn 1986); cultural materialists might examine *Julius Caesar* from the point of view of Cinna the poet (Sinfield 1992: 24–8); post-structuralist psychoanalytic readers might envisage *The Comedy of Errors* as the dream of Aegeon, *The Merchant of Venice* as the posthumous fantasy of Portia's father, or *Hamlet* as the neurotic wish-fulfilment of Claudius (Stockholder 1987).

Another aspect of recent psychoanalytic criticism is also evident in the first-generation case histories by Freud, Jones and Rank, that is, its emphasis on the apparently insignificant or incoherent aspects of the text. Treated as symptoms of an underlying anxiety or desire, the reading of such moments parallels the psychoanalytic interpretation of the dysfunctional limbs of the hysteric: in both cases, those symptoms which speak most loudly to the analyst are precisely those which seem to do just the opposite – the silences, denials, refusals, inconsistencies – just as the hysteric's body, in its very incapacity and muteness, tells a story. The psychoanalytic reader is thereby licensed to read the text against its own grain: in this respect she or he can depart most radically from the Bradleyan imperative to braid contradictory elements into an overall unifying thread of intention. Rank, for example, concentrates on 'the few details Shakespeare freely inserted into the story' of *Julius Caesar*, as well as what he left out, in the process of adapting it from Plutarch and Suetonius – especially the fact that 'Caesar considered Brutus his illegitimate son' (Rank 1992: 168). He therefore proceeds to place enormous weight on a single figure of speech: that moment when Brutus, attempting to convince Antony of the necessity of killing Caesar, remarks that

> Our reasons are so full of good regard
> That were you, Antony, the son of Caesar,
> You should be satisfied.
>
> (3.1.223–5)

For Rank, this brief simile stands as compelling evidence of the repressed Oedipal relation between Brutus himself and Caesar:

> That it is precisely Brutus who says this suggests that Shakespeare was aware of his son relationship to Caesar but eliminated it because of internal inhibitions. For the utterance actually signifies: 'The reasons satisfy me, Caesar's son; they should satisfy you all the more.'
>
> (Rank 1992: 169)

Rank has no trouble admitting that this reading of *Julius Caesar* might 'to a seemingly excessive degree [have] claimed psychological significance for individual, apparently insignificant details, figures of speech, and similes'. However, he asserts,

> If we are really to take seriously the parallels between dream and drama, then . . . [t]he most important thing is to expect,

following our studies of dreams, that the psychologically most important theme of the whole drama may be expressed in an easily overlooked, unobtrusive element. Herein, to an extent, lies of course the aesthetically pleasurable effect. To produce this effect, a 'facade' of innocent, inoffensive elements must be presented.[15]

(Rank 1992: 170)

In this attention to detail – especially to those which might be thought to indicate a repressed or silenced voice speaking between the lines of the text – psychoanalytic practice anticipates, and perhaps shapes, various important modes of recent critical practice, including deconstruction, new historicism and cultural materialism, and of course feminism.[16]

One more legacy appears in 'Freud's Will'. The first generation of psychoanalytic readers of *Hamlet* bequeath, or anticipate, the currently and widely accepted notion that the concept of selfhood which Bradley takes for granted – an interior complexity, a deep layering of experience, memory and affect – is a recent historical invention; and moreover that Shakespeare is one of its creators. Jones, for example, suggests that Shakespeare inaugurates the notion of tragedy as 'inner conflict' rather than external allegory:

In this he shows that the tragedy of man is within himself, that, as the ancient saying goes: Character is Fate. It is the essential difference between pre-historic and civilized man; the difficulties with which the former had to contend came from without, those with which the latter have to contend really come from within. This inner conflict modern psychologists know as neurosis, and it is only by study of neurosis that one can learn the fundamental motives and instincts that move men. Here, as in so many other respects, Shakespeare was the first modern.

(Jones 1949: 151)

Many recent cultural historians of drama – while they might be sceptical about the suggestion that Shakespeare was unique in this respect – would concur that certain kinds of movement from exteriority to interiority can be said to characterise the European epistemological crisis out of which Shakespearean dramaturgy emerges. As Catherine Belsey has argued, late sixteenth- and early seventeenth-century tragedy develops away from a theatre in which characters stood allegorically as external representations of a divine order – for example, in morality drama – and towards a kind of psychodrama which produced, and focused on, the representation of a mental and emotional space internal to the protagonist, whose conflicting psychological tendencies might be projected outwards in the form of separate characters: 'there are in the plays of the late sixteenth and early seventeenth centuries intimations of the construction of a place which notions of personal identity were later to come to fill' (Belsey 1985: 40). For Joel Fineman, it is the sonnets that best illustrate the inauguration of a mode of subjectivity, poetic in its first manifestation, that is 'Built up on or out of the loss of itself, its identity defined as its difference from itself' (Fineman 1991: 111). Similarly, Francis Barker writes of Hamlet's distinction between an authentic inner identity and an inauthentic exterior – 'I have that within which passes show' (1.2.85) – as a moment that anticipates the invention of a 'private' early modern self (Barker 1984: 35), while Michael Neill has argued more recently that in early modern England 'the literal "opening up" of the human body by the new science of anatomy contributed to an emerging discourse of interiority by representing the human body as a multi-layered container of "secrets"' (Neill 1997: 44). And Barbara Freedman suggests that, 'Much as Freud constructed a subject by reference to the unconscious, Shakespeare constructs self-conscious characters by having them refer to an unseen space within' (Freedman 1991: 29). However, all of these critics, in contrast to the fathers of psychoanalysis, see the effect of 'interiority' inaugurated at this time as the effect of cultural practices (such as theatrical representation) rather than as a pre-existing capacity waiting to be accessed; moreover, they insist that it will remain provisional, impressionistic, and conflicted, inasmuch as it functions as an anticipation of – almost an experiment in – a humanistic notion of the self whose time has not yet come.

On the other hand, perhaps the most direct contemporary descendant of first-wave psychoanalytic criticism is Harold Bloom, who echoes Jones by attributing to Shakespeare 'the invention of the human'. Bloom thereby repeats the classic psychoanalytic gesture of re-installing Shakespeare as the founding authority for the psychoanalytic account of human character, of which Freud thus becomes merely an inheritor: 'Shakespeare is the original psychologist, and Freud the belated rhetorician' (Bloom 1999: 714). But, of course, as Michael Bristol points out, Bloom's reading of Shakespeare, and his vast body of critical work generally, owes everything in the first place to that particular version of psychoanalysis to which he subscribes, that is, to 'a way of being in language characterized by a radical self-narration in which self must assume sovereign authority' (Bristol 1996: 125). This privileging of the sovereign self Bloom derives from the humanism of the American ego-psychological tradition and its reading of Freud, rather than from the European structuralist and poststructuralist versions of psychoanalysis that influence the other critics mentioned above. Thus, where the latter would critique the mode of modern subjectivity anticipated in the Shakespearean text, Bloom celebrates its 'invention' by Shakespeare in the most triumphalistic terms: 'When we are wholly human, and know ourselves, we become most like either Hamlet or Falstaff' (Bloom 1999: 745).

To credit the cultural materialist or new historicist version of English dramaturgical history, while remaining suspicious of the universalised and humanistic account of psychological evolution represented by the work of Bloom, requires not only that the paradigm of the self as a deep interior consciousness (and unconsciousness) be seen as an invention which occurs at a particular time, in a particular corner of the world, but also that this invention should be examined in its political, cultural and imperial investments. This hypothesis provides a way to historicise the categories of psychoanalysis – albeit against its own will – and, in so doing, to gain a clearer sense of both their appropriateness and their limitations in the reading of texts. Moreover, if *Hamlet* marks something like the inauguration of that notion of the self as an interior space of drama (or perhaps, an interior space of *trauma* or the interior space of a *dreamer?*), and if Freudian psychoanalysis aims to take that architecture of the self apart, then it becomes apparent why Freudian theory and *Hamlet* appear to have been made for each other all along.

Shakespeare writing Freud

My argument so far has attempted to recognise that Shakespeare precedes psychoanalysis epistemologically, just as he does historically: that is, the modes of narrative, rhetoric, imagery and characterisation that Freud, Rank and Jones encounter in Shakespearean drama help to shape the development of psychoanalytic notions about dreamwork, the operations of the unconscious, and the nature of the self.

Yet this is not perhaps the most commonly held perception of the relation between these two fields of discourse: Shakespearean drama and psychoanalytic theory. More often it is thought that psychoanalysis arrogantly installs itself, historically and epistemologically, prior to Shakespeare, by claiming to 'discover' those universal unconscious tendencies which have characterised human nature throughout history, and have driven the creative expression of artists such as Shakespeare. This allegation, of course, is more than borne out by my reading of Freud, Rank and Jones thus far; but so too is that reverse tendency, according to which the Shakespearean text slips in ahead of psychoanalytic theory, so that at every critical moment of his 'discovery', Freud finds Shakespeare there before him.

Literature can be shown to precede psychoanalysis in other ways as well: Elaine Showalter, for instance, has traced the ways in which the 'case study' of Ophelia was used, during the development of psychiatric practice in the nineteenth century, both in the clinical and in the theoretical setting 'as an account of hysteria or mental breakdown in adolescence' (Showalter 1985: 85–6). Asylum superintendents, such as Hugh Welch Diamond in England and Jean-Martin Charcot in Paris (under whom Freud himself studied), took photographs of their young female patients, encouraging them to adopt the costume, gesture, props and expression of that highly Romanticised version of Ophelia which currently dominated the stage and the pre-Raphaelite canvas alike: 'Charcot's clinic became, as he said, a "living theatre" of female pathology; his women patients were coached in their performances for the camera, and, under hypnosis, were sometimes instructed to play heroines from Shakespeare' (86). It is difficult to imagine a clearer historical instance of the Shakespearean representation of character directing the development of those medical and psychiatric modes of clinical observation out of which psychoanalysis would emerge.

Shoshana Felman approaches the question differently, suggesting that psychoanalytic readings of literary texts can only proceed usefully on the understanding that neither psychoanalysis nor literature can be thought to precede or dictate the other; rather, both fields of discourse supply a major insight that the other lacks:

Psychoanalysis tells us that the fantasy is a fiction, and that consciousness is itself, in a sense, a fantasy-effect. In the same way, literature tells us that authority is a *language effect*, the product or the creation of its own *rhetorical power*: that authority is the *power of fiction*; that authority, therefore, is likewise a fiction.

(Felman 1977: 8)

This shift in the relation between psychoanalysis and literature – so that neither can claim to be 'master' or predecessor or progenitor of the other – destroys the traditional notion that psychoanalytic concepts can be *applied* to literary texts, and replaces it by a process of *implication*:

> bringing analytical questions to bear upon literary questions, *involving* psychoanalysis in the scene of literary analysis . . . the interpreter's role would here be, not to *apply* to the text an acquired science, a preconceived knowledge, but to act as a go-between, to *generate implications* between literature and psychoanalysis – to explore, bring to light and articulate the various (indirect) ways in which the two domains do indeed *implicate each other*, each one finding itself enlightened, informed, but also affected, displaced, by the other.[17]
>
> (Felman 1977: 8–9)

In fact this inter-implication of psychoanalytic and Shakespearean rhetoric is apparent everywhere in Freud. For example, in the notes enclosed with one of his letters to Fliess in 1897, Freud asserts that 'The mechanism of fiction is the same as that of hysterical fantasies.' He goes on to give the example of Goethe, who used a fictional 'fantasy' to protect himself 'from the consequences of his experience', and then comments, 'So Shakespeare was right in juxtaposing fiction and madness (fine frenzy)' (Freud 1985: 251). Of course, this refers to the famous lines from *A Midsummer Night's Dream*:

> The lunatic, the lover, and the poet
> Are of imagination all compact . . .
> The poet's eye, in a fine frenzy rolling,
> Doth glance from heaven to earth, from earth to heaven;
> And as imagination bodies forth
> The forms of things unknown, the poet's pen

Turns them to shapes, and gives to airy nothing
A local habitation and a name.

(5.1.7–17)

A further series of connections – fiction–madness–dream – finds its way into *The Interpretation of Dreams,* again borrowed from Shakespeare:

> Dreams, then, are often most profound when they seem most crazy . . . The Prince in the play, who had to disguise himself as a madman, was behaving just as dreams do in reality; so that we can say of dreams what Hamlet said of himself, concealing the true circumstances under a cloak of wit and unintelligibility: 'I am but mad north-north-west: when the wind is southerly, I know a hawk from a hand-saw!'
>
> (*PFL* 4: 575–6)

And earlier in the same volume: 'the madness of dreams may not be without method and may even be simulated, like that of the Danish prince on whom this shrewd judgement was passed' (*PFL* 4: 126). And again, when debating whether certain 'background thoughts would have sufficed to evoke a dream', Freud once more quotes from *Hamlet*: 'There needs no ghost, my lord, come from the grave / To tell us this' (1.5.131–2; *PFL* 4: 261). What does it mean for Freud to insist that the 'mechanism of fiction is the same as that of hysterical fantasies', and to identify both fiction and mental illness with the 'method' of dreams as well?

For one thing, if the same mechanisms operate in fiction as in dreams and neurotic fantasies, then a Shakespearean play can be psychoanalysed in just the same way that one of Freud's 'real-life neurotics' might be. Conversely, Freud's realisation that dreams and fantasies share the madness and method of literature – itself a Shakespearean notion – must have profoundly shaped both his writing of *The Interpretation of Dreams* and his real-life psycho-analytic practice. Psychoanalysis therefore does not – or it does not only – impose itself on literature; fictional texts – Goethe, Hoffmann, Jensen, Sophocles, but especially and most pervasively Shakespeare – dictate the madness of the psychoanalytic method. All of the dream machineries described by Freud can thus be deployed in the reading of literary texts, because they are at least in part derived *from* literary techniques: condensation and displacement are comparable with metaphor and metonymy; projection, introjection, identification and decomposition have everything in common with various kinds of personification; denial and repression function in a way similar to irony or paradox; and so on.[18] If in this sense, as Felman argues, literature operates as the unconscious of psychoanalysis (Felman 1977: 10), we should not be surprised to discover that there are certain Shakespearean phrases which, in their syntactical form, structure the development of Freud's thought.[19]

As an example, and since Rank can freely associate Polonius (one of Hamlet's 'bad fathers') with Julius Caesar on the basis of the old man's claim to have played the dictator in his youth, I want to examine a condensation that occurs in *The Interpretation of Dreams* between Freud himself and Brutus. For Freud tells us that,

> Strange to say, I really did once play the part of Brutus. I once acted in the scene between Brutus and Caesar from Schiller before an audience of children. I was fourteen years old at the time and was acting with a nephew who was a year my senior.
>
> (*PFL* 4: 552)

This disclosure emerges during a discussion of one of his own dreams, involving an 'evil wish' on the part of Freud's friend Joseph Paneth to have his superior, Professor Fleischl, 'out of the way' and to take his place (*PFL* 4: 623). This wish is compared with Freud's own 'still livelier wish to fill a vacancy' a few years earlier (624), and is further compared to yet another Shakespearean moment, the premature appropriation by Prince Hal of the crown as his father lies dying (*2 Henry IV*, 4.5; cited in *PFL* 4: 624). Both Fleischl and Paneth figure in the dream (along with another of Freud's one-time friends, and later his enemy, Fliess). When Fleischl interrogates him about Paneth, Freud replies '*non vixit*', that is, 'he did not live'. He then turns a hostile gaze on Paneth, who melts into thin air, as does Fleischl: '*I now realized that Ernst Fleischl, too, had been no more than an apparition, a 'revenant' . . . and it seemed to me quite possible that people of that kind only existed as long as one liked and could be got rid of if someone else wished it*' (549). By means of this penetrating and lethal gaze, Freud in the dream wishfully eliminates the two figures who stand in – one as the son, and the other as the father – for Freud's own Oedipalised desire simultaneously to emulate a rival and take the place of a superior.

The only remaining puzzle is the source of this phrase '*non vixit*', which to Freud's bafflement he uses instead of the syntactically more appropriate '*non vivit*' ('he is not alive'). Eventually he locates the word '*vixit*' in an inscription on the bottom of the Kaiser Josef Memorial in the Hofburg in Vienna, and concludes that its occurrence in the dream reflected his unconscious regret 'that the premature death of my brilliant friend P[aneth], whose whole life had been devoted to science, had robbed him of a well-merited claim to a memorial . . . Accordingly, I gave him this memorial in my dream' (*PFL* 4: 551).

These complex displacements manifest, of course, a persistent anxiety that runs through the dreams of the father of psycho-analysis about the credibility of his new discipline in the eyes of its progenitor, science. Killing off those figures in the dream who represent this scientific ego ideal and superego helps, but Freud's analysis requires an alternative identification as well. Thus he continues his concern, in this analysis, with syntax, and this brings him home, at last, to Shakespeare:

> By the rules of dream-interpretation I was even now not entitled to pass from the *Non vixit* derived from my recollection of the Kaiser Josef Memorial to the *Non vivit* required by the sense of the dream-thoughts. There must have been some other element in the dream-thoughts which would help to make the transition possible. It then struck me as noticeable that in the scene in the dream there was a convergence of a hostile and an affectionate current of feeling towards my friend P[aneth], the former being on the surface and the latter concealed, but both of them being represented in the single phrase *Non vixit*. As he had deserved well of science I built him a memorial; but as he was guilty of an evil wish . . . I annihilated him. I noticed that this last sentence had a quite special cadence, and I must have had some model in my mind. Where was an antithesis of this sort to be found, a juxtaposition like this of two opposite reactions towards a single person, both of them claiming to be completely justified and yet not incompatible? Only in one passage in literature – but a passage which makes a profound impression on the reader: in Brutus's speech of self-justification in Shakespeare's *Julius Caesar* . . . 'As Caesar loved me, I weep for him; as he was fortunate, I rejoice at it; as he was valiant, I honour him; but, as he was ambitious, I slew him'

[3.2.24–6]. Were not the formal structure of these sentences and their antithetical meaning precisely the same as in the dream-thought I had uncovered? Thus I had been playing the part of Brutus in the dream . . .

Strange to say, I really did once play the part of Brutus.[20]

(*PFL* 4: 551–2)

It becomes clear that Freud attributes a fundamental importance not so much to the *content* of such 'Speeches in Dreams' (as this section of the treatise is entitled), nor even to their *interpretation*: the main impact that Brutus's lines have on the dream is that they provide a syntactical structure which knits the dream logic together. Even in its apparent absence – the lines are not present in Freud's memory of the dream, but are only recalled after several layers of analysis – Shakespearean rhetoric provides a crucial unconscious syntax, a structure of organisation and articulation, for the dream language.[21]

At this point, therefore, it is possible also to identify various aspects of the Freudian emphasis on language and on vision which will be taken up by Jacques Lacan, the French analyst whose combination of structuralist linguistics with psychoanalytic theory will be the subject of my next chapter. In the first place, the dream clearly marks out a desiring and aggressive relationship between the individual and the rival, the ego and the ego-ideal which it identifies with and desires to replace, assimilate or destroy. This structure of aggressive rivalry will provide the basis for Lacan's development of what he calls 'The Mirror Stage' (Lacan 1977b: 1–7); also for his later discussion of the gaze (Lacan 1979) and his reading of *Hamlet* (Lacan 1977a), in which he focuses on the relation between Hamlet and Laertes.[22] In the second place the Shakespearean rhetoric shapes both the dream and its interpretation; the antithetical syntax of Brutus's lines provides a model, both in Freud's dream and in his theory, for the paradoxical yoking together of love and hostility. Once again, a linguistic and literary figure organises the development of psychoanalytic thought. To rephrase Lacan's famous aphorism that 'the unconscious is structured like a language', I would say instead that in this instance, as elsewhere, the unconscious of psychoanalytic theory is structured exactly like Shakespeare's language.[23]

Shakespeare's femininity

My survey of the initial engagements between Freud, Rank, Jones
and Shakespeare allows me to venture a preliminary assessment
of the advantages and limitations of reading between – or, in
Felman's phrase, 'inter-implicating' – psychoanalytic theory and
Shakespearean drama.

To begin with, the invitation by psychoanalysis to read the
dramatis personae of any given play as projections of unconscious
anxieties or desires can be taken as a corrective to the nineteenth-
century (or Bradleyan) tendency to treat them as 'real people'. But
beyond this, at certain moments the analyses of Freud and his
colleagues also gesture towards the ways in which psychoanalytic
reading will eschew a simple or reductive psychologism; a later
generation of psychoanalytic critics will deliver out of the embry-
onic state in which it inhabits Freud's writing a mode of reading
which, rather than simply inviting the reader to look through the
play into the mind of the protagonist, and thence to the psyche
of the author, instead concentrates on the operation of those
unconscious modes of representation which inter-implicate author,
reader and text alike. Furthermore, emphasis on the unconscious
licenses the psychoanalytic reader to distrust manifest coherencies,
to see texts as sites of struggle between competing meanings and
their contradictory motivations, and also to find new and vital kinds
of significance in those aspects of the text which literary criticism
might be thought most highly qualified to analyse; figures of
speech, rhetorical flourishes, syntactical forms, as manifestations
of possible repressed meanings, can be rescued from their
marginalisation by readings that focus on organic unity of form
and meaning, and thence ramify into entirely different alternative
readings of the texts from which they derive.

Against these putative advantages, opponents of psychoanalytic
reading have put forward a range of objections: that it continues
to 'psychologise' both dramatic characters or the author; that it
pathologises the psyches of its subjects; that it imposes a pre-existing
(Oedipal) interpretive schema, thereby ensuring that it can repeat,
over and over again, its own supposed discoveries; that its privileging of latent rather than manifest meaning brings interpretive
chaos, while its theories of repression and denial, by making
opposites signify the same thing, reduce texts to nonsense; that it
confuses 'reality' with 'fantasy'; that it tends to de-historicise and

depoliticise the plays; and that it reinstalls a phallocentric or masculine-centred model of sexuality.[24]

Some of these objections have been discussed already, if not answered; others will be addressed in subsequent chapters. To my mind, however, the most significant challenges to the process of reading between psychoanalysis and Shakespeare are the last mentioned: the problems of history, politics, sexuality and gender. In the rest of this volume I will argue, therefore, that a productive understanding of the current relation between psychoanalysis and Shakespeare cannot be achieved without a close consideration of the allegations of universalism and ahistoricism. In this regard, the developments during the 1980s and 1990s in new historical, cultural materialist and postcolonial approaches to reading Shakespeare have much to offer psychoanalysis – and perhaps something to gain from it, too. Moreover, it is in this process – whereby psychoanalysis may seek to recognise the cultural and historical specificity of its own 'fantasies' (in particular, the Oedipal family romance) – that familiar assumptions about 'normative' (and therefore about 'pathological') psychology and sexuality are most thoroughly called into question. In this respect psychoanalysis also has the potential to enter into dialogue with both feminism and queer theory.

To foreshadow these last-mentioned developments, it is worth concluding this chapter with some hints about what happens if the avowed psychoanalytic fascination with the peripheral, the scarcely mentioned or the silenced is turned back on these three psychocritical forefathers themselves. One notion that emerges as a result is that of an underlying femininity in Hamlet or – more disturbingly – in Shakespeare. Thus when at one point Jones remarks that 'The maternal influence may also manifest itself by imparting a strikingly tender feminine side to the later character' (Jones 1949: 77), he directs the reader to 'Vining's suggestion that Hamlet really was a woman', and describes the 'femininity' of Shakespeare himself as a critical fact that is 'well known', attested to not only by Bradley but by Harris: 'Whenever we get under the skin, it is Shakespeare's femininity which startles us' (cited in Jones 1949: 77–8, n. 2).[25]

These peculiar and very marginal hints – confined in this text to a footnote – about Shakespeare's or Hamlet's 'femininity' take the place of a far more extended discussion of homosexuality and bisexuality, which constituted nearly the entire second half of the original version of Jones's essay on the play, first published in 1910 and then included in his *Essays in Applied Psycho-Analysis*. There, Jones suggests that because 'the ear is an unconscious equivalent for anus', the means by which Claudius murders Hamlet's father constitutes 'a homosexual assault' (Jones 1951: 326); he then cites the sonnets as proof that 'In a more or less veiled form a pronounced femininity and a readiness to interchange the sexes are prominent characteristics' of Shakespeare's personality (326–7). And he concludes that Hamlet demonstrates towards his father two aspects of the psychoanalytic view of homosexuality: the first is 'mirror-love; Hamlet's father would therefore be his own ideal of himself'; and the second is a 'feminine attitude towards the father' (328). Curiously, when Jones extensively rewrites and expands his study of the play into book length, this discussion of homosexuality and effeminisation disappears almost entirely.

Rank, moreover, replaces the suggestion of Hamlet's or Shakespeare's 'femininity' with the assertion of their misogyny: he suggests that Shakespeare, working through the death of his father immediately prior to writing *Hamlet*, produces a reaction-formation in which his infantile desire for the death of the father is replaced by an overestimation of his value and a corresponding 'disappointment' with the mother: 'Here we find a cause of the playwright's homosexual tendencies' (Rank 1992: 175) – and also, presumably, a cause of *Hamlet*. He goes on to apply this standard psychoanalytic pathologisation of same-sex male desire in relation to *Coriolanus*.

Many recent critics, of course, have turned away in disappointment from psychoanalytic theory precisely because of this tendency to conflate homosexuality either with effeminisation or with misogyny, and in either case to view it as an abnormality, a retardation of the individual's sexual development at an immature phase. But Chapter 5 of this volume will consider some more recent exchanges that have occurred between the psychoanalytic corpus and those bodies of work produced by queer theorists and critics who refuse to read their Shakespeare straight.

As for the question of femininity itself, Jones goes on to describe a close attachment between Hamlet and Gertrude prior to the play's beginning, emphasising Claudius's judgement that the Queen 'Lives almost by his looks' (4.7.12), and suggesting that Ophelia represents the Prince's choice of a chaste, innocent opposite to his mother (Jones 1949: 77–100). In this account, then, the rest of the play constitutes a repression of this prior maternal intimacy in favour of the all-important relation to the father, so that once again psychoanalytic theory takes its cue from Shakespeare, insofar as Freud's Oedipal theory normatises the replacement of the maternal relation by the paternal. Each of my subsequent chapters will address the implications of this repression of the maternal feminine for the psychoanalytic reading of the Shakespearean text. In particular, the next chapter will consider the link between femininity and the more radical aspects of Lacanian theory, and how this association is first explored in Lacan's reading of *Hamlet*, and then foreclosed by his move to *King Lear*.

2
In Paris

If a single scene could function as a paradigm for the first generation of psychoanalytic criticism of Shakespeare, it would be Hamlet's writing on his 'tables' in response to the Ghost's injunction to remember him – a moment that in Freudian terms represents the inscription upon the psyche of the superegoic law of the father. It also demonstrates that focus upon the written word which will preoccupy psychoanalysis and literary criticism alike: certain post-Freudian psychoanalytic readings of Shakespeare will be characterised precisely by their attempts to trace the composition and transmission of the *letter*, in every sense of that word.

As I discussed in the preceding chapter, though, Hamlet's repetition of the paternal command is not entirely faithful: he does not write a literal translation of the words uttered by his ghostly father, but rather a substitute phrase. Similarly, French psychoanalytic theory during the 1950s and 1960s concerned itself with the misappropriation or reappropriation of the 'letter' of the Freudian law. The tenor of this post-Freudian reading is thus equally well expressed by the scene – not enacted on stage but only recounted by the Prince – in which a letter from Claudius sending Hamlet to his execution is substituted for another that brings about the deaths of Rosencrantz and Guildenstern. And it is this scene, of the reinscription and redirection of the lethal letter of the paternal name and law, that captivates the dominant figure in French post-Freudian psychoanalysis, the theorist and clinician Jacques Lacan. This chapter will outline the main features of Lacan's theory of the subject by means of an exegesis of his reading of *Hamlet*, while at the same time demonstrating the ways in which the reading of Shakespeare once again serves as an occasion and as a strategy for the epistemological and institutional development of psychoanalytic thought. As I will argue, Hamlet's redirection of the letter functions as an allegory not only for Lacan's own theory, but also of his own position as a filial reader – a reinterpreter and rewriter – of the letter of the Freudian law.

A digression: ego trips

Lacan, of course, designated his project the 'Return to Freud', claiming not to be countersigning the Freudian text, or giving it a new direction, but rather insisting that he was returning it to (and returning to it) the destination or destiny originally intended by its author. For him, an intervening generation of Freudian 'interpreters' had misappropriated Freudian psychoanalysis, sending it down the wrong track altogether. As Lacan rewrites both Freud and Shakespeare, therefore, he simultaneously writes off the dominant traditions of North American psychoanalysis.

The Second World War precipitated a diaspora among psychoanalytic theorists and practitioners. In the United States, in particular, a revised psychoanalysis took hold, under the auspices of Rudolph Loewenstein, Erik Erikson and Heinz Hartmann, which reversed Freud's early and late emphasis on the primacy of the unconscious over the ego. The dominant North American psychoanalytic movements tended to focus on the formation and strengthening of the ego (Roudinesco 1990: 167), believing that the 'psychic health' of the 'individual' depended upon the absorption, aided by the therapeutic process of analysis, of unruly unconscious elements into an ever-expanding consciousness.

This 'ego psychology', as it came to be called, had a considerable impact upon the psychoanalytic reading of Shakespeare. Erik Erikson, one of the leading figures in the development of American ego psychology, at one point found it productive, like his psychoanalytic predecessors, to press *Hamlet* into the service of his emerging theoretical corpus: in his discussion of identity formation during youth, he reads Hamlet as a delayed adolescent, dealing with his developmental crisis by trying out different identities (Erikson 1968: 236–60). Norman Holland demonstrates how dominant the ego-integrative focus had become by 1964, the year in which he compiled his massive survey of psychoanalytic Shakespeare criticism, when he argues that the psychoanalytic critic 'can help, as no other critic can, an audience to experience an essential function of works of art – the transmutation of grotesque unconscious fantasies into meaningful social, moral, or intellectual wholeness' (Holland 1964: 323).

The application of ego-psychological method specifically to *Hamlet* is more recently represented by the work of Avi Erlich, whose study of *Hamlet's Absent Father* aims 'to describe the ways in which Shakespeare's conscious and unconscious creativity weave together to determine the form and content of *Hamlet*' (Erlich 1977: vii). In agreement with both Holland and Erikson – the latter is cited with approval (199–200) – Erlich aims to press the unruly elements of the drama into the service of 'moral transcendence' (42) and conscious unity, 'viewing the play as the product of Shakespeare's whole mind' (vii).

Along with Freud, Rank and Jones, Erlich reads the psychic conflicts of the protagonist as a reflection of those of its author; moreover, he identifies the two most closely by seeing Hamlet as characterised, above all else, by a preoccupation with writing. He thus perpetuates the psychoanalytic and literary critical concern with the representation of writing itself, which, according to his theoretical paradigm, however, is considered primarily a strategy for the strengthening and maturation of the ego. Thus in his chapter on 'Managing the Unconscious' he comments that 'For Shakespeare, writing was a successful adaptive mechanism against being overwhelmed by the unconscious' (Erlich 1977: 208). The production of the play becomes a kind of psychotherapy, by which Shakespeare can learn from Hamlet's inability to deal with his unconscious conflicts: 'the portrait of failure *was* a success for Shakespeare – and for us. He was able to watch from a distance Hamlet's self-destruction and thereby to gain mastery from it.' And the audience can derive a similar benefit: 'We too can distance Hamlet's familial vicissitudes, and wish . . . and thereby help create, our own psychic health' (251–2).

In many respects, the influence of ego psychology had much in common with that of Carl Jung, who also considered that Freud overemphasised the power of the unconscious, and thus espoused instead the agency of what he called the 'Self', which could be 'realised' by means of the recognition and assimilation of the unconscious aspects of the psyche (the shadow, the anima/animus, the id and so on).[1] Thus, for example, Alex Aronson applies Jungian theory in *Shakespeare and the Ocular Proof* (1995) when he explores the imagery of perception and blindness in the plays as manifestations of the poet's 'evanescent Self' which dissipates and becomes fused with a transpersonal self. In an earlier and more extended work, *Symbol and Psyche in Shakespeare* (1972), Aronson discusses Jung's break with the Freudian emphasis on pathology and neurosis, and his alternative emphasis on the human quest for 'wholeness' (Aronson 1972: 30). Jungian theory thus binds together therapy, transcendence, and psychic unification; the Jungian literary critic aims to trace, in Shakespeare's works, the process of 'individuation' or 'self-realization', the integration by consciousness of those instinctual, libidinal and unconscious forces most opposed to it (29).

Aronson appears to find it rather difficult to assimilate *Hamlet* to this project. His most extended comment on the main plot of the play reads as follows:

> On the level of primeval mythology, Hamlet's 'revenge', his killing both uncle and mother, may then be interpreted as one of the most significant events in a personalized history of the evolution of human consciousness: 'In contrast to the passive, self-absorbed and narcissistic resistance to the mother, the fleeting defiance and self-destruction, this strengthening of masculine consciousness leads the ego to pit itself against the supremacy of the matriarchate'.[2]
>
> (Aronson 1972: 236)

Aronson is here citing with approval a work by Erich Neumann entitled *The Origins and History of Consciousness* (1962). Another characteristic of the Jungian reading of Shakespeare can be clearly identified here: a grandiose universalism, according to which dramatic characters are seen not merely as reflections of the author's psyche but as manifestations of primeval 'archetypes' existing in a 'collective unconscious' shared by the entire human race. According to Aronson's version, the mascu-line ego thus can only achieve self-realisation by means of its transcendence of the 'narcissistic' and destructive feminine

principle, the anima. At times this conflict between the masculine
ego and the anima will be resolved as their mutual assimilation into
the overall unity of the self; the anima can even be the means
by which the ego comes to 'wholeness' (Aronson 1992: 304). But
very often it seems that the feminine principle represents 'an
archetype of evil basically matriarchal in nature' (229), which
for 'human consciousness' to evolve must be repressed altogether,
or killed, as in the final scene of *Hamlet*. The foreclosure of
a primordial feminine relation (in Freud the maternal, in Jung
the matriarchal) provides a troubling undercurrent running
through psychoanalytic theory from Freud, to Jungian and ego
psychology, to Lacan, as I will show.

Along with a striking degree of misogyny, Jungian rhetoric
clearly demonstrates a thoroughgoing humanism: Aronson
concerns himself with the 'evolution of human consciousness'
and the development of the Self as the archetype of wholeness. In
a comparable way Erlich, like the ego psychologists, searches for
'moral transcendence' and 'psychic health' in the assimilation
of unconscious conflict into conscious mastery. Both projects
repress those anti-humanist and anti-Enlightenment tendencies
which, as I argued in the preceding chapter, constitute an alternative strain in Freudian thought. It is these alternative elements,
however – in direct opposition to the ego-psychological and
Jungian tendencies – that the theory and practice of Jacques
Lacan will claim to 'return to Freud'.

The Lacanian return

It would be misleading to suggest that an emphasis on rationality
and the assimilation of unconscious elements into consciousness
is altogether lacking in the first generation of psychoanalytic
readings of Shakespeare. Indeed, Rank's description of drama as
a kind of 'psychic' hygiene (Rank 1992: 50) comes very close to
the therapeutic and integrative imperatives of both Erlich's ego-
psychological and Aronson's Jungian programmes. Similarly,
Jacqueline Rose has argued that the reading of *Hamlet* by Ernest
Jones

> belongs to that psychoanalytic project which restores to ration-
> ality or brings to light, placing what was formerly unconscious
> or unmanageable under the ego's mastery or control. It is a

project which has been read directly out of Freud's much contested statement '*Wo Es war, soll Ich werden*', translated by Strachey 'Where id was, there ego shall be'.

(Rose 1986: 132; citing *PFL* 2: 112)

Freud's English translator, James Strachey, uses the Latin *id* in place of the German term *Es*, which in fact simply means *it*. *Das Es* is Freud's designation, in his later work (sometimes called his 'second topography'), for the instinctual aspects of the unconscious; the second component is the *Ich*, the *I* (or in Strachey's translation the *ego*), which constitutes the collected defensive mechanisms that the psyche brings into play in response to anxiety; the third is the *Uber-Ich*, the *over-I* (Strachey's *superego*), comprising internalised parental prohibitions and demands, acting as judge or censor of the ego and id.[3]

In this topography, the ego actually remains very dependent on, and reactive to, the id and superego, and Freud emphasises the passivity rather than the agency of the subject, commenting that he gives the name 'it' to that part of the mind that produces the impression that 'we are "lived" by unknown and uncontrollable forces' (Freud *PFL* 11: 362; citing Georg Groddeck, following Nietzsche). However, many of Freud's followers – including Jung and the ego psychologists, and also, in Rose's account, Ernest Jones – tended to conflate the ego with Freud's earlier notion of the 'conscious-preconscious system', which he defined against the unconscious in his first topography. Such a conflation transfers to the ego a capacity to act as an overall organising principle, thereby attributing to it considerably more agency and mastery than Freud himself allows. It is in this regard that Rose highlights the integrative interpretation given by an ego-based psychoanalysis to the phrase cited above. 'Where it was, there I shall be' is translated, in this context, as meaning that where there was unconscious conflict and instinctual demand, (ego-driven) analysis shall produce agency, organisation and individuation.

Always, though, the letter of the Freudian law proves peculiarly liable to redirection. Lacan appropriates this aphorism, rereading it not as a guarantee of the attainment of conscious mastery by the ego, but rather as an ethical obligation of psychoanalysis to bring the subject, the 'I', back to its dependence upon the unconscious, *das Es*, the 'it' or 'that'. So, at one point, Lacan translates the phrase as 'I must come to the place where that was'

(Lacan 1977b: 171) – 'that', of course, being the Lacanian version of the id: the symbolic order or Other.

In this sense, Lacan either restores to psychoanalysis or implants in it a radical anti-humanism denied by ego psychology and Jungianism alike. Where ego psychology fantasises about conscious mastery and self-realisation – about something Lacan sarcastically calls 'the sociological poem of the *autonomous ego*' – Lacanian psychoanalysis aims to discover 'the self's radical ex-centricity to itself' (Lacan 1977b: 171), thereby reiterating Freud's own emphasis on the modern subject's dis-ease, its neurotic maladaption to and dislocation from its own place in society and culture (*PFL* 12: 338; Lacan 1977b: 28).

Lacan conducted his campaign against ego psychology throughout the 1950s, in his writings and in the famous fortnightly seminar he gave in Paris for trainee analysts. In the second series of this seminar, for example, he explicitly criticises the attempt to produce an illusory consolidation of the ego in the 'therapeutic mirror': 'The subject reconcentrates his own imaginary ego essentially in the form of the analyst's ego' (Lacan 1988b: 245). For Lacan, this pursuit of integrity by analysis replicates precisely those defensive and retrograde fantasies that are characteristic of the ego itself. The ego – and its acolytes, the ego psychologists – thus remains caught in the realm that Lacan calls the 'imaginary', a realm of illusory narcissism typified by the potential for mutual fascination between analysand and analyst.

In contrast, Lacan's method (at least during the 1950s) focuses on narrating the analysand's experience of her/his subjection to the unconscious, which Lacan calls the Other, and which he relates to the symbolic order, the system of signification or language: 'That is the final relation of the subject to a genuine Other, to the Other who gives the answer one doesn't expect' (Lacan 1988b: 246). He thus moves away from the conception of an individuated *ego* or a *self* which aims to integrate its own psychic components, instead propounding a theory of the *subject*, which comes into being as a signifier, a function within the symbolic order, like the grammatical subject of the sentence. This allows him to produce another version of the Freudian aphorism: punning on the French pronunciation of the letter *S*, standing here for 'subject', and on the German *Es* or id, Lacan signals a movement from an *ego* possessing an imaginary agency to a *subject* defined by its *subjection to* a symbolic order that precedes, encompasses and constitutes it: '*Wo Es war,*

soll Ich werden. This *Es*, take it as the letter *S*. It is there, it is always
there. It is the subject . . . Where the *S* was, there the *Ich* should
be' (246). Lacan thus introduces a split within Freud's *Ich*, which
the German term does not admit, but which French does: between
the *moi* (the *me* or *ego*, which remains within the imaginary) and
the *je* (the *I*, the *subject* of the unconscious, which inhabits
the symbolic).[4] The new translation thus describes an obligation
on the part of psychoanalysis to help the ego (*Ich, moi*) to approach
(although it will never quite get there) full realisation of its status
as subject (*S, je*) to the Other.

Lacan's 'linguistic turn' at this point – his emphasis on the
constitutive role played by language in the constitution of human
subjectivity – reflects the influence of structuralism. That is to
say, Lacan combines a determination to (re)read Freud as rigorously as possible with an interest in the theories of Swiss linguist
Ferdinand de Saussure, as expounded in the latter's *Course in
General Linguistics*, published in 1916 – written not by Saussure
himself but, as with most of Lacan's works too, by his students,
based on their notes from seminars. Saussure considered that
each of the signs that comprise any signifying system is constituted
by a *signifier* (or what Saussure called the sound-image; for example,
the word) and a *signified* (the concept to which the word attaches).
For the French structuralists (the early Lacan, Claude Lévi-Strauss,
Roland Barthes, the early Michel Foucault, Louis Althusser)
Saussure's key insight was the suggestion that for any given
sign, the association between signifier and signified – between word
and meaning, for example – is *arbitrary*, that is to say it is not natural,
not determined by any real, inherent or consistent relation.
The operation of language thus depends not on the fixity of
the union between particular signifiers and their signifieds; the
ability to signify consists solely in the *differences* between signifiers:
'signs function, then, not through their intrinsic value but through
their relative position . . . in language there are only *differences
without positive terms*' (Saussure 1966: 118, 120).[5]

In his seminars during the 1950s, Lacan often displays his debt
to Saussure – at one point, for example, using the most famous of
all Shakespearean speeches to rehearse the structuralist theory
of the sign:

This *To be or not to be* is an entirely verbal story. A very funny
comedian tried showing how Shakespeare came upon it,

scratching his head – *to be or not* . . . and he would start again –
to be or not . . . *to be*. If that's funny, that's because this moment
is when the entire dimension of language comes into focus.

(Lacan 1988b: 233)

It's not very funny, of course, but if nevertheless 'the entire
dimension of language' is embodied by this joke, it is because even
the most crucial of signifiers (the verb 'to be', signifying existence
itself) achieves meaning only by virtue of its difference from
another signifier – in this case its opposite or negation (the phrase
'not to be'). For Lacan, this 'difference without positive terms'
of the linguistic system brings meaning into being, and, with it,
the speaking subject. Hamlet, like any 'subject' in the psychoanalytic sense of that word, comes into existence in this difference
between signifiers.

Lacan's debt to both structuralism and to literature for the
itinerary of his 'return to Freud' comes into focus most clearly and
concisely in his revised version of a seminar first delivered during
the season of 1954–5, which involves his exegesis of Edgar Allan
Poe's 'The Purloined Letter'. Set in Restoration France, the story
became popular in that country after its translation by Baudelaire,
and subsequently provided the occasion for a psychoanalysis of
its author by the prima donna of French psychoanalysis, Freud's
friend and one of his heirs (and Lacan's 'phallic mother'), Marie
Bonaparte. The narrative rests upon an incriminating letter written
by the Queen to some undisclosed other party, which is stolen
in her full sight by a machiavellian Minister, during an audience
with the royal couple – at which moment, as the Minister realises,
the Queen cannot possibly accuse the thief for fear of exposing
herself to the King. The police, having searched the Minister's
apartment thoroughly, enlist the help of Poe's hero, the detective
Dupin, who in the course of a series of mathematical digressions,
reveals that he has already reappropriated the letter. Having
deduced that the Minister would hide it where he thought no one
would look – that is, in a location a 'little *too* self-evident', turned
inside-out and readdressed and then 'carelessly' propped up on
an otherwise bare mantelpiece – Dupin makes a visit to the criminal
and, during a pre-arranged diversion, substitutes for the purloined
letter another identically disguised envelope.

Lacan's seminar uses the tale to illustrate 'that it is the symbolic
order which is constitutive for the subject – by demonstrating in
[Poe's] story the decisive orientation which the subject receives

from the itinerary of a signifier' (Lacan 1972: 40). His reading of 'The Purloined Letter' argues, at every point, that the positions of the various characters, their relative power and agency, depend not upon any agency inherent in them but upon their 'Falling in possession of the letter' – an ambiguous phrase which suggests that each act of 'purloining' of the letter involves a concomitant possession *by* the letter, and by the system within which it circulates (60). The letter, which Lacan calls a 'pure signifier' – in Saussurian terms, it is determined only by its position in the system and not by its 'positivity' or contents, which the reader never discovers – holds and places each character within the symbolic system of the narrative (45). Thus it is the signifier that assigns to each character her or his ultimate itinerary:

> If what Freud discovered and rediscovers with a perpetually increasing sense of shock has a meaning, it is that the displacement of the signifier determines the subjects in their acts, in their destiny, in their refusals, in their blindnesses, in their end and in their fate . . . and that, willingly or not, everything that might be considered the stuff of psychology . . . will follow the path of the signifier.
>
> (Lacan 1972: 60)

As I will show, Lacan's rereading of Freud's rereading of *Hamlet* enacts a structuralist revision that corresponds in all its major points to his reading of 'The Purloined Letter'. Thus, where the Jungians turned psychoanalysis into a universal mythology, and the ego psychologists used it as a personalised psychology, Lacan exposes the arrangement of Freud's 'family romance' and produces from Shakespeare's play not a positive content, but rather a set of relations that are shown to be constitutive of the psychoanalytic account of subjectivity and inter-subjectivity. However, it is also necessary to understand how Lacan's structuralism, his 'linguistic turn', functions as a key strategy in his long war against his rivals in the French psychoanalytic establishment for a pre-eminent claim to the Freudian legacy.

The Lacanian desire

Throughout the 1950s and 1960s, Lacan was fighting to perpetuate the establishment of psychoanalysis as a discipline in its own right, 'reducible to neither neurobiology, nor medicine, nor pedagogy, nor psychology, nor sociology, nor the study of institutions, nor ethnology, nor mythology, nor the science of communication, nor linguistics' (Roudinesco 1990: 238). He was also, of course, concerned to consolidate his own controversial position as the leading Freudian theorist of the post-war scene.

In particular, he opposed Sacha Nacht's attempts, as president of the Société Psychanalytique de Paris (SPP), to facilitate the integration of psychoanalysis with medicine – this move being supported by Marie Bonaparte, whose power within French psycho-analysis Lacan opposed institutionally, as well as specifically attacking her analysis of Poe in his 'Seminar on "The Purloined Letter"'. As the result of a series of complex disciplinary and personal battles, Lacan and his supporters seceded from the SPP, and co-operated in the establishment in 1953 of the Société Française de Psychanalyse (SFP) with another of Lacan's peers, Daniel Lagache.

During the ensuing decade, Lacan's institutional desire was directed towards the inauguration of the SFP, by means of the inter-implication of structuralism and Freudianism, as 'the political seat of the new Freudian orthodoxy: a Counter-Reformation movement in the face of the adaptive ideals from across the Atlantic' (Roudinesco 1990: 254) – that is to say, in the face of North American ego psychology.

Ultimately, though, the SFP did not address itself with sufficient dedication to the Lacanian return to Freud. Lagache, for instance, still favoured a rapprochement between psychoanalysis and psychology; others in the Société continued to resist and criticise the Lacanian innovations. After ten years – still subject to a sentence of excommunication from the International Psychoanalytic Association, which would not recognise the SFP as long as he continued to train its members – Lacan announced, during the inaugural seminar of his series on 'The Four Fundamental Concepts of Psychoanalysis' on 15 January 1963, his intention to found his own school, which would eventually become known as the École Freudienne de Paris (Roudinesco 1990: 361–9).

Thus, over the course of a decade, Lacan defined himself and his theory – by a combination of institutional secession and epistemological incorporation – against the two disciplines that he believed threatened the development of psychoanalytic 'science' proper, namely medicine and psychology, and simultaneously against their prospective proponents, his closest rivals in France,

Nacht and Lagache. All three men had once been in analysis with Loewenstein, a progenitor of North American ego psychology; in this way, of course, Lacan was also abandoning the theory and practice of one 'father' – his former analyst – in favour of the grand(er)father, Freud himself.

In this highly charged institutional context, it becomes vital for Lacan to stand in the place of Freud by rereading the texts through which psychoanalysis was first articulated: especially *Oedipus Rex* and *Hamlet*. Lacan's title for his 1958–9 seminars, 'Desire and its Interpretation', deliberately echoes the title of Freud's own foundational text, *The Interpretation of Dreams*, inasmuch as Lacan's notion of 'desire' replaces the Freudian notion of wish-fulfilment, which was supposed to motivate the dreamwork (Lupton and Reinhard 1993: 67).

Moreover, literature, as the privileged field within which structuralist linguistics was currently being promulgated, also enabled Lacan to pursue his other main project, the transposition of Freudianism into a structuralist key. And so, repeating Freud's strategy half a century earlier in the midst of his institutional wars of secession and independence, Lacan stakes out Shakespearean tragedy as the field of contest that best favours his tactics; hence his particular concentration upon those sections of *The Interpretation of Dreams* which were devoted to Shakespeare's play. These parts of the seminar were later published in French under the suggestive title of '*Hamlet, par Lacan*' (Lacan 1981–3), and translated into English as 'Desire and the Interpretation of Desire in *Hamlet*' (1977a).

In this work Lacan announces that 'The drama of Hamlet makes it possible for us to arrive at an exemplary articulation of this function' – that is, of his theory of the relations between subject, object and desire – 'and this is why we have such a persistent interest in the *structure* of Shakespeare's play' (Lacan 1977a: 28, emphasis added).[6] The seminar goes on to read *Hamlet* as an exemplary structure, focusing on four paradigmatic moments, corresponding to four fundamental components of the Lacanian topography: the encounter between Hamlet and Ophelia in her closet demonstrates the ego's captivation within an imaginary fantasy; Hamlet's redirection of the letter from Claudius on the ship allegorises his subjection to the symbolic order; the scene of rivalry between Laertes and Hamlet at Ophelia's grave identifies the emerging place of the real in Lacanian theory; the final duel with its resulting four deaths stages the interrelationship of the three aforementioned schemas.

Insofar as Lacan's reading of the last scene of the play thus sums up those developments by which he was mobilising his theoretical apparatus against his foremost enemies and competitors, it is worth examining first.

Points of exchange

In a move that echoes Freud's favourite lines from *Julius Caesar* about an ambivalent relation of love and hostility towards the idealised other, Lacan emphasises Hamlet's relationship of rivalry with Laertes.

In doing so he congratulates Shakespeare on a unique psychological acumen – another echo of an earlier psychoanalytic generation – evidenced by the playwright's discovery in advance of what the psychoanalyst wishes to install as fact: 'We cannot help pausing for a moment to consider the soundness of the connection advanced by Shakespeare, in which you will recognize the dialectic of what is already a long-familiar moment in our dialogue, the mirror stage' (Lacan 1977a: 31). Lacan refers here – as does Shakespeare, he suggests – to his own early theory of the captivation of the six- to eighteen-month-old infant by its first sight of its own image in a mirror:

> Unable as yet to walk, or even to stand up, and held tightly as he is by some support, human or artificial . . . he nevertheless overcomes, in a flutter of jubilant activity, the obstructions of his support and, fixing his attitude in a slightly leaning-forward position, in order to hold it in his gaze, brings back an instantaneous aspect of the image.
>
> (Lacan 1977b: 1–2)

According to Lacan, what makes this moment paradigmatic is that, for the first time, the child has recognised its own image. The child sees its 'self' and in the process initiates the formation of an 'I', insofar as its relation to the reflected image constitutes '*an identification*, in the full sense that analysis gives to the term: namely, the transformation that takes place in the subject when he assumes an image' (Lacan 1977b: 2). The infant 'assumes' its specular image in several senses of the word: first, the child assumes or presumes that what it sees is indeed itself as it is now; second, it takes on the attributes of that image (as in the phrase 'to assume responsibility'); and third, it pretends to be identical with that image (as in the phrase 'to assume a false identity'). Lacan wants to stress primarily that in all these aspects the child's identification with the image is inevitably a false assumption, characterised by what he calls *méconnaissance*, 'misrecognition'. The image isn't really the child at all, very obviously, because it's just a reflection, but also because the mirror-image appears to be grown up and well co-ordinated, and to have mastery over its own body – to a far greater degree, that is, than the infant itself, which although it appears to be standing by itself, is actually held up to the mirror by 'some support, human or artificial', and is thus 'still sunk in . . . motor incapacity and nursling dependence' (2). The mirror stage, then, turns out to be a case of mistaken identity, which, for Lacan, provides a 'primordial' scene, a dress-rehearsal for the way in which the subject will eventually come into being as utterly dependent upon language for (self-)representation and therefore always lacking, always alienated.

It is important to stress that, for Lacan, this scene constitutes not so much a phase in developmental psychology as a mode of functioning that will characterise the subject's relations to the objects of desire throughout her or his existence. Rather than a stage in time, the mirror relation provides a spatial stage in which subjectivity is performed; the formation of the 'I' thus occurs continually and 'in a fictional direction', like a series of roles being played, or, as Lacan says elsewhere, the superimposition of a series of coats from the props department of the ego (Lacan 1988b: 155). 'The *mirror stage* is a drama whose internal thrust is precipitated from insufficiency to anticipation' (Lacan 1977b: 4).

The specular scene thus exemplifies a precipitate, insufficient and anticipatory form of the subject of language; precisely, in fact, the qualities of that fantasised and misrecognised ego, whose therapeutic over-valuation by ego psychology Lacan attacks so determinedly. This mirror stage 'manufactures for the subject . . . the armour of an alienating identity' (Lacan 1977b: 4). This fictional identity provides a fantasy of power or agency, as well as a defence, weaponry or armoury. Thus Lacan associates the mirror identification with aggressivity: because the ideal image is desired, and because it cannot be reached, it also becomes the focus of the ego's insecurity and hostility: 'the impotence of a pure consciousness to master any situation; a voyeuristic-sadistic idealization of the sexual relation; a personality that realizes itself only in suicide; a consciousness of the other that can be satisfied only by Hegelian murder' (6). Each of these attributes will be applicable to Lacan's reading of *Hamlet*, but in particular, the reference to 'Hegelian murder' reveals Lacan's important debt to Hegel's dialectic of 'lordship and bondage' in which each term remains locked for its self-definition on an aggressive dependence on the other: the slave cannot be a slave without the master, and vice versa; the only possible outcome is either a continuation of the dialectic, or its dissolution in a murder of the other that would simultaneously be a suicide for the self (Hegel 1977: 111–19).

This aspect of aggressivity provides a point of entry into Lacan's reading of the specular relations in Shakespeare's play. Hamlet, he asserts, agrees to the final duel with Laertes – and here Lacan returns to the search for that which motivates the protagonist's action or inaction – because he remains caught in an imaginary identification with his rival, who thus occupies the place of the ideal ego in the mirror stage:

> He is interested for the sake of honor – what Hegel calls the fight for pure prestige – interested for the sake of honor in a contest that pits him against a rival whom he moreover admires . . .
>
> What is expressly articulated in the text – . . . within a parody – is that at this point Laertes is for Hamlet his double [*semblable*] . . . : 'I take him to be a soul of great article, and his infusion of such dearth and rareness as, to make true diction of him, his semblable is his mirror, and who else would trace him, his umbrage, nothing more' [5.2.116–20].
>
> The image of the other, as you see, is presented here as completely absorbing the beholder . . . The playwright situates the basis of aggressivity in this paroxysm of absorption in the imaginary register, formally expressed as a mirror relationship, a mirrored relation. The one you fight is the one you admire the most. The ego ideal is also, according to Hegel's formula which says that coexistence is impossible, the one you have to kill.
>
> (Lacan 1977a: 31)

Lacan goes on to point out that Hamlet's attitude to the duel, as illustrated by his parodic response to the ludicrous messenger

Osric, appears 'fictive'; he regards this specular aggressivity as 'sham, a mirage' (Lacan 1977a: 32). In this way, Lacan suggests that Hamlet remains, at this stage, captivated within an imaginary order of relations: he cannot see the danger. The imaginary – the first of Lacan's three 'registers' – will always be characterised by a degree of blindness: in its intense focus on the idealised specular image, the 'I' remains unaware that it is itself subject to a gaze from elsewhere. Hamlet thus 'does enter into the game . . . The foils are blunted only in his deluded vision' (32).

The implication that Hamlet is not conscious of the rules of the game he now enters implies the introduction of another, a third term which dictates the position of the duellers, embodying the function of the second of Lacan's three 'registers', the symbolic. 'The tournament puts Hamlet in the position of being the one who, in the wager, takes up the side of Claudius, his uncle and stepfather. He thus wears another man's colors' (Lacan 1977a: 29). Hamlet thus stands in the place dictated by the Other, represented here by the one who has plotted the co-ordinates of the conflict. In clinical terms Lacan suggests that Hamlet's condition in the play corresponds to that of the obsessional neurotic, who, like the ego caught in imaginary captivation, is characterised by preci-pitancy, lack of maturation: 'Hamlet is constantly suspended in the time of the Other, throughout the entire story until the very end' (17). This is the Lacanian explanation of his incapacity to kill Claudius when he finds him praying after the Mousetrap scene – it is not the 'hour of the Other' (18). Bondage to the 'time of the Other' is a synonym for Lacan's notions that subjectivity is in thrall to the unconscious and the symbolic order.

In the final scene, then, still deluded, Hamlet 'rushes into a trap laid by the Other' (Lacan 1977a: 19); that is, the duel with Laertes. He has gone into the fight, as Lacan puts it, 'without, shall we say, his phallus' (32). In Lacanian theory, the phallus does not mean the penis – although the latter may, metonymically, function as a signifier of access to the phallus. The phallus, to put it simply, is the transcendental signifier of power, that term which remains beyond the play of the signifying chain but which guarantees the meaning of each of its signs. The phallus thus embodies the subject's desire, that is, in Lacanian terms, 'the desire of the Other' – mastery over the symbolic order, over meaning, over the unconscious. In this context Lacan puns, in his reading of *Hamlet*, on the word 'will', which functions just as it did for Shakespeare both as phallic synonym and as a word for the supposed capacity of the individual subject to intend and effect change. Hamlet lacks this 'will', this access to symbolic mastery, insofar as he remains at the beck and call of his two very phallic fathers, the Ghost and Claudius.

During the final scene, however, the positions change. Like the analysand during the process of Lacanian analysis, Hamlet is able to move from a position of blindness and incapacity to one of agency; he moves, that is, out of the imaginary captivation of the duel and into a realisation of his position within the three-way structure of symbolic order, bringing both Claudius and Gertrude into the game. Hamlet can move from his position of imaginary blindness and into the apparent mastery of the symbolic order as a result of what Lacan, in his discussion of Poe's 'Purloined Letter', called 'falling in possession of the letter': the exchange of rapiers gives him momentary possession of the 'phallic' signifier, the rapier tipped with poison:

> In their scuffle after Laertes scores the hit from which Hamlet will die, the point changes hands . . . Hamlet can receive the instrument of death only from the other, and that it is located outside the realm of what can actually be represented on the stage. The drama of the fulfillment of Hamlet's desire is played out beyond the pomp of the tournament, beyond his rivalry with that more handsome double, the version of himself that he can love. In that realm beyond, there is the phallus. Ultimately the encounter with the other serves only to enable Hamlet to identify himself with the fatal signifier.
>
> (Lacan 1977a: 32)

Lacan's description of that 'fatal signifier', which the poisoned rapier represents, recalls a number of important features of his theory of the symbolic order. First, access to phallic agency, for the subject-as-signifier, derives only from the Other, the symbolic order, which is always located somewhere else, 'in that realm beyond'. Second, just as in 'The Purloined Letter', the position of mastery apparently granted by the phallic signifier proves as illusory and as ephemeral as that imagined by the ego in its mirror fascination. Third, the phallus turns out to be 'fatal' – remaining, that is, in the service of the death drive. Every object of desire is phallic; every one, looked at another way, is also a stand-in for death, a memento mori, like the famous elongated skull in Holbein's painting of *The Ambassadors*, with which Lacan becomes so entranced in his later seminars (Lacan 1979: 85–92).

When discussing the invitation that Claudius makes to Hamlet to engage in the duel with Laertes, therefore, Lacan emphasises the stakes, the quantity and value of objects wagered:

> These precious objects, gathered together in all their splendor, are staked against death. This is what gives their presentation the character of what is called a *vanitas* in the religious tradition. This is how all objects are presented, all the stakes in the world of human desire – the objects *a*.
>
> (Lacan 1977a: 30)

The high monetary and cultural value of these objects, which Hamlet might win, identifies them for Lacan as *objets a* (with a pun in French on *objets d'art*). In Lacan's algebra, the *objet petit a*, the object as other-with-a-small-o (in French, *autre*), is so called to distinguish it from the capitalised Other (*Autre*), the symbolic order, or elsewhere, the unconscious. These little-o other objects stand in for the phallus, which in turn represents the big-O object of desire, the Other, and hence the mastery of the symbolic order. When Hamlet says to Laertes, 'I'll be your foil', then – a pun to which Lacan devotes several pages of detailed linguistic analysis – he moves beyond an imaginary identification with his *semblable* and towards a symbolic form of 'identification with the mortal phallus', which, however, 'will be able to appear only with the disappearance of the subject himself' (Lacan 1977a: 34). The apparent mastery promised by possession *of* the phallus comes at the cost of possession *by* the phallus. When phallic power 'appears' within the symbolic order, it eclipses the position of the subject itself. To put this in Freudian terms, when the unconscious manifests, the individual sense of will vanishes; the conscious self finds itself (dis)located in the domain of the id. Perhaps now *Wo Es war, soll Ich werden* could be (mis)translated as: 'the "me" arrives at the point where "I" appears and disappears'. Or in other words: language speaks in the place of the speaking subject.

The section of Lacan's seminar that expounds this theory of the phallus is entitled 'Phallophany', a word that captures this sense of phallic power as an apparition, transient and ephemeral, which the subject desires but cannot command. After his close encounter with this phallic apparition, therefore, nothing remains for Hamlet – certainly not speech, mastery of the symbolic having proven both illusory and lethal. And so 'the rest is silence' (5.2.363).

At one level, Lacan's ternary structure – his triangular formulation of real, imaginary and symbolic – represents a structuralist reinvention of the Freudian Oedipal schema: the relation to the mother (real) gives way to narcissistic fantasy (imaginary), which in turn gives way to the Oedipal complex and its resolution in castration anxiety (symbolic). In leaving the seminar with the 'nothing' of the phallus, or the 'silence' of the symbolic order, however, Lacan opens the way for something beyond either imaginary captivation or symbolic subjection. At this moment – the moment at which both the realm of the imaginary and the symbolic order falter, and have nothing to offer – there re-emerges Lacan's third register, the 'real'.

Of the three registers fundamental to Lacanian theory, it is the 'real' that changes its position most radically. During the 1950s, with his clinical emphasis on the movement from an imaginary ego to a subject of the symbolic, Lacan's use of the term 'real' simply seems to designate an inaccessible referent outside of either register and therefore beyond any possibility of apprehension by the psyche – the pre-Oedipal union between the subject and its object, between infant and mother, or between the ego and its environment, which by definition cannot be regained. However, Lacan's emphasis in the seminar on *Hamlet* on the phallus as nothing, and on the phallus as 'real', can be seen as the production of a gap which his later increasing emphasis on the real will come to occupy, or to be preoccupied with.

In the year after his work on *Hamlet*, for example, during the seventh seminar series, on *The Ethics of Psychoanalysis*, he returns repeatedly to the Heideggerian notion of *das Ding*, the Thing, in another attempt to account for the real (Lacan 1992). In these seminars, moreover, Lacan moves away from *Hamlet* and towards an engagement with *King Lear*, which along with *Antigone* becomes, as Lupton and Reinhard (1993) have argued, the key text in his reply to the Freudian reliance on *Oedipus Rex* and *Hamlet*. A few years later, continuing this movement of his clinical practice beyond an emphasis on symbolic narration, Lacan formulates the notion of the real as the *tuché*, a word he glosses as signifying an encounter or appointment that cannot but be missed; he does so in the seminars entitled *The Four Fundamental Concepts of*

Psychoanalysis, which also move the Lacanian return to Freud beyond both the Société Française de Psychanalyse and the International Psychoanalytical Association, and aim it in the direction of the more purely Lacanian (despite or because of its claim to the Freudian title) École Freudienne. The movement beyond imaginary and symbolic to the real, then, anticipated in his reading of *Hamlet* and followed through in his reading of *King Lear*, constitutes for Lacan a turning point, both institutionally and theoretically; his work henceforth demonstrates a decreasing emphasis on structuralist linguistics and an increasing reliance upon phenomenology, and thus the annexation of another discursive field, the claim to another form of authority.

In order to trace the outlines of this emergence of the real, it is necessary to look more closely at those other moments in *Hamlet* upon which Lacan's reading concentrates: the relation between Ophelia and Hamlet, the trick that sends Rosencrantz and Guildenstern to die in Hamlet's place, and the fight over Ophelia's grave. These other 'scenes' provoke various important problematics of psychoanlytic theory: sexuality, femininity and the maternal; repetition; mourning and melancholia.

The object Ophelia

Lacan opens his seminar on Ophelia with a hook that has not failed to provoke critical bites. Referring to his title, 'The Object Ophelia', he comments that 'As a sort of come-on, I announced that I would speak today about that piece of bait named Ophelia, and I'll be as good as my word' (Lacan 1977a: 11). As Elaine Showalter suggests, this reduces Ophelia to an object, a 'come-on', a 'piece of bait' (1985: 77ff.). Why should Lacan want to repeat such a cliché?

One reason would be that a certain kind of objectification plays a fundamental role in the Lacanian theory of the subject. A generous reader might deduce that Lacan is identifying – even critiquing – a kind of masculinism intrinsic to the constitution of this mode of subjectivity. Given the arrogance of Lacan's own pronouncements on femininity, perhaps it is more accurate to say that his psychoanalytic schema reveals a mode of objectification so fundamental to the constitution of this subjectivity within language that psychoanalysis itself cannot help but perpetuate it. Psychoanalysis can only ever be 'as good as [its] word'; like a purloined letter, it cannot itself get beyond the itinerary prescribed for the signifier; at best it can only attempt to mark the route it follows.

Lacan's Ophelia, moreover, exemplifies a particular kind of object, namely, the Lacanian *objet petit a*, the object as other-with-a-small-o, as distinct from the capitalised Other, the system of signification itself. Lacan explicitly defines this *objet a*, in this seminar, not as the 'object *of* desire' but as the 'object *in* desire' (Lacan 1977a: 28, emphasis added). According to this formulation, something is constituted as an *objet a* by its placement within the structure of desire, within the symbolic order or Other.

For this reason, it is vital for Lacan to locate Ophelia – and thereby to place Hamlet – within his clinical topography: he wants to use Hamlet's proximity to or distance from various 'objects in desire' to reconfigure the relationship between his notion of the subject and the three 'registers' upon which his theoretical apparatus rests. The trajectory of the seminar thus moves Hamlet from an imaginary or fantasised relation to the object, through desire of an other located in the symbolic, and towards an impossible encounter with the 'thing' that resides in the real; in the process, Lacan's own clinical and theoretical emphases are being vigorously realigned. This itinerary can therefore be traced by concentrating on the redefinition of the *objet a*, according to which of the three registers it occupies. As others have suggested, *Hamlet* thus provides the object in Lacan's desire, offering him a privileged cultural site on which to redraw his claim to the psychoanalytic high ground (Lupton and Reinhard 1993: 1–7): 'It would be excessive, perhaps, if I were to say that the tragedy of Hamlet took us over the entire range of those functions of the object. But it definitely does enable us to go much further than anyone has ever gone by any route' (Lacan 1977a: 29).

His reading of the play begins with Ophelia's description of her closeted tryst with Hamlet:

> He took me by the wrist and held me hard.
> Then goes he to the length of all his arm,
> And with his other hand thus o'er his brow
> He falls to such perusal of my face
> As a would draw it. Long stay'd he so.
> At last, a little shaking of mine arm,
> And thrice his head thus waving up and down,

He rais'd a sigh so piteous and profound
As it did seem to shatter all his bulk
And end his being. That done, he lets me go,
And with his head over his shoulder turn'd
He seem'd to find his way without his eyes,
For out o' doors he went without their helps,
And to the last bended their light on me.
                            (2.1.77–100)

What Lacan emphasises in this second part of Ophelia's account is Hamlet's wordless and melodramatic miming of separation from the former object of his affection:

> This distance from the object that Hamlet takes in order to move on to whatever new and henceforth difficult identification, his vacillation in the presence of what has been until now the object of supreme exaltation, gives us the first stage, which is, to use the English word, one of 'estrangement'.
>
> (Lacan 1977a: 21)

Hamlet's encounter with the Ghost constitutes, according to the Lacanian reading, a crisis in the register of the imaginary. As a fantasy of narcissistic plenitude, the imaginary attempts to incorporate otherness within the mutuality of a perfect specular love between the ego and its idealised image of itself. The 'object' of desire becomes a kind of mirror surface, reflecting the ego back to itself. The onset of a gaze from outside of this fantasy, however – the irruption of the menacing viewpoint from the Other that cannot be subsumed into the fantasy – disrupts and dissolves this dual relation. When the Ghost fixes his eyes on Hamlet 'most constantly' (1.2.233–4), he first embodies this irrepressible gaze from beyond, which cannot be recuperated by the imaginary order. The eye finds itself subject to a gaze not its own, as if, looking in the mirror, the viewer were to see another face than her or his own uncannily glaring back.[7]

Such moments, when an imaginary unity splits into a threatening duplicity, represent the Lacanian version of what Freud described as the 'uncanny', the unconscious feeling of depersonalisation produced by instances of doubling (*PFL* 14: 336–76). Hamlet mimes this incomplete transition between unity and duality as he grasps Ophelia and pushes her away in the same movement:

'He took me by the wrist and held me hard. / Then goes he to the length of all his arm'. The temporal switch between lines indicates a tense passage between (lost) possession and (current) separation, and the incomplete movement from the imaginary fantasy of mutuality to the symbolic consciousness of distance and difference:

> I assure you that without reference to this pathological schema it is impossible to locate what Freud was the first to elevate to the level of analysis under the name of *das Unheimliche*, the uncanny, which is linked not, as some believed, to all sorts of irruptions from the unconscious, but rather to an imbalance that arises in the fantasy when it decomposes, crossing the limits originally assigned to it, and rejoins the image of the other subject.
>
> In the case of Hamlet, Ophelia is after this episode completely null and dissolved as a love object.
>
> (Lacan 1977a: 21–2)

The fantasy becomes unbalanced and decomposed because of a change in the status of the object. Instead of remaining in the specular suspended animation of the imaginary, the object of desire shatters the limits imposed by the mirror relation and 'rejoins the image of the other subject'. When Hamlet encounters his own status as a subject-signifier within the symbolic order, the *objet a*, instead of remaining a locus for the narcissistic fantasy of the ego, becomes an other in its own right, that is, another subject-as-signifier. The problem for Hamlet at this point is not the objectification of Ophelia – that would be conventional, and proper – but rather the possibility of her transposition from object to subject-in-language.

In the second part of Ophelia's account, then, Hamlet's movement 'out o' doors', finding his way 'without his eyes', indicates this redirection of the subject within a pre-existing itinerary; he is no longer the origin of an imaginary desiring gaze, but manifests instead the blindness of the subject within the symbolic order, an object of other gazes. Sighs and other signifiers of mourning accompany this process, which in fact in a certain way functions to 'end his being' – or at least to dissolve his stable existence as a conscious ego. 'That done, he lets me go': in Shakespearean usage, 'lets' can mean either 'allows' or 'prevents': either 'he prevents me from escaping' or 'he abandons me'. These antithetical possibilities accurately describe Ophelia's subsequent situation: in fact, she remains trapped by her objectification within the abandoned fantasy, which is why the play now abandons her to two forms of dissolution, madness and drowning:

> In short, what is taking place here is the destruction and loss of the object. For the subject the object appears, if I may put it this way, on the outside . . . he rejects it with all the force of his being and will not find it again until he sacrifices himself. It is in this sense that the object is here the equivalent of, assumes the place of, indeed is – the phallus.
>
> This is the second stage in the relationship of the subject to the object.
>
> (Lacan 1977a: 23)

Ophelia, as the object of the abandoned fantasy, takes on, according to Lacan, the same position as the castrated genital object, 'the phallus, exteriorized and rejected by the subject as a symbol signifying life' (Lacan 1977: 23). Freud saw castration anxiety as the result of the Oedipal rivalry between parent and child, representing the father's threatened punishment for the rivalrous love the son feels for the mother. In Lacan's structuralist translation of this Oedipal bargain, entry into language and the concomitant constitution of subjectivity as such also come at a price: that subjection to the Other which is his version of castration. Ophelia, as an *objet a* cast out from the imaginary, now comes to function within the symbolic only in negative terms:

> The object takes the place, I would say, of what the subject is – symbolically – deprived of.
>
> . . . What is it that the subject is deprived of? The phallus; and it is from the phallus that the object gets its function in the fantasy, and from the phallus that desire is constituted with the fantasy as its reference.
>
> (Lacan 1977a: 15)

From here it is a short step to the most egregious of Lacanian puns: Ophelia, he says, is *O-phallos* (Lacan 1977a: 20).

It is, moreover, within this symbolic register that Ophelia functions as what Lacan begins the seminar by calling 'a piece of bait': her father, of course, deploys his daughter as an object in order to lure Hamlet into the game whereby he, in conjunction with those other 'bad parents', Claudius and Gertrude, can spy on Hamlet without his knowledge: a clear enough playing out of the relation between subject and *objet a* under the structuring gaze of the symbolic order, or what Lacan elsewhere calls the *nom-du-père*. Ophelia

> thus becomes one of the innermost elements in Hamlet's drama, the drama of Hamlet as the man who has lost the way of his desire. She provides an essential pivot in the hero's progress toward his mortal rendezvous with his act – an act that he carries out, in some sense, in spite of himself.
>
> (Lacan 1977a: 12)

The rhetoric here – Hamlet's 'mortal rendezvous', his carrying out of the act 'in spite of himself' – emphasises that Ophelia's role is within the symbolic order, which in a sense scripts Hamlet's actions for him, as well as casting her in a role with even less agency: she has taken on, in this register, the purely structural role of an element in the mechanism, a kind of pivot.

It is the vacillation between Ophelia's position as an object and her status as a subject-in-language that returns to trouble the Lacanian reading of the play. To trace this return, however, it is necessary first to follow Hamlet's own digression through the postal route of the symbolic.

Hamlet's purloined letter

As I have argued already, Lacan's reading of *Hamlet* develops some of the positions developed a few years earlier in his seminar on Poe's 'Purloined Letter', in particular his notion of dependence upon the signifier:

> Our purpose, as you remember, is to show the tragedy of desire as it appears in *Hamlet*, human desire, that is, such as we are concerned with it in psychoanalysis.
>
> We distort this desire and confuse it with other terms if we fail to locate it in reference to a set of co-ordinates that, as Freud showed, establish the subject in a certain position of dependence upon the signifier. The signifier is not a reflection, a product

pure and simple of what are called interhuman relationships –
all psychoanalytic experience indicates the contrary.

(Lacan 1977a: 11)

'Interhuman relationships' do not produce the signifier, according
to Lacan; the reverse is true. Psychoanalysis should aim to expose
the structure of desire within which the subject finds her/himself
captivated, and 'The story of *Hamlet* reveals a most vivid dramatic
sense of this topology' (Lacan 1977a: 11). Lacan uses the play to
redraw psychoanalysis as a topology or graph of desire mapped out
onstage, a drama played out in the relationships between changing
positions:

> There is a level in the subject on which it can be said that his
> fate is expressed in terms of a pure signifier, a level at which he
> is merely the reverse-side of a message that is not even his
> own. Well, Hamlet is the very image of this level of subjectivity.
>
> (Lacan 1977a: 12)

Like the purloined letter in Poe's story, turned inside-out and
readdressed by the Minister, Hamlet becomes in Lacan's exegesis
a demonstration of the subject's dependence upon or derivation
from its attachment to the chain of language, the sequence of
letters, the alphabet of signification: 'we also encounter *a* plus *b*
plus *c* and so forth: the most elaborate combinations of sequelae,
of lingering traces combined by chance' (Lacan 1977a: 16). Clearly,
the Lacanian rereading departs radically from Bradleyan criticism
and ego psychology, both of which would consider character as
a form of psychic interiority. For Lacan, in contrast, character
as subjectivity functions as a purloined letter, constituted not by
character as a form of internal motivation or psychology, but rather
by character as a letter or cipher, a set of external structural
relations between subjects.[8]

Early seventeenth-century drama provides an especially rich
resource for the Lacanian rewriting of psychoanalysis as a drama
of the letter, in two distinct but related ways. For one thing the
notion of 'character' exists on the cusp of two meanings at the time
Shakespeare writes: it can mean both 'countenance' or external
aspect, and internal attributes or moral disposition.[9] The early
modern notion of dramatic character thus foregrounds external
signification to a far greater extent than does a modern notion of

character as internal motivation. The word 'character' can also, in Shakespearean usage, signify a typographical symbol or letter, a point relating to the second way in which the drama of this period proves conducive to Lacan's brand of psychoanalytic structuralism.

Early seventeenth-century theatre reflects the mystique and power attributed to writing by a predominantly oral culture. In *King Lear*, Edmund's forged note from Edgar, which Gloucester intercepts, is only one of a series of missives that go astray;[10] in *Twelfth Night*, Malvolio takes Maria's faked letter to be from Olivia; in *Love's Labour's Lost*, the comic effect turns repeatedly on the misappropriation and misreading of successive messages. In these and other plays, the untimely or digressive letter can redirect or reverse the action. Clearly, for Shakespeare's audience, both comedy and tragedy can derive from that characteristic of the written word which also preoccupies Lacan: its capacity for redirection, for interception and for misrepresentation or reinterpretation.

Hamlet is, of course, riddled with such letters, either sent or read always at the direction of one or more of the paternal figures in the play: the 'sealed compact' which grants Old Fortinbras's lands to Old Hamlet (1.1.89); Hamlet's inscription on his tables of the ghostly injunction to 'remember' (1.5.97–110), paralleled by the moment at which Polonius instructs his son Laertes to 'character' paternal precepts on his mind (1.3.58–9); Claudius's greetings to England and to Old Norway (1.2.27–39, 4.3.61–8), and their replies (2.2.59–80, 5.2.372–6); Polonius's 'notes' sent via Reynaldo to Laertes (2.1.1–2); the books read by both Hamlet and Ophelia (2.2.168, 3.1.44–6); Hamlet's love letter to Ophelia, read by Polonius (2.2.109–23); the lines interpolated into *The Murder of Gonzago* by Hamlet, to be interpreted by Claudius (2.2.534–6); Hamlet's own letters home to Horatio (4.6) and to the court (4.7.36–51).

After so many digressive, delayed and reversed inscriptions, the final scene – during which all wayward 'characters' will reach their destinations – opens with Hamlet's account of another such interception and redirection. On the ship bound for England, unable to sleep, he purloins the letters from Claudius to the English monarch, carried by Rosencrantz and Guildenstern:

> Sir, in my heart there was a kind of fighting
> That would not let me sleep . . .
> Up from my cabin,

My sea-gown scarf'd about me, in the dark
Grop'd I to find out them, had my desire,
Finger'd their packet, and in fine withdrew
To mine own room again, making so bold,
My fears forgetting manners, to unseal
Their grand commission.

(5.2.4–18)

Discovering that they command his own execution by the English, Hamlet rewrites the letters as instructions for the deaths of the two messengers instead; he reseals and replaces them:

Being thus benetted round with villainies –
Or I could make a prologue to my brains,
They had begun the play – I sat me down,
Devis'd a new commission, wrote it fair –
I once did hold it, as our statists do,
A baseness to write fair, and labour'd much
How to forget that learning, but, sir, now
It did me yeoman's service. Wilt thou know
Th'effect of what I wrote?
Hor.   Ay, good my lord.
Ham. An earnest conjuration from the King . . .
That on the view and knowing of these contents,
Without debatement further more or less,
He should those bearers put to sudden death,
Not shriving-time allow'd.
Hor.   How was this seal'd?
Ham. Why, even in that was heaven ordinant.
I had my father's signet in my purse,
Which was the model of that Danish seal,
Folded the writ up in the form of th'other,
Subscrib'd it, gave't th'impression, plac'd it safely,
The changeling never known.

(5.2.29–53)

From the outset, Hamlet stresses that this nocturnal act of misappropriation is impelled by some force, within or without, that he doesn't understand or control: his best approximation of it is the conviction that 'There's a divinity that shapes our ends, / Rough-hew them how we will –' (5.2.10–11). Yet his rhetoric also suggests another kind of agency at work: that of the brains themselves, which have devised, scripted and enacted this drama – 'begun the play' – before Hamlet has time to think out a 'prologue'.

Like a surrealist engaged in 'automatic writing', who thereby becomes the agent of the unconscious, Hamlet gives himself up to his fears, and the network of villainies from which they derive: the circuit of these anxieties imbues his actions and dictates his reinscription of the letters. Even the 'fair' handwriting he employs arises from a repressed part of his mind, one he had previously 'labour'd much / How to forget'. For Lacan – once heavily influenced by surrealism and now proponent of a theory of the subject's subjugation to an unconscious structured like a language – this account proves irresistible.[11] He imagines Hamlet

> awakening in the dead of night on the storm-tossed ship, going about almost in a daze, breaking the seals of the message borne by Rosencrantz and Guildenstern, substituting almost automatically one message for another, and duplicating the royal seal with his father's ring. He then has the amazing good luck to be carried off by pirates, which enables him to ditch his guards, who will go off unwittingly to their own execution.
>
> (Lacan 1977a: 24)

The actors in this miniature drama play their parts 'in a daze', 'almost automatically', or 'unwittingly'. Hamlet is then himself purloined, carried off by pirates, according to the kind of 'amazing good luck' that he himself would most likely attribute to divinity or heaven. Insofar as Lacan can envisage this episode as a kind of dreamwork, an automatic (re)writing, this little scene functions as an allegory for the subject's engagement by the unconscious, and for the determination of the fate of the subject (Hamlet or Rosencrantz and Guildenstern) according to its falling in possession of the letter. Lacan does not mention the contents of the message, concentrating instead on its redirection, and on the crucial effect played by its external surface – Hamlet's use of the royal seal which comes from his father's ring – just as his seminar on 'The Purloined Letter' emphasised the addressing and readdressing of the envelope.[12] Rosencrantz and Guildenstern, characters in the service of the symbolic, are ciphers of the letter and so liable to lethal redirection; as a signifier himself, Hamlet is also, via this exchange, returned to his proper destination. In this sense, the reinscription of the subject-as-signifier within a prior network of signification functions as the Lacanian version of the Freudian notion of the death drive, which inscribes the organism within a digressive itinerary (a 'circuitous path', as Freud calls it) that must be followed in preference to any alternative short-cuts, forcing it 'to make ever more complicated *détours* before reaching its aim of death ... Hence arises the paradoxical situation that the living organism struggles most energetically against events (dangers, in fact) which might help it to attain its life's aim rapidly – by a kind of short-circuit' (*PFL* 11: 311–12).

Like Erlich, Lacan emphasises the play's thematisation of writing. Like Bradley, he also points out Hamlet's capacity for wordplay. But Erlich puts the play of writing in the service of ego integration – perceiving it as a conscious strategy for 'managing the unconscious' (Erlich 1977: 209–10) – while Bradley, as discussed in the preceding chapter, reads linguistic facility as a manifestation of the transcendent genius of the author. Where both of these readers thus channel the waywardness of Hamlet's 'character' towards a direct access to the mind of Shakespeare himself, Lacan insists repeatedly that the digressiveness of both letter and duplicitous speech disseminate the play of meaning:

> those substitutions of signifiers whose essential function I have been stressing ... lend Shakespeare's theater a style, a color, that is the basis of its psychological dimension ...
>
> This constant ambiguity is one of the dimensions in which Hamlet's tension is achieved, a tension that is concealed by the masquerade-like side of things ... It is in this playfulness, which is not merely a play of disguises but the play of signifiers in the dimension of meaning, that the very spirit of the play resides.
>
> Everything that Hamlet says, and at the same time the reactions of those around him, constitute as many problems in which the audience is constantly losing its bearings. This is the source of the scope and import of the play.
>
> (Lacan 1977a: 33–4)

When Hamlet, sarcastically bidding Claudius farewell on his departure for England, calls out 'Farewell, dear mother', the phrase functions as a Freudian slip that dislocates the position of the King, whose correction is in turn subject to correction:

King. Thy loving father, Hamlet
Ham. My mother. Father and mother is man and wife, man
and wife is one flesh; so my mother.

(4.3.52–5)

This exchange represents a knotting together of various of the
key terms by which Lacan brings his analysis to its conclusion – or
rather its inconclusive ending.

The hole in/of the real

If, as I have argued, Lacan uses his reading of *Hamlet* to move his
psychoanalytic doctrine past an emphasis on the transition of the
subject from imaginary captivation to symbolic narrativisation, and
towards the identification of a (redefined) category designated
as the real, this necessitates a reconfiguration of the Freudian
counterparts of the Lacanian symbolic and real registers – namely,
the paternal and maternal functions – as well as of the object of/in
desire.

As discussed above, the object in desire – or, in Lacan's terms,
the *objet a*, the other – functions within the imaginary realm as
a constituent in the formation of the ego or self-image. This
function Ophelia fulfils, as Hamlet's celestial 'soul's idol' (2.2.109),
at least until this idealised and dualistic mirrored love relation
decomposes as the result of the intrusion of the gaze of the
Other, when Polonius, Claudius and Gertrude act as audience,
first reading Hamlet's love letter to Ophelia, and then using her
as 'bait' for their observation of Hamlet's mental condition.[13]
The intrusion of the parental gaze indicates, in Lacanian terms,
the move from the imaginary to the symbolic order. At this stage,
the *objet a* becomes redefined as a stand-in for the phallus, the
guarantee of mastery of the Other, the symbolic order.

However, the price of entry into the symbolic order is castration,
which for Lacan means at least two things. The subject, for its
existence as such, pays a double price: it remains subject to a
linguistic order that precedes and speaks (for) it, and it loses direct
or immediate access to that pre-linguistic 'reality' of which it was
once an undifferentiated part. Hence, the phallus as symbolic
object of desire manifests two altogether antithetical aspects, as a
privileged or fetishised signifier of the power of the Other, but also
as the disgusting, rejected residue, the cut-off bit of decomposing

flesh that recalls that the price of symbolisation is an irremediable distance between the subject and the 'real':

> through his relationship to the signifier, the subject is deprived of something of himself, of his very life, which has assumed the value of that which binds him to the signifier. The phallus is our term for the signifier of his alienation in signification . . . Something becomes an object in desire when it takes the place of what by its very nature remains concealed from the subject: that self-sacrifice, that pound of flesh which is mortgaged [*engagé*] in his relationship to the signifier.
>
> (Lacan 1977a: 28–9)

The scene between Hamlet and Ophelia, during which this symbolic transaction occurs under the parental gaze, therefore demonstrates a fluctuation between over-valuation and detestation of the flesh as the object in desire, summed up by the 'nunnery' – which could in Shakespeare's day mean either a house of religion or a brothel – to which Hamlet directs Ophelia. The distance which Hamlet began to put between himself and the object of his fantasy has widened and become imbued with the reactive disgust that forms the underside of an over-valuation of the phallic object:

> *Ham.* For if the sun breed maggots in a dead dog, being a good
> kissing carrion – Have you a daughter?
> *Pol.* I have, my lord.
> *Ham.* Let her not walk i'th'sun. Conception is a blessing, but
> as your daughter may conceive – friend, look to't.
>
> (2.2.181–6)

In figures of bestial and corrupt procreation, such rhetoric binds together feminine sexuality and the maternal as the inevitable dual loci for what psychoanalysis names 'castration anxiety'; Hamlet's invective designates Ophelia as a worthless piece of flesh, a reminder of the lost immediacy of the pre-symbolic real, which parallels the Freudian notion of castration as the threat that enforces that separation between (male) child and mother which is the outcome of the Oedipal process.

Because it cannot offer immediate access to the 'real', but can only represent it from a distance and in a delayed form, Lacan's symbolic order or Other itself comes to seem lacking. Not even the *nom-du-père* – the patriarchal, executive or legislative form of the symbolic – has possession of the phallus, which after all is only ever an apparition, an illusion of presence, a nothing. Similarly Hamlet's 'fathers' prove to be respectively a ghost, a 'wretched, rash, intruding fool' (3.4.31), and a 'king of shreds and patches' (3.4.103); the relation between subject and this lack in the symbolic order

> is embodied by the Father, since he is the expected source of the sanction from the locus of the Other, the truth about truth. The Father must be the author of the law, yet he cannot vouch for it any more than anyone else can, because he, too, must submit to the bar, which makes him, insofar as he is the real father, a castrated father.
>
> (Lacan 1977a: 44)

According to Lacan, *Hamlet* therefore embodies a decadent form of the Oedipal situation, a moment of decline in which 'The Other reveals himself from the beginning as the barred Other' (Lacan 1977a: 44). Reading *Hamlet* according to Freud's papers on 'Mourning and Melancholia' – in which Hamlet features explicitly as model of the melancholic (*PFL* 11: 251–68)[14] – and on 'The Dissolution of the Oedipus Complex' (*PFL* 7: 313–22), Lacan continues his movement beyond an emphasis on the transition between imaginary and symbolic, and towards his nascent activation of the notion of the real. Thus he also moves away from Freud's privileging of the paternal–filial axis and towards an emphasis on the relationship between Hamlet and Gertrude:

> The omnipotence of which we are always speaking in psycho-analysis is first of all the omnipotence of the subject as subject of the first demand, and this omnipotence must be related back to the Mother.
>
> The principle subject of the play is beyond all doubt Prince Hamlet . . . How is the desire of the Other manifested in the very perspective of this subject, Prince Hamlet? This desire, of the mother, is essentially manifested in the fact that, confronted on one hand with an eminent, idealized, exalted object – his father – and on the other with the degraded, despicable object Claudius, the criminal and adulterous brother, Hamlet does not choose.

His mother does not choose because of something present inside her, like an instinctive voracity. The sacrosanct genital object . . . appears to her as an object to be enjoyed . . . in what is truly the direct satisfaction of a need, and nothing else. This is the aspect that makes Hamlet waver in his abjuration of his mother. Even when he transmits to her – in the crudest, cruellest terms – the essential message with which the ghost, his father, has entrusted him, he still first appeals to her to abstain. Then, a moment later, his appeal fails, and he sends her to Claudius' bed, into the arms of the man who once again will not fail to make her yield.

This fall, this abandon, gives us a model that enables us to conceive how it is that Hamlet's desire – his zeal with respect to an act that he so longs to carry out that the whole world becomes for him a living reproach for his perpetual inadequacy to his own will – how this zeal always flags. The dependence of his desire on the Other subject forms the permanent dimension of Hamlet's drama.

(Lacan 1977a: 12–13)

The object, in this move away from its role in the imaginary and symbolic, begins to function less as a passive element in the construction of the subject, and more as a locus of active enjoyment in its own right – a scandalous, 'primordial' mode or source of subjectivity outside of the symbolic order. Rather than reading Gertrude as an adjunct to the character of Hamlet, Lacan makes the protagonist's agency entirely subject to its desire of ('of' here meaning 'for', but also 'on the part of') the (m)Other. Between one paragraph and the next, Lacan elides Hamlet's failure to choose into his mother's failure to choose, due to her 'voracity', 'something inside her' that partakes of an outrageous form of enjoyment. Hamlet's desire, as Lacan stresses, 'is far from being his own. It is not his desire for his mother; it is the desire of his mother' (Lee 1990: 113; translation and citation from Lacan 1982a: 20).[15]

During the scene of greatest intimacy between son and mother, in Gertrude's bedchamber, Hamlet responds to her question 'What shall I do?' with an unusually dense configuration of negatives: 'Not this, by no means, that I bid you do: / Let the bloat King tempt you again to bed' (3.4.182–4), followed by a detailed description of the amorous tactics by which Claudius might elicit from his wife the secret of her son's imposture. As Janet Adelman comments of this exchange, 'There has to be an easier way of asking your mother not to reveal that your madness is an act . . . Hamlet cannot stop imagining, even commanding, the sexual act that he wants to undo' (Adelman 1992: 32). His prohibition to his mother thus corresponds to what Lacan calls *denegation*, a term which he uses to supersede the Freudian notion of *Verneinung*, according to which the subject's consciously expressed negation of a desire betrays an unconscious affirmation of it.

Hamlet's subject position within the symbolic – his 'zeal', agency, will and ability to act – proves to be pre-empted and negated by his incapacity fully to abjure or foreclose an identification with the 'omnipotence' of the pre-symbolic, that 'instinctive voracity' or object-enjoyment endemic to the real. The *objet a* at this point no longer functions as the product of desire, as in other moments of Lacanian theory; rather, it is the cause of desire. The recalcitrance of the real to symbolisation brings about the lack which desire seeks, vainly, to fill. This, then, is the final destination in the seminar of the object in desire or *objet a*: from an idealised fantasy object in the imaginary, to a foreclosed phallic signifier in the symbolic, to the locus of an impossible enjoyment: 'Ophelia, whom Hamlet rejects by equating her with the overbearing corporeality of his mother, comes to embody for Hamlet the flagrant grossness of the real phallus as *objet d'une jouissance*' (Lupton and Reinhard 1993: 77). During the middle sections of the play, the role initially played by Ophelia – idol, piece of bait, rejected piece of flesh – dissolves into that taken by Gertrude.[16]

It is therefore only after her death, during the graveyard scene, that Ophelia becomes once again for Hamlet an object in desire: 'we see something like the reintegration of the object *a*, won back here at the price of mourning and death' (Lacan 1977a: 24). As an imaginary idol she may be lost; as a phallic signifier in the symbolic she may be cut off; all the more reason for her now to appear most desirable to Hamlet, in the form of a gap in representation: 'only insofar as the object of Hamlet's desire has become an impossible object can it become once more the object of his desire' (36). This impossibility of the object as real is manifested in physical terms by her open grave, and in cultural terms by her suicide, which renders her burial in sacred ground out of place:

Where is the gap, the hole that results from this loss and that calls forth mourning on the part of the subject? It is a hole in the real, by means of which the subject enters into a relationship that is the inverse of what I have set forth in earlier seminars under the name of *Verwerfung* [repudiation, foreclosure].

Just as what is rejected from the symbolic register reappears in the real, in the same way the hole in the real that results from loss, sets the signifier in motion. This hole provides the place for the projection of the missing signifier, which is essential to the structure of the Other. This is the signifier whose absence leaves the Other incapable of responding to your question, the signifier that can be purchased only with your own flesh and your own blood, the signifier that is essentially the veiled phallus.

(Lacan 1977a: 37–8)

The phallus, symbolic object of desire, representative of that lost relation to the real that must be repudiated or foreclosed when the subject enters into language, now becomes superseded by 'the hole in the real' – a paradoxical term according to one definition of the real as a (pre)condition of impossible plenitude. Laertes and Hamlet plunge into the grave in their attempt to regain the absent object of their mutual desire; Ophelia can now function as an object of desire in the real – that is, in Lacan's terms, a cause of desire in the symbolic – precisely because she is now permanently lost. As Hamlet's dialogue with the gravedigger reveals, Ophelia's death has taken her beyond the categories by which the symbolic represents human subjects: like the Lacanian real, she is, in the terms of the symbolic, nothing; or else she is something else, that very 'thing' which is outside the ken of the symbolic. The real 'object Ophelia' now becomes 'the signifier whose absence leaves the Other incapable of responding to your question', which can only be represented negatively, as a gap:

Ham.   What man dost thou dig it for?
Grave.   For no man, sir.
Ham.   What woman then?
Grave.   For none neither.
Ham.   Who is to be buried in't?
Grave.   One that was a woman, sir; but rest her soul, she's dead.

(5.1.126–32)

The rediscovery of Ophelia as a totally unassimilable object of desire produces either this 'absolute' breakdown of language into negation, or else its frenzied proliferation into nonsense and hyperbole, as in Hamlet's outrageous elegy, which far more clearly signifies his continuing rivalry with Laertes than it does his relation to Ophelia:

> I lov'd Ophelia. Forty thousand brothers
> Could not with all their quantity of love
> Make up my sum. What wilt thou do for her? . . .
> Woo't weep, woo't fight, woo't fast, woo't tear thyself,
> Woo't drink up eisel, eat a crocodile?
> I'll do't. Dost come here to whine,
> To outface me with leaping in her grave?
>
> (5.1.264–73)

Dissolution and decay, at this point, most clearly characterise the symbolic texture of the play; something remains rotten in the state of Denmark, insofar as the court cannot properly complete those rituals of mourning by which the symbolic order normally compensates for loss: 'The work of mourning is first of all performed to satisfy the disorder that is produced by the inadequacy of signifying elements to cope with the hole that has been created in existence' (Lacan 1977a: 38). As Lacan goes on to point out, 'from one end of *Hamlet* to the other, all anyone talks about is mourning' (39), because the rituals in every case are corrupt: Old Hamlet's funeral was interrupted too rapidly by his widow's remarriage to his brother; Polonius is buried 'hugger-mugger' to prevent scandal; Ophelia is interred in contradiction of ecclesiastical law. The impotence of the symbolic, manifest in these decayed rites, returns in the form of the 'veiled phallus', the disruptive effect of a real which betrays what remains lacking: Old Hamlet's ghost, Polonius's misplaced body, Ophelia's fought-over corpse.[17]

Lacan's confusing – and arguably confused – terminology in the seminar on *Hamlet* thus indicates an incomplete transition from one theoretical emphasis to the next. The phallus, for example, signifies power in the symbolic, whereas the 'veiled phallus' – the phallus as 'real' – stands for the incapacity of the symbolic. At the end of the seminar he represents the phallus as 'nothing', as a phantom, by which he means to stress that the signifier of symbolic mastery disguises an Other which is itself lacking or 'castrated':

> Replace the word 'king' with the word 'phallus', and you'll see that that's exactly the point – the body is bound up [*engagé*] in this matter of the phallus – and how – but the phallus, on the contrary, is bound to nothing: it always slips through your fingers . . .
>
> Hamlet: The king is a thing –
> Guildenstern: A thing, my lord?
> Hamlet: Of nothing.
>
> (Lacan 1977a: 52; citing 4.2.27–9)

The emphasis on the ghostliness of the phallus entails another set of references to 'the real phallus', a phrase that occurs always in the context of feminine sexuality; specifically, to that troubling association between enjoyment and the maternal represented by the character of Gertrude:

> in the tragedy of Hamlet, unlike that of Oedipus, after the murder of the father, the phallus is still there . . .
>   Claudius' real phallus is always somewhere in the picture. What does Hamlet have to reproach his mother for, after all, if not for having filled herself with it? And with dejected arm and speech he sends her back to that fatal, fateful object, here real indeed, around which the play revolves.
>
> (Lacan 1977a: 50)

Anticipated here is the movement, in Lacan's theory, towards a feminine desire conceived *on its own* terms, rather than a femininity envisaged in the first instance as the object of masculine desire; of course, this conceptual shift cannot be completed until that desire is no longer inevitably expressed in the language of the phallus – or at least until the phallus no longer signifies a specifically masculine mode of power. Hence Lacan's later insistence that the phallus is not reducible to 'the organ, penis or clitoris, that it symbolizes' (1977b: 285).

For Lacan, then, Hamlet's condition arises less from his identification with the Other-as-Father (good and/or bad), and more from his identification with the desire of the Other-as-Mother. This remains, of course, an impossible identification, insofar as it desires an object outside of the symbolic order in which the subject as such is constituted. This 'real' object – the object in/as the 'real' – produces a double mourning: for the lost illusion of the omnipotence of the symbolic order, and for the impossibility of (re)gaining the lost relation of intimacy with/in the real. *Hamlet*, according to Lacan's reading, turns on the ritualisation of this mourning, the necessary counterpart of desire:

> Ritual introduces some mediation of the gap [*béance*] opened up by mourning. More precisely, ritual operates in such a way as to make this gap coincide with that greater *béance*, the point *x*, the symbolic lack. The navel of the dream, to which Freud refers at one point, is perhaps nothing but the psychological counterpart of this lack.
>
> (Lacan 1977a: 40)

In Freud's reading of the play it is Hamlet's own desire, his sexual feeling for his mother, that provides the 'navel' or unplumbable origin of the play. In contrast, Lacan's seminar, despite itself, opens up the possibility of a feminine pleasure – non-symbolisable, unimaginable – which features as the inaccessible kernel of the real, the impossible gap in representation around which the text of *Hamlet* is woven.

Something rotten in the state of Britain

In the seminar series immediately following the one on *Hamlet*, Lacan turns to *King Lear* in order to discuss *The Ethics of Psychoanalysis* (1959–60; Lacan 1992). Here, the incipient emphasis that I have described in his reading of *Hamlet* – on the real as a radical alterity, and as some kind of productive positivity rather than as a purely negative 'gap in the symbolic' – is developed in relation to the Heideggerian notion of the Thing, *das Ding*.

Lacan argues that Lear encounters the radical alterity of the real because he renounces the 'goods' and the 'duties' that mark his position within this symbolic order (Lacan 1992: 305), and thereby enters the 'zone between-two-deaths' (320), which comprises the difference or hiatus between 'natural' or biological death and what Lacan calls the 'second death', the substitution of thing-for-word that comes about through representation in the symbolic.[18] It would seem from Lacan's examples that entry into this zone between two deaths can occur in two ways. An interruption of mourning or the failure to complete correct funeral rites, as occurs in *Hamlet* and *Antigone*, will result in an incomplete transition from the first death to the second. On the other hand, if, as occurs in *King Lear* and *Oedipus Rex*, the protagonists renounce of all those goods, honours and titles that grant them their privileged place in the symbolic order *before their natural deaths occur*, they will incur the second death before the first, and hence continue to haunt and disrupt the representational system: the body is not with the King, but the King is with the body.

So, after his abdication, Lear and those who follow him, and indeed the entire realm they inhabit, become haunted by a thoroughgoing misalliance between the symbolic and the 'real', defined now by Lacan as an inaccessible and traumatic referent: he remarks that Lear 'makes the ocean and the earth echo because he tried to enter [the zone between-two-deaths] in a salutary way with everyone agreeing' (Lacan 1992: 310). This description is Lacan's paraphrase of Lear's contention 'with the fretful elements' during the storm scene, when he 'Bids the wind blow the earth into the sea, / Or swell the curled waters 'bove the main, / That things might change or cease' (3.1.3–6). Here the divisions put in place in the first verses of Genesis are dissolved, exemplifying Lacan's notion of the 'second death', that is, 'death insofar as it is regarded as the point at which the very cycles of the transformations of nature are annihilated' (Lacan 1992: 248).

This reading of *King Lear* – as a representation of that which exceeds the symbolic order, or undoes it – offers Lacan another way of theorising the 'real', which also helps to propel his theoretical machine beyond its reliance upon a surrealist version of structuralism, and towards an engagement with the phenomenology of Heidegger, Sartre and Merleau-Ponty. It is this philosophical discourse, moreover, that will provide crucial epistemological capital during his imminent secession from the Société Française de Psychanalyse and his foundation of the École Freudienne de Paris. The importation of phenomenological theory also, however, has the effect of masking or replacing Lacan's reconsideration of Freud's model of the place of femininity with the Oedipal scenario, and in particular within the intersubjective structure of *Hamlet*. Yet the return of the feminine as a disruptive effect – so evident in Lacan's late work, during which he moves away from phenomenology and into an increasingly idiosyncratic and obscure mathematical 'algebra' – is fleetingly anticipated during his brief comments on *King Lear* in *The Ethics of Psychoanalysis,* which clearly address themselves to Freud's reading of the play in 'The Theme of the Three Caskets'. For Freud, the silent Cordelia figures as both the mother and the goddess of death, the earth from which 'man' is born and by which he is swallowed at burial:

> Lear carries Cordelia's dead body over the stage. Cordelia is Death. If we reverse the situation it becomes intelligible to us ... It is in vain that the old man yearns for the love of woman as he had it first from his mother; the third of the Fates alone, the silent Goddess of Death, will take him in her arms.
>
> (*PFL* 14: 246–7)

Lacan, notably, reverts to the Shakespearean stage direction, commenting that Lear 'appears at the end as still not having understood a thing and holding dead in his arms the object of his love, who is, of course, misrecognized by him' (Lacan 1992: 310).

These two alternative stagings of the final moments of *King Lear* by Freud and Lacan rehearse, I would suggest, the vicissitudes undergone by the 'feminine principle' in psychoanalytic theory: either the feminine features as a silenced object, rendered lifeless by the very system of signification within which the patriarchal order attempts to hold it, or else it manifests as that embrace which is itself both silencing and lethal, because it exists utterly beyond the masculinist symbolic order of language and representation. For both Lacan and Freud, femininity becomes therefore the limit of representation, the unthinkable or thoughtless underside of psychoanalytic thought. Hence Freud famously describes feminine sexuality as the 'dark continent' (Freud 1966, vol. 20: 212), as a 'riddle' (*PFL* 2: 149), or as 'veiled in an impenetrable mystery' (*PFL* 7: 63). And Lacan, late in his career, devotes whole seminars to the notion of a feminine *jouissance* (pleasure, orgasm) as that which can neither be spoken by another nor speak itself, because it takes place beyond the phallus, outside of the symbolic order, and in opposition to masculine desire: 'the woman does not exist,' he announces, for it is 'elsewhere that she upholds the question of her own *jouissance*' (Lacan 1982: 141, 121). According to feminist psychoanalytic critics like Jacqueline Rose, this aspect of Lacan's work aims to critique the construction of femininity as an object in both psychoanalysis and in patriarchal culture generally; on the other hand, as Rose admits, Lacan cannot help but repeat that consignment of 'the feminine' to a realm outside of the symbolic, from which position the attainment of any kind of voice, agency or power would seem to be problematic, to say the least (Rose 1986: 78–80).[19]

The Lacanian remains

In the battle over the psychoanalytic heritage, Freud's descendants read his will and testament according to very different critical modalities. Where Jungians mythologise the Oedipal schema – turning mother, father, rival and love object into archetypes – the ego psychologists allegorise, producing a kind of 'pilgrim's progress' through which the individual, as hero, must triumph. Lacan, in contrast, structuralises the Freudian paradigm, so that the maternal and paternal functions, and the roles of rival and lover, give way to a complex topography of three inter-related registers – imaginary, symbolic, and real – in which terms such as *objet a*, phallus, desire, and subject play out their parts. *Hamlet*, in the Lacanian account, dramatises this interplay of all of these psychoanalytic elements.

For readers of Shakespeare, the two most significant challenges to a Lacanian-influenced critical method derive from the various brands of feminism, on one hand, and of new historicism and cultural materialism, on the other. Feminist critics, for example, have suggested that Lacan's theory repeats the narrative structure of the Freudian family romance: the relation to the feminine is repressed as the subject moves into the imaginary and symbolic; thus, in the very process by which the (male) subject is constituted, 'woman' becomes an object (Showalter 1985). However, my reading of the seminar on *Hamlet* suggests the emergence of a tendency within Lacanian theory away from this simple 'objectification' of femininity by means of the imaginary and symbolic constructions of the subject, and towards an emphasis on a feminine *jouissance* conceived on its own terms, as an otherness beyond the patriarchal symbolic order, and deeply challenging to it. Hamlet's reproaches to his mother become the occasions for psychoanalytic reapproaches to the maternal. It is hardly surprising, given Lacan's

infamous and ongoing antagonism towards feminism, that this
tendency remains at best an always-conflicted possibility within the
Lacanian theoretical apparatus, and thus drops largely out of sight
in the following year's seminar when he deals with *King Lear*
– although it will re-emerge in the last stage of his career.[20]

   As for the historicist and materialist challenges, there is no doubt
that Lacan's critical practice repeats the universalism evidenced by
Freud, Rank and Jones, demonstrating the same unwillingness
to recognise the psychoanalytic version of subjectivity as culturally
and historically specific – that is, as a European, twentieth-
century, late modern, post-Enlightenment anti-humanism. This
is not to say, however, that all attempts to read between Lacan
and Shakespeare must perpetuate this ahistoricism. One corrective, as many critics have argued, is to examine the role played
by Shakespearean texts as representational mechanisms in the
construction of Lacan's theory. His dependence on Renaissance
texts and sources – *Hamlet, King Lear,* Holbein's *The Ambassadors*
– for the ongoing reformulation of his theoretical apparatus
during the late 1950s and early 1960s suggests a certain kind of
historical identification being enacted between his particular brand
of post-humanism and the pre-humanism of the sixteenth and early
seventeenth centuries.[21]

   Hence, a major project of Lacanian-influenced Shakespeare
critics has been to destabilise the relationship of mutual reinforcement that ties together the grand narratives of literary criticism
and humanist modernity; this aim is of course consistent with
the kind of historicism that searches for the ways in which
'Shakespearean culture' manifests an alterity or foreignness
altogether incommensurable with modernity. The investigation
of some of the possibilities of this latter project constitutes
a substantial aspect of the second half of this volume. But first,
in the next chapter I will conclude my examination of the ways
in which the reading of *Hamlet* has served the expansion and
establishment of the psychoanalytic empire – this time in a rather
less predictable location, that of pre-apartheid South Africa.

3

In Johannesburg

Analysis in the contact zone

Freud's *Hamlet* gets around, of course. He travels well enough within Europe – Vienna, Paris, London – and eventually makes it big in the USA as well. His adventures on the margins of empire have also been documented: this chapter explores what happens to the Oedipal Dane when he lands up in Johannesburg, in the midst of that most conflicted and persistent of colonial contact zones, segregationist South Africa.[1] What emerges is one instance of the ways in which culturally specific modes of subjectivity reproduce themselves across political and ethnic divides (or fail to do so, or do so in hybrid forms), via the co-operation between literature and psychoanalysis.

The South African contact zone provides a context in which the political and cultural stakes involved in the establishment of psychoanalysis become unusually apparent. Finding its accent out of place, and thus estranged from its own tone of authority, the psychoanalytic Shakespeare cannot help but engage with the speech of the other, a tongue it cannot apprehend but finds itself repeating.

This chapter will focus on two texts by Wulf Sachs: *Black Hamlet* (first published in 1937) and *Black Anger*, the sequel, or rather a version of the same story revised and extended by its author ten years after the first book. These are not especially well known texts to readers of either Shakespeare or psychoanalytic theory, so some contextualisation is required.

Wulf Sachs emigrated to South Africa in 1922. A medical doctor, he soon established a flourishing general practice among Johannesburg's affluent middle class. Lithuanian by birth, Jewish by ancestry and a Zionist on nationalist rather than religious grounds – belonging, as he puts it himself, to 'a people ceaselessly driven from pillar to post' (Sachs 1996: 286) – he felt an affinity with South Africa's growing population of dislocated, disenfranchised and detribalised urban blacks. His radical sympathies led him to associate with other white liberals, including Ellen Hellman, an anthropologist working among urban blacks in Johannesburg's Rooiyard slums. It was through this connection that he first met John Chavafambira, an immigrant from Manyika (the eastern part of what was then called Rhodesia) living in the Rooiyard tenements with his wife Maggie, and trying to build up his practice as a traditional healer-diviner or *nganga*. This is the man who becomes the subject of these two books, the man cast by Sachs in the role of 'Black Hamlet'. Sachs's title refers, of course, primarily to Freud's version of *Hamlet*. Because alongside his work as a physician, Sachs pioneered the establishment of Freudian psychoanalysis in South Africa in the 1930s and 1940s: *Black Hamlet* both documents and advances this enterprise.

In the 1930s South Africa's recovery from the depression led to a labour shortage which drew vast numbers of the rural black population into the cities. The policies regulating relations between urban blacks and whites therefore struggled with a necessary ambivalence – requiring on one hand an increasing mobility of black labour within the white economy, and on the other a corresponding rigidification of social, sexual, spatial and cultural segregation (thereby laying the foundations for the post-war establishment of apartheid) (Dubow 1996: 8–10).

Various kinds of discursive authority helped to manage the play of this ambivalence; for instance, throughout the 1930s and 1940s, segregationist policy was reinforced by the anthropological and psychological notion of 'deculturation', which tended to attribute all difficulties suffered by blacks in white cities – crime, poverty, mental and physical disease – to the supposed inability of the urbanised black 'to cope with the breakdown of tribal restraints and . . . the demands of western education and cultural values' (Dubow 1996: 16).

It is in this context then that psychoanalysis emerged in South Africa. In some ways, psychoanalytic theory underwrote ideologies of colonial domination – by asserting, for instance, that the widespread practice of so-called 'sudden weaning' by African mothers resulted in a lifelong infantilisation in their children, a liability to dependency and a lack of individual initiative. Sachs himself stated that 'the Bantu mother's practice of nursing the babies whenever they want the breast and until an advanced age' explained why 'even the educated Bantu today has a tendency to look for favours, for care and protection to the government and the white man' (Sachs, cited in Dubow 1996: 13–14). On the other hand, psychoanalytic theory decried the continued under-privilege of blacks, and in particular their poor access to education, diagnosing a bifurcation in black subjectivity which could only be remedied by their more equal sharing in the economic and cultural fruits of the now prospering Union of South Africa.

The engagement between Sachs and Chavafambira, then, carries from the outset a heavy political and epistemological freight. For Sachs, the implications of his study include the establish-ment of psychoanalysis as a science with universal validity, but also the production of a popular and academically viable argument against the psychological and anthropological bases for the Union's continued pursuit of racial segregation. *Black Hamlet* begins with Sachs's 'startling discovery' in his work at the Pretoria mental hospital in 1928 that 'the manifestations of insanity, in its form, content, origin, and causation, are identical in both natives and Europeans':

> This discovery made me inquisitive to know if the working fundamental principles of the mind in its normal state were not also the same. I had difficulties in approaching this prob-lem, for many reasons. To begin with, it was difficult to find a native who would be willing to become the object of a deep and protracted psycho-analytical study.
>
> (Sachs 1996: 71)

In John Chavafambira, Sachs met a man willing to collaborate in this project: psychoanalytic universalism deployed as an episte-mological guerrilla tactic, an attempt to sabotage the historical road that would eventually lead South Africa to apartheid.

One of the most powerful weapons in this campaign is Sachs's use of what this chapter will refer to as the 'Hamlet narrative': that interpretation of the play, inaugurated by Freud and developed by Jones and Rank, that was the subject of the opening chapter of my discussion.

What happens in *Black Hamlet*

Most evidently, the Freudian version of *Hamlet* offers Sachs a robust and flexible – and unequivocally Eurocentric – narrative mechanism by which to recuperate the apparent foreignness of Chavafambira's psychological experience and background. Freud's Hamlet provides the measure according to which the appropriate details of the subject's case history can be selected, arranged and privileged: Sachs narrates for his reader in a suitably dramatic order the death of John's admired father, Chavafambira, whose name he inherits; and, following this, a deterioration of the son's close relationship with his powerful and charismatic mother Nesta, due to her remarriage to her dead husband's brother Charlie, with whom John is in ceaseless conflict, and whom he suspects of 'poisoning' his father.

It's easy enough to imagine how this narrative processes extravagant differences between Manyika and European kinship structures in order to assign Chavafambira the Hamlet role in an Oedipalised, Western, nuclear family. To take a couple of imme- diate examples: when Chavafambira speaks of 'poisoning' he means, of course, not the kind practised by Shakespeare's Claudius, but rather the Manyika custom of spiritual malediction by means of 'pointing the bone'; more importantly, while the taint of incest between Claudius and Gertrude might have seemed stronger in Freud's Vienna than it would have in the context of the royal families of either Shakespeare's England or Hamlet's Denmark, in the Manyikan context the scandal disappears altogether, due to an indigenous cultural imperative for the brother of a dead man to marry the latter's widow – this protocol presumably offering the best way for the extended family to fulfil its responsibilities to the children (Sachs 1996: 288).

It might be thought that this absence of the incest theme fundamentally incapacitates the psychoanalytic interpretation of Chavafambira's situation; in fact, of course, it is the Hamlet narrative that allows this integral feature to be inserted into the account. Ernest Jones, following Freud, diagnosed Hamlet as suffering from a 'specific aboulia', a failure in will which, deriving from a specific cause – his incapacity to revenge himself upon his stepfather because, in killing Hamlet's father and marrying his mother, Claudius has fulfilled the Prince's own unconscious desire – produces a generalised indecision and melancholia, a decomposition of the Oedipal complex that manifests as a generalised irresolution. Identifying the same complaint in his Manyika analysand, Sachs demands the admission of the black African to the psychoanalytic Family of Man (united in its Oedipal psychopathology) while simultaneously providing another explanation for his infantilism, and further justifying his continued dependency on white patronage.

Thus another mainstay of the Freudian Hamlet is (re)discovered in Chavafambira's attitude: the injunction of the dead father to be remembered by his son. As Sachs puts it, 'I was struck by the fact of how little John, throughout his life, gave himself a chance of thinking out a problem for himself and making his own decision. Always his mother or his father came to his help. In this direction he remained an infant throughout life' (Sachs 1996: 87). By the time Sachs meets John, his mother and father are *both* dead; in describing John's parents helping him, Sachs is referring to the customary practice of the diviner, 'talking inwardly to his family *mudzimu* [ancestral spirit], to his father, Chavafambira's, spirit' (81). In the practice of his divination Sachs goes on to repeat, 'John feels his father right inside himself when he talks to him' (82), which the psychoanalyst describes as 'an interesting form of what psychologists call an introjection of an object' (83). Hamlet, as Sachs expects his reader to know, sees his dead father in his mind's eye (1.2.184–5), and later, on hearing the Ghost's injunction to 'Remember me', responds with a promise to inscribe the paternal commandment 'all alone . . . / Within the book and volume of my brain, / Unmix'd with baser matter' (1.5.91–104).

The Oedipalisation of the Manyikan psyche proceeds, therefore, by means of this omnipresent – albeit most often implicit – comparison with a text which, if a Hollywood movie were made of it, would be called *Sigmund Freud's William Shakespeare's Hamlet.* It's a game of double gestures. For the two-part manoeuvre by which he adopts Black Hamlet into the psychoanalytic Family of Man, and at the same time guarantees his infantilisation, Sachs claims a joint authorising signature: the first provided by the Eurocentric psychoanalytic institution, the second by the considerable cultural capital of Shakespeare (still at its peak, in the late imperial first half of the twentieth century, and clearly as viable in Anglo-Afrikaaner South Africa as it was in Vienna).[2] Meanwhile, another linked pair of aims – the reinforcement of the claim to scientific status of psychoanalysis, and the solidification of its tenuous institutional authority within South Africa – are pursued by means of two excursions into alien territory: the first crosses the boundary of racial difference to retrieve a universal (Oedipal) humanity; the second enters the field most distinct from science, that of the arts, to appropriate one of its most privileged symbolic objects. Sachs's claims to authorisation are clear enough when he asserts that

> the situation which occurs in *Hamlet* is common to all humanity, and this is the primary reason why Shakespeare's tragedy appeals to men of all races and nations. In *Hamlet*, Shakespeare, with the intuition of genius, penetrated the depths of man's innermost conflicts and illustrated in an unprecedented and unexcelled manner the tragic outcome of such conflicts.
>
> (Sachs 1996: 237)

The Hamlet narrative's organisation of Chavafambira's experience into a necessarily Oedipal structure becomes most explicit when it is working hardest to bridge the cultural gap. The only time Sachs quotes Shakespeare's text, for example, is when he needs to interpolate a crucial detail lacking from Chavafambira's own account of his experience, namely, in relation to the mutuality of the essential Oedipal relationship between mother and son. Chavafambira's cited comments, while they do bespeak his own intense attachment to his mother, do not give direct testimony to his mother's especial love for him. Consequently Sachs supplies this from Shakespeare: speaking of Hamlet, he writes that 'The mother, for her part, was passionately fond of him. "The Queen his mother lives almost by his looks," Claudius says to Laertes. We know already how much John loved his mother' (Sachs 1996: 239). While the Shakespeare quotation describes Gertrude's feelings for Hamlet, the following sentence, presented as a parallel, speaks of John's love for his mother. Sachs's elision functions to hide (or reveal?) precisely the maternal difference: that is, those aspects of the power and position of the woman in the Manyika kinship structure which might prove incommensurable with the Western Oedipal template, because, in fact, Chavafambira's comments about his mother say less about his individual affection for her, and more about his intense respect for her own potency as a medium for the ancestral spirits. Not only does this disrupt somewhat that exclusive and libidinised mutuality required for the Freudian account, the evidence of Nesta's own spiritual authority has the potential to allow her a rather different role in this drama from that played by Gertrude in Shakespeare's play. Therefore, some recasting is required, easily achieved by means of rehearsing a line from the source script.[3]

Other specific aspects of the Hamlet narrative fulfil particular functions in Sachs's account. When Chavafambira articulates a very powerful attack on white society –

> 'You say the white people want to help us. Who will believe it? Who will believe the white devils? . . . You say they want to help us, but I say they want to get rid of us! Well, let them give us back our land, then we will gladly go away, live by ourselves, away from you all. We don't want white devils.'
>
> (Sachs 1996: 234)

– Sachs frames his comments as a 'furious tirade', an 'uncontrolled fury', which however fails to result in action: 'as usual, he collapsed as suddenly as he had flared up. His tragedy was that of so many Africans' (Sachs 1996: 234). And the elements of this 'tragedy', as Sachs now goes on to specify, are lack of 'will-power', 'inner division'. It is this moment that Sachs takes as his cue to expound explicitly for the first time the theory of 'Hamletism' that has structured his analysis so far; Chavafambira's outburst constitutes the same kind of hesitancy and mock-madness that Shakespeare's Danish prince displays. When Chavafambira says that blacks want 'white devils' to give back their land, Sachs hears an expression of deep interior indecisiveness. An express desire for total decolonisation, heard via the stereophonic audio equipment of psychoanalytic theory and Shakespearean theatre, sounds in Sachs's ears like a longing for greater participation in white society. The Hamlet narrative enables the translation of a political challenge frustrated by material and ideological disenfranchisement into an individual hesitancy produced by internal psychic ambivalence.

In apparent contrast to this depoliticising effect, the Hamlet narrative elsewhere – in an earlier book by Sachs – permits him to experiment with a certain degree of politicisation of the Oedipal relation. In *Psychoanalysis: Its Meaning and Practical Applications*, he concentrates – as Rank and Jones had before him – on the throwaway association between Julius Caesar and Polonius, who of course tells Hamlet that in his days at university (typically, both birthplace and grave of political radicalism) he once enacted the role of the Roman dictator himself. This hint is enough for psychoanalysis to identify Polonius with Caesar-as-tyrannical-father, and to take Hamlet's creaky pun on the name of the conspirator most favourably presented in Shakespeare's version of the assassination – 'It was a brute part of him to kill so capital a calf there' (3.2.104–5) – to identify the Prince, in turn, with Brutus-as-rebellious-son. Emphasising this connection, Sachs allows the explicit politics of the Roman play to infuse his reading of the Oedipalised Hamlet; to imply that, in his later killing of the hidden Polonius in his mother's chamber, Hamlet acts as a kind of closet revolutionary, a double for Brutus struggling heroically against paternalism and imperialism:

> In other words, the original father, as so often happens in the fantasy of the child, is split into two fathers, one good and the other bad, corresponding with the division in the son's feelings. In Hamlet's unconscious, Polonius was identified with the tyrant aspect of Caesar, the Caesar who had to be killed by a revolutionary.
>
> (Sachs 1934: 205)

In its most manifest application of the Shakespeare narrative, *Black Hamlet* clearly identifies Chavafambira's 'bad' father, the correlative of Polonius/Claudius/Caesar, as his uncle Charlie. But when, in a chapter entitled 'Revolt', Chavafambira challenges and triumphs over this wicked stepfather/uncle, *and yet remains dissatisfied and unresolved*, it almost becomes evident in the text that there are other candidates for the role of paternal tyrant: white imperial rule in Rhodesia and South Africa, perhaps; or even the white liberal patron, Sachs himself, imperiously intervening in John's life and constantly demanding affiliation.

The end of *Black Hamlet* suggests that John can only succeed in attaining some measure of Oedipal resolution by, once again, a double operation. First he must return to his kraal – with Sachs in attendance – and engage in a struggle for prestige with Charlie, his uncle and stepfather, who of course is also a *nganga* (healer-diviner). Chavafambira proves capable of overruling his uncle, owing (according to Sachs) to a newfound authority deriving from his syncretic approach to healing – traditional skills honed in the urban environment, in addition to his access to Western medical practices and pharmaceuticals; and also an expanded ability to interpret the psychological distress of his patients, learned, of course, from his psychoanalytic sessions with Sachs.

Hamlet's work is not done yet, however. Despite his victory over Charlie, and his triumphant accession to the *nganga* legacy of his father, Chavafambira remains anxious and depressed. 'The dreams of my childhood are fulfilled', he comments to Sachs:

> 'I am in the place prepared for me by my father. My life-long enemy Charlie has been laid low . . . Now my way is clear before me to become the famous *nganga* in Manyikaland, even the whole of Rhodesia. Then why is my heart heavy within me? Is it because my friend, the doctor, is leaving me? Perhaps I should not have come back to the kraal. I have learned new ways in the big town. Life in the kraal is rough. Will I be happy here?'
>
> (Sachs 1996: 335)

The Oedipal conflict, worked out in the native Manyikan context, now becomes transposed to the cross-cultural register, in the form of that psychological split which Sachs describes as characteristic of all Africans living between the worlds of the native kraals and the white cities; a tension between love for the mother-culture and a latent hostility combined with a manifest obedience to a paternalistic colonial culture.

The final chapter of the book continues the working out of this other Hamletic relation, by recounting how, in a state of depression following Sachs's departure, John gets drunk and sleeps with a Junia, a stranger in the kraal, forgetting first to ask to which *mutupo* or ritual animal group she belongs. When he remembers to ask later in the night, she replies, 'Soko' – monkey: *the same as his own.*

> Slowly he released her as he realized what he had done. He had slept with a woman of his own *mutupo*. It was the incestuous

crime of which he had been warned so often in dreams . . . To
a strange woman a man's first question is always, 'What is your
mutupo?'

(Sachs 1996: 337)

As well as returning to the narrative once again that incest motif
(and motive) upon which the authority of psychoanalysis relies,
this moment strengthens the association between the Oedipal
structure and Sachs's continued adherence to the 'deculturation'
thesis: Chavafambira has forgotten to ask the question demanded
by the precepts of his mother-culture because of his now-habitual
possession of and by the culture of the paternal coloniser: John
knows he cannot now remain in the kraal because

> he would remain a laughing-stock: the *nganga* who went to towns
> and became so civilized that he had been intimate with a
> girl without asking her *mutupo*! . . . What confidence would the
> people have in the bond between the ancestors and the new
> *nganga?*

(Sachs 1996: 337–8)

He resolves to leave the kraal once more, and to return to the city.
It only remains for this post-Oedipal accession to the paternal-
colonial symbolic at the cost of the relation to the maternal-native
culture to be validated in Manyikan terms: Chavafambira propi-
tiates his ancestors because on the way back to South Africa he
happens upon a mother monkey with a baby crossing the road
and about to be killed by a car full of whites. He saves the monkey
family from being killed and is in the process assaulted by the
whites: 'But I was happy. To suffer through and for your *mutupo* is
the highest thing a man can do' (Sachs 1996: 339).

In this state of double Oedipal resolution, Chavafambira
continues his journey to the Union, back to his wife – with whom
his relationship has been, to say the least, problematic – dedicating
himself to the enculturation of his son: 'The boy must be educated,
for life as it is now, and not as it was when I was a boy. Daniel must
be able to look an educated African in the face. Our ancestors will
help him. They have sent me a sign.' To this, in the final paragraph
of *Black Hamlet*, Sachs adds his avuncular support: 'now he could
see the way to reconcile the past with the future, life in the kraal
with that in the town' (Sachs 1996: 340).

What relation exists between this resolution and that provided by the Hamlet narrative? For the Freudian Hamlet, the mass murder and suicide of Shakespeare's play constitutes the only means by which the Prince can take revenge not just against the bad father and the rival Laertes, but against himself for harbouring the desire for incest and parricide. Only thus is the way left clear for the post-Oedipal scenario represented by the entry of Fortinbras, the strong arm of the law-of-the-good-father. Sachs, in a comparable but less overtly violent manner, demonstrates the working out of the Oedipal dilemma in an act of culturecide that masquerades as integration, a relinquishing of the maternal relation and an accession to the paternal symbolic, with its promise of agency and subjectivity on European terms.

The tidiness with which *Black Hamlet* applies the Shakespearean narrative, and the rapid conclusion of the account after Chavafambira's return to Johannesburg, comes undone when Sachs returns to the story, rewriting and extending his account of his relationship with Chavafambira ten years later. In the version of the text published as *Black Anger*, as the new title suggests, either the Hamlet narrative seems to have loosened its grip or else the more radical possibilities for its application have become more evident. But that hypothesis requires closer examination.

Rewriting *Black Hamlet*

After his return to Johannesburg from Manyikaland, Sachs loses touch with Chavafambira for over a year, owing to a period of illness and a trip to Europe. During this time he completes *Black Hamlet* and sends it to publishers in England. Years later he rewrites the story as *Black Anger*, and in doing so adds a chapter recounting the renewal of the relationship after he returns to South Africa.

As suggested by the change in title, the second book seems to move away from the psychoanalytic interpretation of Chavafambira's life, and towards an emphasis on the need for direct political consciousness and activism. Thus the new chapter begins with statements such as the following:

John's greatest need was not to know more of his repressed unconscious, but to know the society he lived in, to recognize its ills and to learn how to fight them. If I could no longer be his companion, if I could do little for him as his physician, I could at least teach him what he had to know and to do.

(Sachs 1947: 275–6)

The resolution in Oedipal terms of John's inner tensions – as a subject caught between two parent cultures – has been replaced as a goal by the imperative to learn about and to struggle against the external injustices of white-dominated society. Moreover, their relationship has changed correspondingly: no longer styling himself Chavafambira's analyst, Sachs is determined to be his teacher. But the nature of the knowledge required for the struggle, and its modes of propagation, remains to be defined.

The reorganisation of material between the two books, moreover, demonstrates that psychoanalysis continues to play a pivotal role in mediating Sachs's relationship with Chavafambira, and that the Hamlet narrative maintains and extends – in a very explicit manner – its function as an instrument by which to complete the Oedipal colonisation of Manyikan experience.

To argue this, I need to go back to *Black Hamlet*, to an incident before Chavafambira's return to Manyikaland, when he is arrested for being on the streets without the special pass required for blacks to be out at night. While in custody he is questioned about the recent deaths of a pair of twin babies in the Rooiyard. He repeats the details of this interrogation to Sachs:

'The stout man with dark glasses suddenly asked me what do I know about this murder. "Nothing, baas", I said. "Twins are bad luck – aren't they?" he asked me. "So you *ngangas* kill them. Well? – you are a witch-doctor, aren't you?"'

(Sachs 1996: 207)

After his release Chavafambira falls ill, and becomes depressed and anxious:

An idea tortured him. He came out with it one morning after a sleepless night. 'It sprang suddenly on me when I tossed in bed. It was painful. The thought came to me that you and the detective were very alike. So alike that you both looked like one man, not two. It was a terrible thought. You must not be cross with me, Doctor. I pushed it away, but back it would crawl, like a beaten dog.'

(Sachs 1996: 211–12)

Sachs explains that, while counselling Chavafambira after his arrest, he had also questioned him about the custom of killing twins:

> Day after day I had questioned him, and John had done his best to satisfy my curiosity, explaining that the Manyika people regarded twins as coming from two fathers . . . But I was still not satisfied, seeking all the time for more detailed information. 'And the stout detective,' John said, 'did he not do the same?'
>
> (Sachs 1996: 212, 213)

In the face of this interrogation, Chavafambira cannot help but recognise the continuity in form and function between his experience of the South African repressive state apparatus in action, and the interpellative function of psychoanalysis: 'It seemed to John as if these white people put their meddlesome hands into his very thoughts, ruthlessly tearing and digging out information. The two men, the detective, and myself, thus fused in John's mind into one voice, one set of features' (Sachs 1996: 213). It seems clear, then, that Sachs's psychoanalysis of his subject installs that Oedipalised subjectivity which it requires for its political agenda; but at the same time, Sachs's psychoanalytic imperative to represent the resistance of his subject opens a space in the text for Chavafambira's own knowledge of that process – which clearly demonstrates the implication of the psychoanalytic relation in colonial politics. These two claims require spelling out before my argument can continue, since they underlie its further development.

In the first place, then, the *Black Hamlet* narrative facilitates the installation or incitement in this Manyika healer-diviner of an interiorised, Oedipalised subjectivity on the Freudian model: ego, id and superego. It's a familiar enough allegation that what psychoanalysis looks for, it tends to find, because the psychoanalytic search engine functions as a mechanism of implantation. Or, to use another metaphor, irresistible in this context: like a policeman planting a weapon, the psychoanalyst discovers the smoking gun of Oedipal guilt at the scene of the crime, every time.

This reproach, which seems amply borne out by Sachs's description of the operation of psychoanalysis in the colonial contact zone, is perhaps best represented by Deleuze and Guattari in *Anti-Oedipus*, according to which the presence of Oedipal structures in non-European cultures is precisely the legacy of colonisation:

> an Oedipal framework is outlined for the dispossessed primitives: a shantytown Oedipus . . . Oedipus is always colonization pursued by other means, it is the interior colony . . . even here at home, where we Europeans are concerned, it is our intimate colonial education.
>
> (Deleuze and Guattari 1977: 169–70)

As these two anti-Oedipalists also insist, however, 'the colonized resists oedipalization' (Deleuze and Guattari 1977: 169). And in *Black Hamlet* resistance is certainly in evidence. Sachs produces a style of case history in which the techniques, the investments and the limitations of the process are articulated with a clarity not usually present in psychoanalytic practice on its home territory. This is the second aspect of my discussion in the rest of this chapter: that in this context the exchange of knowledges succeeds in dislocating the promulgation of psychoanalytic authority at its point of inception. With the transcultural investment so high, the critical viewpoint of the analysand assumes an authority that cannot be altogether assimilated (as transferential 'resistance', for example) by the psychoanalytic interpretation.

To return to the text of *Black Hamlet*: on a later occasion Chavafambira is once again taken to prison, and this time faces trial for his work as a *nganga*. Three of his friends visit Sachs and urge him to help:

> I found the visit of these three men distinctly embarrassing. I read in their faces, in their tone of voice, in the manner of their speech, thinly disguised under their servility before a white man, the accusation that they dared not put into words . . . Now, when danger threatened one of their men, I was held responsible . . . Yes – I was on trial now.
>
> (Sachs 1996: 285–6)

What is Sachs's response? When the men leave his house, he decides to read back through his psychoanalytic notes, but with different eyes:

> I tried for the first time to see John the human being and not the subject of psycho-analytical studies. It seemed to me that in

spite of my sympathy and external freedom in relationship with him, he nevertheless had remained chiefly a psycho-anthropological specimen . . .

Now in the stillness of the night my main concern was for John's safety and well-being. A new man separated himself from the pages I was reading. The human: the real John. And the whole panorama of his life unfolded itself vividly before me.

John's birth and christening. His mother Nesta never stopped talking of the great affair . . . he was the baby son, mother's darling, father's choice as his perpetuator. Carefree life with practically no illness.

The first drama in little John's life. His mother's remarriage with the hateful Charlie, his uncle, when the six-year-old John, bitterly jealous and protesting, he had to go to sleep with other boys in the boys' hut. The origin of Hamletism to which I have previously referred.

. . . John never liked Charlie. 'It is time Charlie began to teach me,' he would say with annoyance. Nesta was worried . . .

Growing pains. The missionary school, to which he went together with his lifelong competitor, Nathan . . . Charlie was as cruel as the teacher in the mission . . .

1917. Charlie forced him to leave school . . .

1918. The terrible epidemic, and the death of his mother . . .

After that he went to Umtali, Salisbury, Bulawayo, wandering from one place to another. Always restless, always discontented, always lonely, like an African Odysseus.

(Sachs 1996: 287–9)

Going beyond his psychoanalytic perspective of John as an object of study, Sachs claims to see a new man separating himself from the pages of his case notes: 'The human: the real John'. To round out this three-dimensional figure who arises from the psycho-analytical stereotype, Sachs presents the vivid panorama of John's life in dramatic terms, which, however, replicate once more the characteristic moments of the Hamlet tragedy. His search for the real John returns to Sachs his Freudo-Shakespearean original. The final phrase, 'an African Odysseus', only just misses full recognition of this in its swerve from the expected formulation 'an African *Oedipus*'.

In the revised book, *Black Anger*, however, this same epiphanic recognition of the key determinants of John's psychobiography occurs at a different moment, fulfilling an equally vital function. Sachs cuts the summary of John's life from this part of the story in the version that he updates and publishes in 1947 and pastes it in, nearly word for word, at a crucial moment in the renewal of his relationship with the Manyika after their separation at the end of *Black Hamlet*.

So when Sachs returns from his trip to Europe to find Chavafambira living in a Soweto slum, full of suspicion and resentment of him, and unwilling to resume their relationship, he describes how

> I was . . . faced with the necessity of establishing a relationship between us that would enable me to assume my newly chosen role of teacher. Frequent visits to John failed to break down the resistance I felt in him. The solution came in a way I had not foreseen. A newly published psychological study I had made of John arrived one morning from my English publishers. I took two of the copies, giving one to John and the other to Maggie. I volunteered to read it for him, and Maggie, since it was obviously too difficult for them. I asked him to make comments as we read along. The book made a tremendous impression on John. I had often told him I intended to write a book about him, but he had never believed me. Now here was the printed book with his picture on the first page.
>
> As we read John would make comments, sometimes recapturing a memory or mood that he had forgotten at the first telling. He would declare himself puzzled by some of the psychological interpretations I had made in the book, and there would ensue long discussions about the influence of childhood on the adult behaviour.
>
> Gradually the whole panorama of his life unfolded itself vividly before him.
>
> (Sachs 1947: 282–3)

It is to *this* location, then, in *Black Anger*, that Sachs transfers that list of crucial moments in (his narrative of) Chavafambira's life:

> His birth and christening . . . Mother's darling, Father's choice as his perpetuator . . . The first drama in his life . . . His mother's

remarriage with the hateful Charlie, his uncle . . . Always restless, always discontented, always lonely, an African Odysseus.

(Sachs 1947: 283–4)

Black Hamlet – the book itself – at this moment invites the ultimate introjection, by the analysand, of that narrative, scripted by psychoanalysis, which returns to him/returns him to the pivotal points of the Hamlet myth. John now experiences verbatim the same epiphany, the same panoramic realisation that Sachs attributed to himself in *Black Hamlet*. No wonder he experiences it verbatim: John is hearing the author read from the newly published copy of *Black Hamlet* the very words that Sachs now uses in the *second* book to describe this act of reading. Sachs's production of *Black Hamlet* folds in upon its reception in *Black Anger*, a moment of reading that is at once both catechism and confession writes John Chavafambira into the Hamlet narrative – and in turn inscribes that narrative in the book and volume of his brain, to quote 'white Hamlet'.

Hamlet, repressed by the title of the second book, returns in this narrative, and in his unfamiliar guise as Odysseus (whose geographical digressions parallel the Prince's psychic indecisions). The same account is called upon to manage, in each book, the two moments when Sachs's involvement in Chavafambira's life is most subject to challenge. At these critical junctures the Hamlet narrative, by its effortless transcendence of three centuries and at least two disparate cultures in the name of a single human nature, reinstalls at once Sachs's capacity for insight, Chavafambira's own Hamlet-like failure of will, and the corresponding and necessary authority of the psychoanalytic discourse organising both terms.

But what takes place on the other side of that black mirror in which Sachs makes out the contours of psychoanalytic man? Chavafambira, it is clear, interrogates the image Sachs holds up, demonstrating 'puzzlement' at some of the book's psychological interpretations. Sachs implies that all these discussions confirm his subject's assent to the tragic portrait offered him in *Black Hamlet*. Unquestionably, Chavafambira has learned to act that part for all it's worth. But what other roles might he be playing out concurrently? What alternative knowledges and interpretations may he be articulating, to himself if not to Sachs?

Noting that Chavafambira sees his picture on the first page of the text, Sachs plainly envisages his identification with that image.

Two pictures are given in the updated text, each showing a strikingly different version of the man. In the first he stands alongside Sachs himself, appearing every inch the colonial mimic man; his European style of dress and his rigid posture display a desire to please, by imitating, the dapper Sachs on his right (Sachs 1996: frontispiece). In the text Sachs has described how, in spite of the warnings of his friends,

> John was already too much under my influence. Besides, unknown to himself, civilization had penetrated into his innermost being. He loved the town . . . he loved the suits and shirts and ties that he could buy in the shops . . . it would have been difficult to find a European with a tie as neatly made as his.
>
> (Sachs 1996: 200)

In the photo, however, John's shoes are missing, his pants are over-large, and the lack of a waistcoat and jacket put him in a different sartorial category from that of his patron, comfortable in a well-cut three-piece suit. Rather than illustrating that jubilant assumption of the white man as his ego ideal which Sachs describes, this image embodies instead the kind of colonial mimicry described by Homi Bhabha, which, by demonstrating a gap between the signs of European civility and their adoption by the other, functions simultaneously as an instrument of surveillance and a reversal of it; a sign of domination and a locus of resistance; 'a desire that reverses "in part" the colonial appropriation by now producing a partial version of the colonizer's presence; a gaze of otherness' (Bhabha 1994: 88–9).[4]

The second of the two photographs, upon which the pencil sketch on the cover of the original edition was based, is very different. It is a picture of Chavafambira by himself, squatting comfortably on his haunches, with his right arm extended. He looks nothing like his image in the first, but not much like the figure we expect from Sachs's comments either. He is stylishly dressed, with shoes and a jacket on this time, a shirt casually open at the neck and a chic hat; his choice of European clothes combines with an altogether non-European habitus to produce an image quite different from that dictated by the colonial relation (Sachs 1996: 9). His posture and the gesture he is making – is he in the act of throwing the bones for a client? – bespeak the kind of authority that, deriving from a knowledge outside of the discourses of white South Africa, inhabits that European apparel with a hybrid style absolutely distinct from either figure – Sachs or himself – in the other photograph. The look directed by Chavafambira at the camera in each photograph, moreover, demonstrates still further the difference between these two modes: in the first he responds obediently, smiling directly into the camera; in the second he stares over the photographer's shoulder, with an expression simultaneously knowing and unrevealing.

This difference offers a paradigm for the rest of my reading of the text. According to one mode, John is the obedient colonial who accedes to the subjectivity offered him by the psychoanalytic relation, but in this act of mimicry subverts that perspective from within, making evident its ill-fit with the Manyikan habitus. According to the second mode, Chavafambira incorporates a cultural capital unassimilable by psychoanalysis or anthropology, but which, in its hybridised inhabitation of those discourses, produces another knowledge of their norms and challenges the bases of their epistemological authority.

Mimicry and hybridity

How, then, does Chavafambira inhabit his sessions with Sachs?

> As I found out later, he was originally coming to me, not to please me, but to extract all he could get out of me concerning my medicines and Europeans in general. He was careful not to arouse my suspicions, and copied me to an amazing degree . . . he was carefully noting our speech, actions, dress, and especially anything connected with my medical work. 'It seemed to me, Doctor, that I was again learning the medicine, as in my young days with my father Charlie. Only Charlie taught me better.'
>
> (Sachs 1996: 199)

By means of his mimetic participation in the psychoanalytic relation, Chavafambira hopes to gain access to white authority, both epistemologically and pharmaceutically. But in doing so he does not renounce the primacy of Manyika knowledge: his step-father Charlie (Sachs's version of Claudius) taught him medicine better, and, by implication, taught him better medicine:

As for the white man, clever as he was, he failed even to cure the ills of the body. Of 'poisoning' [that is, causing psycho-physical illness caused by 'pointing the bone'] and witchcraft of course he knew nothing . . . 'How can such people cure when their hearts know no sorrow for the sick?' John demanded of me . . . How could a man be treated by a doctor who did not know his name nor the name of his father? He thought of the intimate contact obtained by a native doctor as he throws the bones, when he finds out the luck of his patient, which is finally the deciding-point in the treatment.

(Sachs 1996: 161–3)

In its emphasis on the intimate relationship between mental and physical distress, and its interrogation of the patient's life history, the methodology of the Manyika healer-diviner has more in common with psychoanalysis than with conventional European medical practice. As Jacqueline Rose points out, Sachs and Chavafambira are both proponents of a 'talking cure', which in each case depends for its efficacy upon the capacity of the practitioner to elicit and interpret the speech of the client (Rose 1996: 42). The emergence of these resemblances between the Manyikan methods of divination practised by Chavafambira and the clinical techniques practised by Sachs himself further estrange the bases of the white man's authority.

The disciplines of both men, for example, give primacy to the rites of interpretation as they occur within the consultative context, in the intimacy of the 'session'. Chavafambira's practice centres upon 'throwing the bones', 'an art', Sachs remarks, 'which turned out to be very interesting from a psychological point of view' (Sachs 1996: 216):

John explained to me that it was necessary to rub the horns thoroughly on his hands and on the patient's forehead so as to establish a contact between the patient and his ancestors. Then, after all this ceremony, he would interpret the movement of the horns entirely at random, for each time, no matter how they moved, he would give a totally different reading.

Actually, his interpretation depended solely upon infor-mation gleaned from the patient and from the patient's reactions to his suggestions.

(Sachs 1996: 217)

The interpretive technology, reliant as it is upon the establishment of a dialogic relationship between diviner and client, has enough in common with the psychoanalytic method that Sachs cannot resist the temptation to try out for the role of *nganga* himself:

> After witnessing a number of his sessions, I soon found myself as proficient a witch-doctor as he, and to his delight and amazement I proved it to him on several occasions, with the advantage, of course, that my medical knowledge of the case and a deeper psychological insight than John's helped me to obtain from the bones a more correct interpretation than his.
>
> (Sachs 1996: 219)

Sachs's self-satisfaction at the superiority of his medical and psychoanalytic knowledge over John's Manyikan discipline remains blind to the extent to which his performance undercuts the authority of those modes of knowledge he is trying to privilege. His skill at divination demonstrates the extent to which the Manyikan practice occupies in large part the same interpersonal epistemology as his own: it relies, at any rate, to an equal extent on skills of interpretation and the rapid transmutation of this into an authority that wins the patient's confidence. The result, in the meetings between Sachs and Chavafambira, is a double-sided mimicry that produces an inextricably hybridised knowledge. Again, this conforms to Bhabha's notion of the hybrid object which troubles the authority of Enlightenment discourse by reversing the formal process by which colonialism seeks to disavow other knowledges:

> Hybridity is a problematic of colonial representation and individuation that reverses the effects of the colonialist disavowal, so that other "denied" knowledges enter upon the dominant discourse and estrange the basis of its authority – its rules of recognition.
>
> (Bhabha 1994: 114)

The hybrid object, Bhabha writes, 'retains the actual semblance of the authoritative symbol but revalues its presence by resisting it', leading to 'questions of authority that the [colonial] authorities . . . cannot answer' (Bhabha 1994: 115).

The destabilisation of psychoanalytic authority by its relation to Manyikan divination has much in common with an example given by Deleuze and Guattari from a different African context. They recount a case described by Victor Turner among the Ndembu, of a man whose complaint, 'to our perverted [that is, Oedipalised] eyes . . . appears Oedipal. Effeminate, insufferable, vain, failing at everything he tries, the sick K. is preyed upon by the ghost of his maternal grandfather, who cruelly reproaches him' (Deleuze and Guattari 1977: 167). Instead of the therapeutic internalisation of this problem, according to the psychoanalytic mode, it is worked out by means of a form of divination which proves effective precisely according to its capacity to trace and repair the components of what Deleuze and Guattari refer to as the sick man's 'desiring machine', that is, the circuit of micro-cultural filaments connecting him to his environment:

> the soothsayer and the medicine man launch into a social analysis concerning the territory and its environs, the chief-tainship and its subchieftainships, the lineages and their segments, the alliances and the filiations; they constantly bring to light desire in its relations with political and economic units: 'Divination becomes a form of social analysis in the course of which hidden struggles between individuals and factions are brought to light, in such a way that they can be treated by traditional ritual methods.'[5]
>
> (Deleuze and Guattari 1977: 167)

What is more, an integral element in this investigation is its examination precisely of the local 'colonizer–colonized relations: the English have not recognized the chieftainship; the impover-ished village is falling into decrepitude' as a result of its alienation from the colonial economy (Deleuze and Guattari 1977: 168).

Other kinds of hybrid knowledge are also produced by the exchanges between Sachs and Chavafambira, which will demon-strate this same effect by which analysis overflows the constraints of an interiorised psychoanalytic subjectivity into the ramifying passages of the social, and particularly the colonial, contexts concerned. I will conclude by focusing on two more, because both impact upon psychoanalytic authority as well as upon the function of the Hamlet narrative: the first is the psychopathology of madness, and the second is the question of feminine sexuality.

Madness and colonisation

In the psychoanalytic account, Hamlet's madness arises from the incommensurable demands of his unconscious and of his superego. Freud's *Hamlet* thus demonstrates the psychic disease fundamental to the modern individual, radically undermining the grounds for any secure distinction between reason and unreason. Chavafambira, similarly, deploys his hybrid position within the Manyikan and the psychoanalytic regimes of knowledge to question the authority of a South African psychiatric discipline that uses its policing of the border between reason and unreason as a means to regulate cross-cultural identification.

He accompanies Sachs on his visits to the Pretoria mental hospital, where he sees five hundred native patients confined in a single ward. Initially he attributes their distress to 'poisoners' in the traditional Manyikan way. But it begins to be apparent to him that most often – in every one of the cases Sachs describes in detail, in fact – the delusions owe a great deal to white culture: one man claims to be a chief, but asserts that his brother has taken his wives and cattle 'and keeps me here with these dirty kaffirs' (Sachs 1996: 250); another, 'an elderly Bushman', identifies himself in Afrikaans as King George, threatening his fellow-inmates with disciplinary action from his soldiers and police. Sachs's narrative once again slips the reader into Chavafambira's thoughts: 'John found himself at a loss. Was the old Bushman, his face hatched and cross-hatched with wrinkles, really mad, or just playing the fool?' (Sachs 1996: 250–1). (It is hard not to wonder whether this insight owes more to *Hamlet* or to *King Lear* than it does to Chavafambira's actual comments to Sachs.)

Another patient, a young Xosa boy, claims in quick succession that he is a saint, that he is Satan, that Satan is his mother, that he is God and Satan, that he is their son. At this point, Sachs recounts,

> John remarked to me: 'The Christian religion muddles some native brains. I hear so much silly talk when these people think they are God, Jesus Christ, or Satan. But I have not heard a single one imagine himself to be *Mwari* or a *midzimu* [that is, either the chief god or one of the ancestral spirits of the Manyika]. Yes, the old religion of our fathers is better for us. The Christian religion makes trouble in the native brain. It is the talk of sin that makes all the trouble.'
>
> (Sachs 1996: 251–2)

The text goes on to describe how 'a feeling akin to panic' descends upon Chavafambira in the yard; a fear that he too will be infected with the poison that afflicts these unfortunates. What does Chavafambira most fear contracting – the germ of insanity or the influenza of a white culture that estranges the African mind from its own beliefs? The same anxiety, about the breakdown of the distinction between the psychically diseased and the healer, recurs a page or so later:

> Several patients talk about their sexual troubles to him. One said: 'I am an African. I am afraid of the white people. I am afraid of my own people. My father wants to poison me. I have been fifteen years in this hospital and every night God and judges standing in the sky force me to sleep with my mother.'
>
> These statements worried John. Fears of fathers and brothers! Sleeping with one's own mother! How like his own dreams, and the dreams of his friends and patients! . . . If incestuous dreams were a sign of insanity, was anyone sane?
>
> (Sachs 1996: 253)

This final question encapsulates the most radical aspect of psycho-analytic universality – the commonality of unconscious desires as the disruption of conventional borders between normality and abnormality; perversion as the grounds for acceptance into the Oedipal family of man – and at the same time demonstrates its function as a colonising ideology. Like the patients inside the asylum, John (at least according to Sachs's free indirect style) finds himself rehearsing, consciously and unconsciously, the incestuous dramas of the white Oedipal family structure. These Hamlet-like dreams make trouble in the native brain, just as Chavafambira describes the white religions doing with their talk of sin. Indeed, the colonial functions of Christianity, of juridical power and of psychoanalytic narrative combine in this nightmare image of 'God and judges standing in the sky forc[ing] me to sleep with my mother'.

But ultimately, the authority of psychoanalysis cannot answer the challenge posed to it in this chapter. Where the Freudian reading of *Hamlet* conceives of madness as the sign of an interminable depth in the humanist self, reinstalling the privileges of European bourgeois interiorised subjectivity in the very act of rehearsing its pathologies, the hybrid knowledge produced by

Sachs and Chavafambira reconstitutes madness as the product of socio-cultural forces; in particular, of the colonial conflict between Manyika knowledges of self and those of white South Africa. This perception, of course, undermines the very foundation of Sachs's ostensible project in *Black Hamlet*, and the 'startling discovery' with which the book begins: that realisation of the shared psychopathology of blacks and whites at the mental hospital which first inspired Sachs to attempt analysis of the 'normal' black psyche. The psychoanalyst has no answer to this, except to wonder at Chavafambira's success in eliciting information from the inmates where he has failed: 'And I wonder if it wouldn't be advisable, from a psychological point of view, to employ *ngangas* in the treatment of insane natives. In any case, there is nothing to lose, for our methods fail lamentably' (Sachs 1996: 253).

Black Ophelia

What, in the end, do the protagonists of *Black Hamlet* produce between them?

I could say a unique instance of the practice of psychoanalysis, and of the reading of literature, as registers that prove endlessly deconstructive not simply of their own metaphysics, but of their access to discursive and institutional power, and thereby uniquely capable – as no other forms of Western knowledge at such a time and in such a context could be – of allowing a kind of heteroglossia, of allowing the other to speak through the fractured voice of colonial authority. But surely to designate the exchange between these figures as a radicalised mode of psychoanalytic practice, or a politicisation of the power of literary rhetoric, would be to return this legacy to the same old forefathers, Shakespeare and Freud.

This is precisely the gesture repeated by two major recent critical approaches to these texts – that is, by Jacqueline Rose, in her introduction to the 1996 Johns Hopkins reissue of *Black Hamlet*, and by Andreas Bertoldi, writing about the text in the 1998 collection *Post-colonial Shakespeares*. Both critics reinstate the claims to universality often attributed to psychoanalytic theory. Both accept the transposition of Freud's nineteenth-century Viennese family romance into a structuralist key. Both want to maintain the fundamental validity of this unconscious structured, as Lacan insisted, like a language – and therefore, although inevitably speaking in different tongues across disparate cultures, retaining everywhere the same syntax.

So Bertoldi suggests that

> We understand Oedipus not as some European, Victorian sexual myth, but rather as the fundamental *mechanism* that ensures the transition from nature to culture . . . the question then becomes one of the details or ingredients making up the culturally specific forms of Oedipus.
>
> (Bertoldi 1998: 248–9)

Cultural difference is here reduced to a question of 'detail', superficial material to be processed by the 'fundamental' psychoanalytic mechanism, which adapts to and works within any imaginable localised setting.

The epistemological consequences of this return to psychoanalytic universalism are highly undesirable. Bertoldi finds himself subscribing to a theory of the development of cultures and the psyches of peoples derived in equal parts from the Freudian model of individual psychic maturation on one hand, and, on the other, that history of the (European) subject which takes *Hamlet* as its founding moment:

> what separates the ancients from Hamlet and the moderns is not the absence or presence of a super-ego, but rather the differential nature of the culturally specific forms of the resolution of Oedipus. In other words what separates various social formations is precisely the 'secular advance of repression', the increasing internalization of the super-ego and the psychologization of power. This is what Shakespeare's *Hamlet* represents, and it is this that Sachs reads into the South African colonial context. What we have in *Black Hamlet* is nothing less than a difference and conflict between a modern form of power and a 'pre-modern' social formation where the superego requires external social and cultural resources, such as initiation rituals, 'witchcraft' and 'magic' to ensure compliance.
>
> (Bertoldi 1998: 253)

In an accompanying note, Bertoldi insists with some anxiety that 'The distinction between the modern and the pre-modern as used here *does not* imply any pejorative usage, but is used to suggest different social regimes and organizations' (Bertoldi 1998: 258 n. 13; emphasis in original). A 'pejorative' intention becomes beside the point, however, insofar as the terms 'modern' and 'pre-modern' cannot help but imply a narrative of development out of the 'primitive', in both the psychoanalytic and anthropological senses of that term. This in turn allows only two politically regressive possibilities: either the romanticisation or the devaluation of the 'primitive' culture, which in either case continues to be judged in purely Eurocentric terms.

In Rose's account, similarly, the universalism of the Freudian moment is sternly reprimanded and shown the door, only to sneak back in via the skeleton key of structuralist abstraction. Rose accepts the findings of Marie Cecile and Edmond Ortigues, authors of *Oedipe Africaine*, that 'the Oedipus complex is, if anything, more rather than less present in [Africa] than in the West . . . But it is lived precisely publicly, collectively, mythically' (Rose 1996: 41). The Manyikan emphasis on the voice of the ancestors becomes subsumed under the category of 'conscience'; when Rose comments that 'ancestry, lineage, dead fathers, and ghosts are the touchstones of psychic well-being, [and] the individual suffers – fails at one level to be constituted *as* individual – when her or his sense of inheritance and continuity is out of joint' (Rose 1996: 40), it is clear that she comes to the text already equipped with a psychoanalytic structure, as constituted by Freud, Jones and Lacan via the character of Hamlet, whose comment after an encounter with his own ghostly father haunts Rose's rhetoric: 'The time is out of joint' (1.5.196).

Moreover, the colonial problematics of *Black Hamlet* constantly resolve into psychoanalytic ones for Rose, rather than the other way around: 'we should notice how hostility across the racial barrier, which might seem to be the fundamental problem, is inseparable from the fully psychoanalytic question of what speech, in terms of its internal and external boundaries, is capable of' (Rose 1996: 46). She also argues against the suggestion that Sachs in *Black Anger* abandons psychoanalysis for political engagement, working hard to preserve for psychoanalysis the epistemological – and even the political – high ground over its abandonment in favour of active engagement in political resistance (50).

Just as Rose brings a ready-made psychoanalytic protocol of reading to the text – she begins with the familiar feminist psychoanalytic enquiry, 'whose desire or fantasy are we dealing with here?

What does Wulf Sachs *want* of John Chavafambira?' (Rose 1996: 39) – she also concludes with her model intact. The end of her essay focuses on Maggie and Nesta, Chavafambira's wife and his mother, to demonstrate how the figure of the woman 'carries' or is burdened with a weight of signification foreclosed from the dominant narrative constructed by Sachs and his patient. The final function of the Hamlet theme, according to Rose, is to scapegoat the feminine in the service of the working out of a subjectivity predicated on masculinist terms: 'This is a book about Hamlet (who could not act) and Oedipus (who was lame). But who is it who really drags her leg (her feet) in the text?' (63). Rose is referring here to Maggie, whose lame leg first brought Sachs to the Rooiyard where he met Chavafambira, and whose disability remains a focal point for her husband's frustration with his life. Sachs unquestionably colludes with John's scapegoating of Maggie, writing for example that 'The power the lazy cripple exercised over her husband was amazing' (295). As Rose asks,

> Who becomes the repository of Hamletism, the inability to act, while Chavafambira, under Sachs's tutelage, steps forth into his new world? 'You lame bastard,' Chavafambira is reported as shouting at her in the moment before he poisons her and thinks he has killed her – the moment Sachs reads as signifying that he is at last 'ready for revolt' (298–300). What is the woman carrying for the rest of the players in this tale?
>
> (Rose 1996: 63)

Convincing as it is, Rose's critical strategy here repeats precisely her account of the function played by Gertrude in Freud's, Jones's and Lacan's interpretations of *Hamlet* in her crucial essay 'Hamlet – the Mona Lisa of Literature' (Rose 1986). Even more notably – and less happily, to my mind – this is the insight that paves the way for the final return in triumph of psychoanalytic truth, which supersedes and displaces the authority of an otherwise incisive feminist reading. Rose's argument ends with the remark that the women in *Black Hamlet*

> run rings around psychoanalysis, setting the limits to what it can do in Africa, making it impossible for psychoanalysis to have the last word. That there can be no last word – not

psychically, not politically – is, however, also the fundamental principle of psychoanalysis.

(Rose 1996: 63–4)

By a chiasmatic rhetoric familiar from the writings of Freud and Lacan, Rose banishes the notion of a 'last word', but goes back on her word at 'however', since her last clause returns an ultimate interpretive authority to psychoanalysis as the source of that very insight.

Earlier, Rose mentions that at one point in *Black Anger* Sachs attempts a brief analysis of Maggie, but she dismisses the results of this attempt by asserting that, along with the other African women mentioned in the text, she proves to be 'beyond the analytic pale' (Rose 1996: 63). In fact, this dialogue between Sachs and Maggie deserves rather more scrutiny than Rose affords it. Otherwise, there is a real risk of bequeathing once more to 'Woman' – as I think Rose does – the now-familiar role of the unspoken and unspeakable other of the psychoanalytic narrative. Maggie refuses to be just another instance of that 'dark continent' which cannot be penetrated by the psychoanalytic exploration.

To be sure, at the beginning of her reported conversation with Sachs, Maggie appears to offer the classic psychoanalytic cliché of the inscrutable woman:

Maggie was willing to talk to me, but to make her associate freely was not so easy.

'Just think aloud,' I said to her. 'Let the words slip off your tongue. If you won't look at me when you talk, it will be easier.'

'Why do you want *me* to talk to *me?*' she asked, baffled.

(Sachs 1947: 289)

Maggie is saying a great deal here. Her bafflement at the notion of free association makes it clear that the practices of psychoanalysis depend upon a model of subjectivity – of the self in communion with itself, of a conversation among different agencies (ego, superego, id) – that altogether subsumes the collective and the social within the firmly constituted boundaries of the individual. For Maggie, psychoanalytic 'honesty' is inappropriate precisely because of the real and pervasive presence of others, within her own sense of self, whose confidence she wishes to respect:

She refused to tell me her dreams, saying, 'What I see in my sleep I tell no one. My dead people will be cross.' She went on to say, 'I'm asleep, I'm like dead . . . and the *midzimu* come to talk to you then . . . Bad and silly people forget their dreams. And so they don't know what's going to happen to them; then they come to John and he, through his bones and horns, speaks for them with their *midzimu.* John can talk with dead people any time.'

Her *midzimu*, said Maggie, came to her every night. In the kraal it was different. The dead were in the hut with the living, there was a special place of them. 'But,' said Maggie, 'of course they couldn't live in Blacktown'.

(Sachs 1947: 289)

Far from filling the role of inappropriate revenants, or interlopers from an undiscovered country from where no traveller ought to return, the ancestral spirits have their proper place within the domestic space of Manyikan life, alongside their descendants. It is urbanisation that disrupts this arrangement, necessitating the confinement of the *midzimu* to dreams, to the space of the forgotten, and thence to the 'analytic session' officiated over by the healer-diviner. As Deleuze and Guattari point out, in the colonial context, 'Oedipus is not only an ideological process, but the result of a destruction of the environment, of habitat' (Deleuze and Guattari 1977: 169, n.).

Maggie proves more impervious to analytic interpellation than her husband, and grounds this resistance in the Manyika knowledge of dreams as deriving from the ancestors (which ought therefore to remain subject to their authority) rather than from the unconscious (and therefore subject to the authority of psychoanalysis).

While her resistance proves ultimately inadequate, it does seem justified, for when at last Sachs persuades her to yield some accounts of her dreams, he quickly satisfies himself that he is correct in diagnosing in her an aversion to sex and a hatred of men (Sachs 1947: 290–3). And behind this psychopathology, of course, the psychoanalyst discovers that 'Maggie . . . had a secret of her own. But the compulsion to confess was not strong enough to overcome the feeling of shame' (Sachs 1947: 292). The secret, of which Sachs has prior knowledge, is Maggie's extramarital affairs. The remainder of their dialogue is portrayed as the breaking down of Maggie's resistance to the discovery of this secret, achieved by means of Sachs's tendentious interpretation of her dreams (Sachs 1947: 292–3).

Despite the fact that Chavafambira's own liaisons with women other than his wife have been frequently attested to by Sachs, his analysis of Maggie makes a clear association between femininity, sexual profligacy, shame and deceit – behind which figures, once again, the shadowy outlines of the Hamlet narrative. Shakespeare's Prince famously comments, of his mother's supposed sexual voracity, 'Frailty, thy name is woman' (1.2.146); then to his former love Ophelia, on to whom he projects the same ubiquitous inconstancy, he remarks accusingly, 'I have heard of your paintings well enough. God hath given you one face and you make yourselves another' (3.1.144–6). Despite some of Maggie's explicit assessments of gender politics – her complaint that 'Men are loafers, no good. They want to sleep with you!' (Sachs 1947: 289), her comment that 'I think we shouldn't do it . . . It spoils our nation. What'll happen to our girls?' (292), and Sachs's admission that 'she herself found no joy in sleeping with a man' (290) – it is the psychoanalytically overdetermined presumption of feminine guilt that licenses Sachs to find in her dreams a motivating guilt that derives from her own sexual incontinence: when she dreams of a snake with many heads, Sachs tells her it is 'a sign that many men were tempting her'; regarding a dream involving water, his verdict is that 'you felt unclean and therefore were busy washing' (291–2).

While both *Hamlet* and *The Interpretation of Dreams* are working hard in this chapter of *Black Anger* to produce the required results from the exchange between Sachs and Maggie, here as elsewhere another mode of authority emerges, represented by the Manyikan knowledge of dreams and remaining unassimilable by the psychoanalytic and literary narratives. One of the striking things about Maggie's dreams, as Sachs recounts them, is that they often centre upon the appearance of animals, especially horses and snakes (Sachs 1947: 290–1). Sachs rapidly provides psychoanalytic explanations familiar enough from the psychoanalytic lexicon of dream symbols: animals 'are as a rule employed by the dream-work to represent passionate impulses of which the dreamer is afraid' (*PFL* 4: 536), while snakes, 'those most important symbols of the male organ' (474), are also associated with an entire Judaeo-Christian mythopoeia of feminine sexual perversity going back, as

Sachs reminds Maggie, to 'the story of Adam and Eve' (Sachs 1947: 291). Remarking that Maggie 'accepted my psychoanalytic inter- pretation of symbols quite readily' (292), Sachs ignores altogether a critical point made by Maggie herself prior to her dream accounts: that dreams are not the only, nor even the primary, medium through which the ancestral spirits communicate: 'if [the *midzimu*] are too busy to come, they send a message by a snake, a horse, or some other animal' (289). This suggestion not only challenges the priority given by Freudian theory to the dream as the 'royal road' to the unconscious; more importantly it gestures towards an entire alternative cosmology, or perhaps a bestiary, of Manyikan cultural meaning.

Without access to this other cultural knowledge, it is only possible to guess at other directions for the reading of these dreams. If the authority of Maggie's suggestion that animals are the agents of the *midzimu* is granted, the scenario in which a herd of horses run away at the appearance of a 'white lady' (Sachs 1947: 290), for instance, might suggest the extent to which the cultural and political relations between whites and blacks have already infiltrated Maggie's dreams: 'it is good to dream of an old white lady,' she remarks; 'It is good luck if the white people are good to us' (291). Similarly, in *Black Hamlet*, Sachs was able to deploy the psychoanalytic discourse on 'totem' animals – which I will discuss more fully in the next chapter – to interpret the occasion on which Chavafambira saved a *soko* or monkey (his *mutupo* animal) from its white attackers as a repayment of his debt to the paternal incest taboo, without considering the colonial politics of this act of resistance to white cruelty.

Unlike Rose, then, I am unwilling to give the last word on *Black Hamlet* to either psychoanalysis or Shakespeare. Instead I would prefer to read the exchanges with both Chavafambira and with Maggie described by Sachs in the light of the hybridised moment of healing-divination, the meeting and conflict between European and Manyikan epistemological authorities. These mutually imitative and mutually resistant encounters allow the possibility of a mimicry and a hybridity occurring in the terms, and on the epistemological terrain, of the colonised rather than those of the coloniser. Such a process embodies, moreover, several virtues from which contemporary critical discourse could learn much, demonstrating a mode of enquiry that acknowledges its reliance upon the repeated practices of interpretation (divination) rather than assuming a prior knowledge of either its pharmakon or its subjects; that remains utterly immersed in its reading of the microcultural signifiers of everyday life in their relation to the most localised of possible contexts; and that recognises its debts to domains of cultural knowledge beyond any European episteme.

Moreover, if the specificities and differences of local cultural habitats are respected, as Maggie demonstrates, a refusal to speak no longer has to be read as an inevitably feminised resistance to – and thereby a validation of – the authority of a masculinised governing discourse. Nor does the appearance of an absolute otherness – in the form of the non-human, spirit or animal – simply reflect back to European discourse its own fascinating limits. Rather, Sachs's text foreshadows the possibility – even if it remains unfulfilled – of a politics which, although inaugurated by liberal humanism, breaks into a post-humanist ethics, the recognition of the debt to an absolute alterity no longer circumscribed by the field of culture, or by the boundaries that humanism draws around the figure of the human itself. In other words, the animals in Maggie's dreams could be read for the way they represent the operation of a peculiarly Manyikan negotiation between nature and culture – no longer reducible to the Oedipal mechanism, or that alternative version of Oedipus that constitutes the psychoanalytic understanding of 'primitive' totem and taboo. Such a Manyikan reading of these dreams is well beyond both the scope of the present volume and my own cultural authority, so I can only begin to demonstrate the ways in which the conceptual development of integral aspects of the psychoanalytic apparatus – even 'at home' in Vienna – depends upon cultural knowledges other than those of Europe. In the next chapter I will suggest some of the ways in which Freud's notions of conscience, neurosis, the unconscious, repetition compulsion and even the Oedipal complex itself draw upon anthropological representations of cultures perceived as 'primitive' in European terms – studies which arise out of the multiple colonial 'contact zones' of the nineteenth century: Africa, the Indian subcontinent, the Pacific, Australia, New Zealand. Colonial epistemology thus proves to be an integral element of psychoanalytic thought; even at its European birthplace, Freudianism starts to look like a child of mixed parentage.

To attend to the moments at which both Shakespeare and psychoanalysis release their grip is to treat the protagonists of these texts with certain kinds of respect that seem, to me, not only appropriate but necessary: to recognise both the material courage and the intellectual radicalism of Sachs, as a Jewish immigrant challenging not only the brutal racism of the Union of South Africa but the wider context of escalating European anti-Semitism during the 1930s and 1940s; but also to honour the different kinds of cultural authority of the Manyikan man and woman to whom Sachs owes so much. This entails acknowledging the incapacity, at such a moment and in such a location, of any European epistemology – literary or psychoanalytic – recognising fully its debt to knowledges outside of its own field of vision.

One sign of the blindness that accompanies every insight in this text is that in *Black Hamlet* Wulf always refers to his subjects as 'John' and 'Maggie', insistently forgetting their Manyikan names. It's not surprising, perhaps, that we never hear Maggie's name at all; on the other hand, it seems apposite that the name we do hear, Chavafambira, which her husband inherits from his ancestors, translates from Shona into the English phrase 'the reason you are here' (Dubow, in Sachs 1996: 7).

Part II

Psychoanalysis out of Shakespeare

4
Shakespeare's memory

The memory of the other

A late story by Jorge Luis Borges describes two men meeting at a Shakespeare conference. The first, a German academic by the name of Hermann Sörgel, receives from the second a singular offer: Daniel Thorpe claims to have mental possession of the memory of Shakespeare, complete from childhood to death, and he wants to give it away. Despite his scepticism, Sörgel cannot refuse; uttering his acceptance aloud is sufficient to transmit the memory from Thorpe's mind into his own.

Sörgel does not gain immediate access to the memory, but eventually it emerges – initially in auditory rather than visual terms: stray recollections of previously unknown phrases and melodies, a new facility with Elizabethan pronunciation. Eventually the visual memories follow – faces, rooms – but only initially in dreams. Disturbingly, however, as Shakespeare's memory becomes activated, it starts to obliterate Sörgel's own. He finds himself forgetting his native German; he starts to lose his ability to cope with and understand the modern world around him. One morning he panics at the Bremen railway station, unable to recognise the deafening noises and the gigantic moving shapes of iron, glass and wood that surround him. Eventually, fearing for his sanity, he decides to rid himself of Shakespeare's memory, and does so by dialling telephone numbers at random until he finds a suitable candidate, one who will speak the words that allow the memory to be passed on again.

'Shakespeare's Memory' brings to an ironic summation the Argentine fabulist's lifelong fascination with Shakespeare and also with notions of memory, time and identity. The story also exemplifies key aspects of the psychoanalytic understanding of each of these terms.[1]

The Freudian unconscious, following Lacan's rereading of it, might be thought of as 'the memory of the other': those thoughts, perceptions, impressions, words and so on that seem to emerge, in the subject, from elsewhere. Like Freud, Borges describes the memory of the other (at least in its visual form) emerging primarily in dreams, and also in apparently random and inconsequential perceptions that are only secondarily processed into meaning. Shakespeare's memory, moreover, grasps and manipulates the subject, rather than being under his control: Thorpe warns Sörgel, 'I possess . . . *two* memories – my own personal memory and the memory of that Shakespeare that I partially am. Or rather, two memories possess *me*' (Borges 1998: 510). Similarly, Lacan's observation about each of the characters in Poe's 'The Purloined Letter', that 'Falling in possession of the letter – admirable ambiguity of language – its meaning possesses them' (Lacan 1972: 60), only needs to be interpreted in the context of his famous insistence that 'the unconscious is structured like a language' to become a description of the function of memory (Lacan 1977b: 234; 1979: 20).

Hearing Thorpe's offer, Sörgel feels 'as though I had been offered the ocean' (Borges 1998: 510), and comments when he receives the gift that 'At first the waters of the two memories did not mix; in time, the great torrent of Shakespeare threatened to flood my own modest stream – and very nearly did so' (514). Elsewhere Borges deftly interpolates two other versions of memory: the first, from de Quincey, envisages the brain as a palimpsest in which 'Every new text covers the previous one, and is in turn covered by the text that follows – but all-powerful Memory is able to exhume any impression, no matter how momentary it might have been, if given sufficient stimulus' (512); the second is attributed to St Augustine, who 'speaks, if I am not mistaken, of the palaces and caverns of memory' (513). Each of these metaphors characterises memory according to its contradictory functions: like an ocean or torrent, it combines limitless capacity with the threat of engulfment; like a palimpsest, writing and erasure; like an underground cavern, excavation and burial. The same ambivalence will serve as a focal point in both the Shakespearean and the psychoanalytic accounts of memory.

Sörgel also finds that 'Like our own, Shakespeare's memory included regions, broad regions, of shadow – regions that he willfully rejected' (Borges 1998: 513). These shadowy regions of the Shakespearean memory – overwritten texts, drowned perceptions, buried structures – seem to correspond even more clearly to the psychoanalytic unconscious, the domain of the repressed, until the narrator comments, 'One morning I perceived a sense of guilt deep within his memory. I did not try to define it; Shakespeare himself has done so for all time. Suffice it to say that the offense had nothing in common with perversion' (513). This implied scepticism about the Freudian reading of Shakespeare's Oedipalised psychopathology functions as one of those strategies of faked authenticity typical of Borges: the veracity of the narrative is guaranteed by Sörgel's stated access to a knowledge of Shakespeare's memory beyond that postulated by Freud.

However, any psychoanalytic disavowal serves as well as a confession: Borges's tale owes much to the psychoanalytic account of memory, and in particular to a question that haunted Freud: does memory provide access to authentic perceptions from the past, or can it only perform reconstructions? The story first elicits, then suspends, and finally reactivates the reader's suspicion regarding this question. Thorpe's account of his own acquisition of the memory refuses the kind of detail that would give it verisimilitude: 'The exact date is not important' (Borges 1998: 510); 'I will not say where or when; I know all too well that such specifics are in fact vaguenesses' (509). At first then, Borges skilfully alienates the reader from her or his scepticism by having Sörgel voice it as well: in relation to Thorpe's acquisition of the memory from a dying soldier, he comments that 'the pathetic scene of the bestowal struck me as "literary" in the worst sense of the word. It all made me a bit leery' (510). Because the narrator appropriates the reader's disbelief in this way, though, he also exorcises it; so the reader goes along with his eventual acceptance of the memory and its gradual emergence in his mind. The randomness and inconsequentiality – even the banality – of the recollections vouchsafed also help to convince.

But as the narrative continues, the reader's suspicion re-emerges, entertaining the possibility that the insights could merely be the products of the narrator's own literary-critical and historical erudition. The 'exercises' Sörgel devises to activate the memory – reading Shakespeare's sources (Chaucer, Holinshed, Florio's Montaigne, North's Plutarch) and his sonnets – are no different from those followed by generations of critics seeking access to the mind of Shakespeare. Moreover, those academic 'insights' Sörgel vouchsafes from experience seem nothing more than ancient critical clichés: he discovers that Shakespeare's 'apparent instances of inadvertence' were deliberate, designed to make the plays appear spontaneous rather than 'overly polished and artificial' (Borges 1998: 513), a notion which has been advanced often enough by critics eager to transform Shakespeare's errors into guarantees of his genius; he writes an article arguing that Sonnet 127 refers to the defeat of the Spanish Armada, a knowledge to which the memory allows him authoritative access, while simultaneously making him forget that Samuel Butler advanced the thesis before him in 1899.

The conclusion of the narrative re-engages with its reader's scepticism, albeit in a somewhat unexpected way. A brief italicised postscript is included, ostensibly added by Sörgel after he has relinquished the memory:

> *I am now a man among men. In my waking hours I am Professor Emeritus Hermann Sörgel; . . . but at dawn I sometimes know that the person dreaming is that other man. Every so often in the evening I am unsettled by small, fleeting memories that are perhaps authentic.*
>
> (Borges 1998: 515)

The dubious status of memory returns here overtly, but in an unexpected form: the authenticity of Shakespeare's memory now seems less in question than that of Sörgel's own. In a manner familiar to his readers, Borges suggests that the narrator's own identity and perceptions have proven to be phantasms, the dreams or memories of someone else.

'Shakespeare's Memory' thus concisely recasts the psycho-analytic account of the function of memory in the constitution of the subject. But it also raises a question that haunts any attempt to read between psychoanalysis and Shakespeare: to what extent, and in what ways, are the identifications we make with the subjectivity we find in Shakespearean texts projections, back in time, of our own (psychoanalytically influenced) concerns about, and representations of, identity, history and relationships?

Alternatively, we surely cannot afford simply to dismiss 'psychoanalytic reading(s) of Shakespeare' out of hand – as, say, anachronistic, or as incompetent to recognise the historical differences between early modern and twentieth-century notions of subjectivity. For even a critic determined to honour historical and cultural difference depends, after all, upon certain notions of memory and identity, and I am convinced that our current (Western literary-critical) grasp and deployment of those notions is itself inexorably influenced by psychoanalysis – as was Borges for his own elegant disavowal of Freud's version of Shakespeare. How accurate can our memories of Shakespeare be if the very structure and function of our notions of memory and history are irremediably inf(l)ected by psychoanalytic models? On the other hand, to what extent are these psychoanalytic understandings of memory (and forgetting) dictated by Shakespearean ones? Where do Shakespeare's and Freud's memories come from, and what have they to do with each other?

History's forgetting

> I began with the desire to speak with the dead.

Stephen Greenblatt claims that this opening sentence of his book *Shakespearean Negotiations* expresses 'a familiar, if unvoiced, motive in literary studies'. Confessing that 'in my most intense moments of straining to listen all I could hear was my own voice', Greenblatt claims to have discovered nevertheless that his own voice embodied that of the dead, who had 'contrived to leave textual traces of themselves heard in the voices of the living'. And the most capacious repositories of this ghostly speech proved to be literary texts which 'anticipate and compensate for the vanishing of the actual life that has empowered them. Conventional in my tastes, I found the most satisfying intensity of all in Shakespeare' (Greenblatt 1988: 1).

The same desire, for communication with the speaking memory of Shakespeare, provides Borges with his parable about reading, but it is hardly unique to literary criticism; it thoroughly infuses the theories of Freud and Lacan, too. And surely any mode of literary historical enquiry – such as new historicism – that finds in the present the voice of the past repeating itself, or that seeks to hear in texts those 'lost' or buried 'traces' most difficult to make out, or indeed that can recognise in itself a motivating desire, at once 'familiar' and 'unvoiced', owes a debt to psychoanalysis.[2]

For psychoanalysis as for Greenblatt, speech with the dead therefore provides a primary figure of the constitution of memory, an integral aspect of the processes that bring the subject into being. Formed at least in part upon the model provided by *Hamlet*, the Freudian and Lacanian schema of subjectivity, as I have argued in earlier chapters, takes as its inaugural moment the introjection of the command of the dead father: 'Remember me.' De Certeau argues that this ghostly visitation emblematises for Freud the return of the repressed – the fundamental principle of the psychoanalytic conceptualisation of memory:

> If the past (that which took place during, and took the form of, a decisive moment in the course of a crisis) is *repressed*, it *returns* in the present from which it was excluded, but does so surreptitiously. One of Freud's favourite examples is a figuration of this detour-return, which constitutes the ruse of history: Hamlet's father returns after his murder, but in the form of a phantom, in another scene, and it is only then that he becomes the law his son obeys.
>
> (de Certeau 1986: 3)

This law speaks even in critics who, like Greenblatt, explicitly disavow the psychoanalytic discourse on memory and history – precisely because the psychoanalytic and Shakespearean conceptualisations of memory are at once so intimately linked to each other, and so pervasively present within any critical mode that draws upon structuralist or poststructuralist theory.

Despite the psychoanalytical figuration of his own motive for reading, Greenblatt's attitude to the relation between psychoanalysis and history remains one of thoroughgoing suspicion. In an often-cited article, 'Psychoanalysis and Renaissance Culture', he tries to explain why Renaissance texts so often seem to invite, but always frustrate, a psychoanalytical reading: they do so because 'psychoanalysis is at once the fulfillment and effacement of specifically Renaissance insights: psychoanalysis is, in more than one sense, the end of the Renaissance' (Greenblatt 1990: 131). Early modern identity, he argues, is not defined in the same way that psychoanalysis sees the self, that is, as an interiorised psychic history with inalienable links to infantile life experience and biological traits. Rather, the early modern self manifests primarily as 'the placeholder in a complex system of possession, kinship bonds, contractual relationships, customary rights, and ethical obligations'. Subjectivity must in such a context function as 'the *product* . . . rather than the *producer* of these relations, objects, and judgements' (137). It is the historical transition from the first of these notions to the second – from the early modern to the modern, or in Greenblatt's slick formulations, from property to psyche, from purse to person – that produces the conditions of possibility for psychoanalysis. For the new historicist, then, 'psychoanalytic interpretation is causally belated, even as it is causally linked' to sixteenth- and seventeenth-century representations and practices of social and cultural identity (142). So, although psychoanalytic modes of reading Renaissance texts are not exactly anachronistic, they risk distorting our sense of the past insofar as they do not recognise their own production by the histories they read.[3]

Greenblatt's accusation is therefore that psychoanalysis forgets both historical difference and its own cultural genealogy; it thereby risks both anachronism and universalism when it finds Freudian structures at work in Shakespeare, or in any pre-twentieth-century text. By a kind of retroactive epistemological colonialism, psychoanalysis assimilates the differences of past cultures and events to its own meta-paradigm of the human condition. But the law of repetition respects no one: Greenblatt's own inattention to the recent histories of psychoanalysis allows him to advance a reductive, outdated and overly monolithic (in fact a Jungian or ego-psychological) version of the psychoanalytic notion of the subject, according to which the 'mask' of a person's social identity functions as 'a defensive strategy, a veneer hiding the authentic self beneath' (Greenblatt 1990: 143), which he then contrasts with a Renaissance attitude that perceives the social and cultural representation of a person as the authentic self. His formulation forgets that Freudian and Lacanian psychoanalysis represents a radical challenge to any such model of an 'authentic' deep self; and forgets also that this is the very epistemological breakthrough which allows him to recognise this difference between early modern and the modern 'selves' in the first place. To take this point a step further, I would argue moreover that psychoanalysis can only make this breakthrough because of its own identification with those modes of subjectivity that are outside (because prior to) the modern, which it finds, pre-eminently, in Shakespeare. In several different ways, then, Greenblatt blurs or elides the important investments and inheritances that shape the relation between early modern texts and psychoanalytic theory.

Such a misprision reinforces rather than undermines the necessity of a thoroughgoing historicisation of psychoanalysis, but also illustrates the danger of imagining that such a project could have free access to a notion of history that is not already implicated in the genealogy of the subject, and therefore of psychoanalysis itself. And so the questions advanced earlier return. What kind of memory – what theory of history – could serve the production of a thoroughgoing historicisation of psycho-analytic models and procedures? How to historicise a theory which itself demonstrates the non-innocence of the functions of memory and history?

One response to these issues attempts to spell out a specifically psychoanalytic theory of collective history; most often, however, this attempt repeats blindly many of Freud's most dated short-comings: his Eurocentrism, his masculinism, his heterosexism. Michael Roth, for example, traces Freud's far-flung comments on history to discover a repeated reliance on a linear trajectory history of development from 'primitivism' (from totemism and animism, via monotheism) to civilisation (defined in specifically European terms) (Roth 1987). Although Freud's view of this evolution is pessimistic – he equates the development of civilisation with the advance of psychic repression – it nevertheless remains imperiously Eurocentric in its attribution of cultural value: the greater the repression, the 'higher' (more sublime, more sublimated) the capacity for cultural productivity. Roth fails to notice both this and the banal linearity of his Freudian model of history, which hardly constitutes a radical departure from the teleological default setting programmed into historiography by the nineteenth-century emphasis on progress – of which the evolutionary theory of Freud's hero, Charles Darwin, offers only the most obvious instance.[4]

Moreover, for the most part Roth has to extrapolate his psychoanalytically derived theory of history from Freud's theories of individual memory: the narration of the individual's life experience in analysis, for example. It is a characteristic psychoanalytical vice to prioritise individual psychic history in this way, and to presume that the structures of perception and memory experienced by the individual subject precede and dictate the operations of collective history. For the cultural historian, though, this assumption seems inverted; surely it must be equally valid to claim that the individual's experience of the relationship between past, present and future derives from the representations of memory and history she or he receives from the surrounding culture – in which, of course, both psychoanalytic theory and Shakespearean drama might well be formative influences.[5] In this way, psychoanalytic notions of the 'individual history of the subject', rather than being transferred to the domain of 'group psychology' – the histories of nations, classes, genders, peoples – would need to be seen as deriving from those cultural collectives.

In fact, exploration of the historical and cultural production of psychoanalytic structures and processes has been progressing rapidly, both before and after the first appearance of Greenblatt's essay in 1986. Concentrating only on the aspect of this considerable project that forms the focus of the present volume – the relation between psychoanalysis and the reading of Shakespeare – I would identify two parallel dimensions at work.

The first examines the role played by the deployment of the Shakespearean text in the twentieth-century establishment and maintenance of psychoanalysis as a discourse, an institution of knowledge. The first three chapters of the present volume have been oriented to this project, towards which important contributions have been made by those critics who have analysed the influence of *Hamlet* upon Charcot and other nineteenth-century psychiatric theorists (Showalter 1985); upon Freud himself (Garber 1987); and upon his inheritors, Jones and Lacan (Rose 1986) and Wulf Sachs (Rose, in Sachs 1996).

The second way to historicise the relation between psychoanalysis and Shakespeare involves the genealogical exploration of psychoanalytic concepts, schemata and epistemological structures. Many recent critics have undertaken different aspects of this task, whereby the fundamental constituents of psychoanalytic theory can been traced, via Shakespearean drama, back to Renaissance and classical antecedents. In the 1980s groundbreaking work by Catherine Belsey (1985), Joel Fineman (1986) and Jonathan

Dollimore (1989) began to excavate the literary-cultural origins of the modern subject. More recently, Belsey has concentrated on the historical development of particular sources of the subjectivity described by psychoanalysis, exploring the genealogy of the Oedipal account of gender and sexuality in relation to changing notions of desire (1994) and the emergence of the Western nuclear family (1999). Other recent studies have concentrated on bringing to light the cultural memories of different concepts fundamental to psychoanalysis: mourning and melancholia (Lupton and Reinhard 1993); the superego, conscience or *nom-du-père* (Lukacher 1994); identification, misrecognition and the scopic drive (Freedman 1991; Armstrong 2000). In another field, work on early modern conceptualisations of the body – for example, by Stallybrass and White (1986), Laquer (1990), Traub (1992), Paster (1993), Kahn (1997) and Neill (1997: 139–67) – has explored those histories out of which psychoanalysis draws its representations of relationships between corporeality, gender, class, sexuality and the organisation of individual subjectivities and intersubjectivities.

In what follows, I want to focus on the relationship between the Freudian and the Shakespearean theories of memory – an enquiry which seems to me critical to the development of a well-informed historicisation of psychoanalysis, of literary criticism and of historiography itself.

Freud's memory

Communion with the dead: that which was familiar is lost, and encountered again unexpectedly. As de Certeau suggests, the major insight offered by psychoanalysis into memory is an emphasis on its uncanniness. All Freud's dissertations on the topic manifest that sense of anxious displacement which characterises the return of the repressed.

When Borges cites the remembrancer's descent into 'palaces and caverns', he activates a figure of memory that ought to prove most unproblematic for Freud: archaeology. The image of excavating buried sites combines many aspects of Freud's manifest view of both collective history and individual memory: the progress of 'civilisation' (corresponding to ego autonomy in the individual subject) proceeds in conjunction with the covering over of previous structures and impressions (that is, the repression or burial of prior psychic states). Freud's texts on metapsychology – especially 'Beyond the Pleasure Principle' (1920; *PFL* 11: 269–338) – and on the origins of society and religion – 'Totem and Taboo' (1913; *PFL* 13: 43–224), 'Civilisation and Its Discontents' (1930; *PFL* 12: 243–340), 'Moses and Monotheism' (1939; *PFL* 13: 237–386) – derive their overt models of psychic development from scientific disciplines in the ascendant in the nineteenth century: palaeontology and evolutionary biology on one hand, and archaeology and ethnographic narratives of cultural progress towards 'civilisation', on the other. These discourses combined to produce popular and academic conceptualisations of an evolutionary history that rehearsed a linear progression from the primitive to the complex; in doing so, however, they both derived from and invested in the enterprise of European (and especially British) colonialism. The ethnographies of Cook's voyages in the Pacific, Darwin's observations during his travels on the *Beagle*, the archaeological excavations in continental Europe and Egypt, the Victorian anthropologies of Australian, Pacific, South Asian and African peoples: all were motivated by the imperial mission, and made possible by the opportunities for travel and 'collection' it provided; all in turn extended the possibilities for colonialism by providing it both with an ideological rationale (the advance of civilisation, the eradication of the primitive) and with strategically useful information about other cultures. To the extent that Freud draws upon these discourses, therefore, psychoanalysis invests from the outset in the epistemological functions of the colonial project.

Nineteenth-century archaeology, for example, dreamed of discovering a synchronic snapshot of lived past experience, lying perfectly preserved beneath the feet of the current forgetful inhabitants. Freud first discovered Pompeii as an analogy for analysis in Jensen's short story *Gradiva*, in which an archaeologist becomes fascinated by a relief of a young woman at a museum in Rome, only to see the same figure in the street one day; a dream about experiencing the eruption of Vesuvius prompts him to visit Pompeii, where he again encounters the mysterious woman. It emerges that repressed memories of a childhood friendship between the two were reawakened by the image in the museum, which then provided the unconscious motivation for his journey to the place in which he would find her again. The location for this rediscovery provides the final simile of the tale – that of the 'childhood friend who had been dug out of the ruins' – to which Freud then adds the comment that there is 'no better analogy for repression, by which something in the mind is at once made inaccessible and preserved, than burial of the sort to which Pompeii fell a victim and from which it could emerge once more through the work of spades' (*PFL* 14: 65). This analogy for memory – which cannot be bettered – envisages childhood impressions as fossilised, preserved intact but inaccessible, waiting to be dug out by analysis – a function fulfilled, in Jensen's story, by the extraordinary perspicacity of the young woman in question, and secondarily of course by both the work of the creative writer and the hermeneutics of the reader, Freud himself.

Pompeii comes to light again two years later, in 'Notes upon a Case of Obsessional Neurosis' (1909). Addressing his patient (often referred to as 'The Rat Man'), Freud assures him that

> everything conscious was subject to a process of wearing-away, while what was unconscious was relatively unchangeable; and I illustrated my remarks by pointing to the antiques standing about in my room. They were, in fact, I said, only objects found in a tomb, and their burial had been their preservation: the destruction of Pompeii was only beginning now that it had been dug up.
>
> (*PFL* 9: 57)

The emphasis here is upon the 'relatively unchangeable' status of unconscious memories, their resistance to wearing away – a state of preservation produced by their repression, in the same way that the burial of Pompeii protected it from decay. The passage also demonstrates vividly how Freud's theories about memory are formulated by means of a dialogue between his analytic explorations of individual psyches – in this case the Rat Man's – and his simultaneous engagement with the cultural and historical surroundings – here, the immediate context of his consulting room, in which collected antiques demonstrate his debt to archaeology, but also the broader context provided by his reference to the relatively recent discovery and ongoing excavation of Pompeii.[6]

Two decades later, in *Civilisation and Its Discontents*, Freud reconfigures the metaphor to insist upon the survival of early psychic memory-traces alongside later and 'more developed' forms. He first alludes to evolutionary biology, according to which 'the most highly developed species have proceeded from the lowest; and yet we find all the simple forms still in existence to-day' (*PFL* 12: 256). Yet this analogy does not quite suit, since 'the lower species which survive are for the most part not the true ancestors of the present-day more highly developed species. As a rule the intermediate links have died out and are known to us only through reconstruction.' In the realm of the mind, by contrast, 'what is primitive is . . . commonly preserved alongside of the trans- formed version which has arisen from it'. Freud wants to find a model that avoids the notion of memory as *knowledge through reconstruction*; one that encompasses instead the perfect preser- vation of memory-traces alongside current perceptions: 'Let us try to grasp what this assumption involves by taking an analogy from another field. We will choose as an example the history of the Eternal City' (256). Shifting his rhetorical ground from biology back to ancient history, and his archaeological dig from Pompeii to Rome, Freud now invites his reader to imagine all the successive stages of topographical and architectural modification of that cityscape, from early fenced settlements, to a city bounded by the Servian wall, to the imperial centre surrounded by the wall of Aurelian. His emphasis on the construction of a boundary as constitutive of urban space derives, of course, from the implied analogy with the formation of the individual ego, which, as he has described a page or so earlier, forms via the establishment and maintenance of a separation of itself from the external world (255).

But his next move extends the analogy, and in so doing fantastically dislocates the metaphor from its grounding in standard archaeological practice:

> Now let us, by a flight of imagination, suppose that Rome is not a human habitation but a psychical entity with a similarly long and copious past – an entity, that is to say, in which nothing that has once come into existence will have passed away and all the earlier phases of development continue to exist alongside the latest one . . . And the observer would perhaps only have to change the direction of his glance or his position in order to call up the one view or the other.
>
> (*PFL* 12: 257–8)

Searching for a metaphor to embody his conviction that the function of memory, as described by the theory and activated by the practice of psychoanalysis, admits access to an original and intact psychic artefact – rather than a process of knowledge through reconstruction – Freud designs an archaeological fantasy so elaborate and artificial that he has to conclude that it 'leads to things that are unimaginable and even absurd' (*PFL* 12: 258). It is much easier today than when Freud was writing to envisage a virtual-reality programme that might allow the spectator to superimpose layer upon layer of urban development; computer-generated scenarios can combine the kind of precision and retentiveness that he wants to attribute to memory with the other attributes that his account wants to avoid but cannot help implying: performativity, theatricality and artifice. For Freud, though, this remains a disappointing analogy: too much fiction, too little science. He decides that historical sequence cannot be represented in spatial terms.

And so the scientific archaeology which is at the same time a mental space of performance is overlaid, in later texts, by the figure of a mystic slate, a scene of inscription. But even when Freud chooses to describe memory as a succession of layers of writing and rewriting, rather than of burials and excavations, he still cannot escape the ambivalencies generated by his temporal model. The supposed qualities of writing (materiality, reliability, compatibility with individual agency) continue to dissolve into those of performance (ephemerality, liability to revision, reliance upon the collective).

In a brief sketch made famous by Jacques Derrida, Freud compares the memory to a device (comparable to de Quincey's metaphor of the palimpsest, cited by Borges) upon which succeeding impressions are recorded and then overlaid, but never altogether lost. 'A Note on the Mystic Writing Pad' (1925; *PFL* 11: 427–34) describes an ingenious apparatus consisting of a slab of wax, upon which rests a sheet of paper covered in turn by celluloid. Scratching the top layer with a stylus creates inscriptions rendered visible by the adherence of the paper, wherever pressure has been applied, to the slab beneath; these can be erased by peeling the paper back, leaving the pad once more blank and ready for imprinting. However, lifting the double covering layer altogether reveals that the indentations caused by prior messages remain imprinted upon the wax slab beneath. The mystic pad thereby illustrates two traits Freud considers fundamental to the operation of memory: 'an unlimited receptive capacity and a retention of permanent traces' (*PFL* 11: 430).

Moreover, the separate components of the device can be compared with the different constituents in operation in the mind: the paper layer with the mental function of perception-consciousness (which Freud abbreviates to *Pcpt.-Cs.*), receiving stimuli from the external world; the covering celluloid with the 'protective shield' that diminishes the strength of incoming excitations, thereby avoiding damage to the perceptual apparatus; the wax slab with the unconscious, receiving and preserving the memory-traces; 'and the appearance and disappearance of the writing with the flickering-up and passing-away of consciousness in the process of perception' (*PFL* 11: 433).

This humble analogy concludes with one of those sweeping gestures typical of Freud. The intermittence of the contact between stylus (stimulus), paper (perception) and slab (unconscious) becomes the focus of attention – that feature of the mystic pad which replicates the 'flickering-up and passing-away of consciousness'. Remarkably, Freud proposes that consciousness does not maintain a constant existence in time; even more strangely, that time itself is inconstant, produced by the intermittent 'investments' (the charged impulses which he calls *cathexes*) passing between unconscious, conscious and external perception:

> On the Mystic Pad the writing vanishes every time the close contact is broken between the paper which receives the stimulus and the wax slab which preserves the impression . . . My theory was that cathectic innervations are sent out and withdrawn in rapid periodic impulses from within into the completely pervious system *Pcpt.-Cs.* So long as that system is cathected in this manner, it receives perceptions (which are accompanied by consciousness) and passes the excitation on to the unconscious mnemic systems; but as soon as the cathexis is withdrawn, consciousness is extinguished and the functioning of the system comes to a standstill. It is as though the unconscious stretches out feelers, through the medium of the system *Pcpt.-Cs.*, towards the external world and hastily withdraws them as soon as they have sampled the excitations coming from it . . . I further had a suspicion that this discontinuous method of functioning of the system *Pctp.-Cs.* lies at the bottom of the origin of the concept of time.

(*PFL* 11: 433–4)

A radical challenge to the modern, autonomous, sovereign self emerges here. Seen in this way, the self can no longer be conceived of as an independent collection of consistent impressions, memories, beliefs and thoughts; on the contrary, it becomes an illusory, ephemeral and intermittent effect thrown up by momentary impulses exchanged between the unconscious and the external excitations. This was the position of the narrator at the conclusion of the Borges tale: that of finding himself no more than a by-product of occasional, fleeting and contingent memories deriving from the other. It also, of course, corresponds to the phenomenology of theatrical characters, whose 'consciousness', however engaging an audience may find it, corresponds only to the stitched-together sum of their actual appearances onstage.

Furthermore, if 'the bottom of the origin of the concept of time' (a phrase which itself dissolves the very idea of priority into an endless regression of layers: time into concept into origin into bottom) must be considered a secondary effect of this system, any access to a stable narrative of linear causation or historical progress becomes equally illusory. The Freudian approach to the function of memory – upon which the effect of subjectivity depends – requires us to conceive of the temporal relation between past, present and future impressions as utterly subject on one hand to the motivations and investments of the unconscious, and on the other to the vagaries of the external world from which stimuli arrive.

The processes of the unconscious, as Freud puts it elsewhere, can therefore be considered 'timeless; i.e. they are not ordered temporally, are not altered by the passage of time; they have no reference to time at all' (*PFL* 11: 191). Here, then, is perhaps the most substantial and productive contribution of the psychoanalytic theory of memory: it offers a way of conceptualising effects that occur outside of a conventional linear causality: investments, connections and stimuli that pass back and forth between past, present and future; perceptions of history without regard for rational or conscious causation. It is this 'atemporality' – or, more accurately, this alternative temporality – that allows Freud and Lacan, for example, stimulated by the early modern texts they read, to identify and activate modes and models of thought and identity repressed or forgotten by the dominant culture of the rational within which they work: thus Freud's scientific evolutionism and painstaking archaeology mutate into a spectacular theatre of vision which anticipates virtual reality. Similarly, his mystic writing pad, combining 'unlimited receptive capacity' with the 'retention of permanent traces', reminds me simultaneously of the word processor on which I now write, *and* the early modern scenes of 'mystic writing' that Shakespeare dramatises.

Recalling Hamlet

For the most obvious of these, I return to *Hamlet* (*Hamlet* returns to me). In response to the visit from his dead father, by whom he is enjoined to 'Remember me', Hamlet resorts to a scene of reinscription, writing over all the prior impressions held on his 'tables' – his mystic writing pad – a reminder to fulfil the paternal command (1.5.91–112). One of the things that the Freudian account takes from its memory of *Hamlet* is an attitude to the act of writing-as-memory which, unlike the highly individualised, private and ego-centred culture of writing bequeathed by the eighteenth and nineteenth centuries, retains the communal, performative and ephemeral characteristics of theatre.

For Hamlet's scene of writing simultaneously invests in – cathects with – two kinds of memory: the received or residual function of public theatre as the 'memory bank' of Elizabethan society (communal, performative and open to all) and the future emergence of writing as the dominant mode of record (private, individualistic and tied to a certain mode of education).[7] The cultural function of the early modern public playhouse demonstrates that the performance of historical plays and well-known narratives retained immensely more power than the historiography of written records, both as popular cultural rehearsals of memory and as records of and prompts to monarchical governance. In addition, of course, the player on the Shakespearean stage was in the eyes of the audience 'a hero of memory', as Jonathan Baldo (1995: 143) puts it, and it is literally to these capacious verbal and dramatic memories that we owe our own memory of Shakespeare. In these very material senses Shakespeare's memory, then and now, must be considered primarily oral and theatrical, and only secondarily inscriptive.

Early modern theatrical memory functioned at a more esoteric level too, as Frances Yates makes clear when she describes Robert Fludd's occult 'art of memory', which recommended the use of an image of the theatre (derived, Yates thinks, from the Globe itself) as a mental architecture within which to summon up, organise and retain mnemonic data (Yates 1966). Hamlet evokes this image of his mnemic capacity when he promises to remember 'whiles memory holds a seat / In this distracted globe' (1.5.96–7); moreover, much of his subsequent activity in the play entails the attempt to repair or restore this memory to its proper place, as Michael Neill has argued, by means of repeated re-narration and acting out: 'Aeneas' tale to Dido', 'The Murder of Gonzago', the 'self-consciously theatrical "play" of Hamlet's exhibition bout with Laertes': 'such memorials typically take the form of theatrical fictions whose images of the occluded truth, by making re-enactment the witty instrument of revenge, magically compact together the original crime and its requital' (Neill 1997: 259–60).

None the less, the power of written memory permeates the Shakespearean text as well. The sonnets famously celebrate the power of 'black lines' of writing to keep the memory green (Sonnet 63); and in *The Tempest*, Prospero's mnemic pre-eminence remains closely associated with his possession of mystic 'books'. Moreover, Hamlet, as a scholar, turns often to writing and reading for the management of his troublesome memory, either in order to summon memories or to forget them. The Prince thus embodies the kinds of tension that Shakespeare's culture would have associated with the difference between memory-as-writing and memory-as-performance: between an inward-looking, scholarly, writerly, contemplative figure who might well forget to act, in contrast to a socially responsive, soldierly, performative actor who recollects and justifies the past in action.[8]

Malcolm Evans has described what he calls the 'strong reservations' that characterised the attitudes of Shakespeare's contemporaries towards 'the cultural impact of books and reading . . . Caxton promoted the printing press in England by praising writing – a secure "memory" for cultural and religious truths – at the expense of speech, seen as intrinsically "perisshing, vayne and forgeteful"' (Caxton 1928: 51; cited in Evans 1986: 41–2). As Evans points out, however, these contradictory attitudes to the cultural function of writing-as-memory prove subject to recollection or forgetting according to motivations or investments of both broad cultural developments and the micropolitics of specific occasions: while the dissemination of literacy has been associated in broad terms with the advent of 'print capitalism', the rise of the middle classes, and the emergence of Protestant individualism, nonconformist preachers would increasingly rail against the *letter* of the law and in favour of the *spoken* word of the Spirit descending upon the individual believer (Evans 1986: 44–6). Meanwhile, early colonists such as Thomas Harriot and essayists such as Montaigne could agree on the absence of writing in Native American cultures, but while the former used this 'fact' to demonstrate Europe's superiority over other cultures, the latter offered it as evidence of European corruption in comparison with the innocence of more primitive cultures (Harriot, in Quinn and Quinn 1973: 69; Montaigne 1958: 110).[9]

The association of writing with reliable memory could be diametrically reversed by a notion articulated as early as Plato's *Phaedrus*: 'If men learn this [writing], it will implant forgetfulness in their souls: they will cease to exercise memory because they rely on that which is written, calling things to remembrance no longer from within themselves, but by means of external marks' (cited in Baldo 1995: 120, n. 19). It is perhaps this anxiety that gives rise to the fact that, as Neill observes, 'Hamlet's solemn rite of memory after his first encounter with the Ghost' is at the same time 'an act of oblivion, in which the memories installed by the Ghost expunge "all forms, all pressures past" with their oppressive scripture' (1997: 254, 1.5.100). Shakespeare's predominantly non-literate audience, within their 'distracted globe' of theatrical commemoration, would feel acutely this suspicion of writing as a form of oblivion. However, modernity will replace that attitude with a culture that constitutes the letter as the dominant form of social bond, that privileges the written contract and archive above any other legal or historical memory, and that subjects the notions of performative memory and theatrical re-enactment to a corresponding degree of suspicion and devaluation.

In the writing of Freud, though, the memory of the early modern – memory as rehearsal and theatre – returns to haunt every attempt at definition. Just as his archaeology takes off into a spectacular flight of fancy, his account of mnemic writing cannot repress the functioning of a certain performativity: the 'mystic writing pad' demonstrates not the mechanical constancy of memory, but rather its ephemerality, its dependence upon the construction of particular connections and momentary cathexes. It is also necessary to remember, in this context, that Freud's inaugural account of subjectivity owes everything to theatre – not only because of his

Oedipal debt to Sophocles and Shakespeare, but because the mental apparatus he develops remains theatrical in structure and function.

> Freudian analysis adopts as its system of explanation the structuration of psychic phenomena through the positing of three agencies . . . : The Ego . . . the Id . . . and the Superego . . . The psychic machine echoes a theatrical model. It is constituted in the manner of a Greek tragedy and in that of Shakespearian drama, from which we know that Freud drew structures of thought, categories of analysis and authoritative quotations. Non-human 'role-players' . . . [the ego, id and superego] form a configuration of roles which respond to one another by their opposition; from the beginning of the play, they set forth in synchronic fashion the stages through which the name-bestowing hero (the 'I' for Freud, King Lear or Hamlet for Shakespeare) will pass in order to find himself at the end in the inverse of his original position. At the beginning, an order of agencies yields in topographical form, the 'moments' which will unfold in diachronic form with successive displacement of the 'hero'. Every play or story is the progressive transformation of a spatial order into a temporal series. The psychic apparatus and its function are built on this 'literary' model of theater.
>
> (de Certeau 1986: 22)

The psychoanalytical experience and vocabulary *par excellence* remains that of the stage: analysis concerns itself with a subject whose trauma (drama) derives from being an audience to the 'primal scene'; it seeks that catharsis postulated by the Aristotelian theory of tragedy; its favourite operations (forgettings and rememberings, the working out of emotional angst in action, the compulsion to repeat) are the stuff of drama.

Thus from a theory of memory that seemed to focus on and derive from the inner mental life of the individual, a reading of the 'other scenes' of psychoanalysis produces a theory of memory as a function of cultural and historical collectivity. And so the psychoanalytic quest for the preserved artefacts of an authentic and original past is displaced by an insistent performativity and constructedness that pervade both memory and forgetting. These alternative tendencies emerge, of course, substantially through the so-called 'return to Freud', the name Jacques Lacan gave to that project by which he dedicated himself to – or to himself? – the memory of Freud.

Lacan's recollection of the Freudian theory of memory hinges upon two terms: repetition and retroaction. The first refers to that 'compulsion' or 'automatism' that I described in Chapter 2, by which unconscious memories reproduce themselves in action: the rehearsal of the past rewrites the future. The second term, 'retroaction', in a sense mirrors this operation in reverse. It derives from Freud's term *Nachträglichkeit*, sometimes translated as 'deferred action', a phrase which misses entirely both the function and the significance that Lacanian theory gives the term. According to the Lacanian reading, one of Freud's most far-reaching assertions was that, as Malcolm Bowie puts it,

> in the mind, the present could alter the past. A later event could release new memories of an earlier event; a new desire or intention could cause the mind to rewrite its own prehistory; and the dispositions of the individual upon reaching a new configuration – during therapy, say – could entirely transform the individual's sense of the life he had previously led.
>
> (Bowie 1991: 14)

In this way, memory remains at all times subject to, and modifiable by, the meanings associated with it retroactively in the narratives of the subject's (or the nation's) history.

To this extent, the structure of subjectivity remains outside of conventional time: impressions of historical progress are no more than illusions thrown out by the endless reconfiguration of the narrative imposed upon the past, or anticipated in the future, by the present. The relationships between the memories that constitute the subject, and the meanings with which they come to be endowed, are held, formed and renegotiated in a kind of 'suspended animation' (Bowie 1991: 178). In this way Lacan rejects 'developmental models of subjectivity and the "mythology of instinctual maturation" [Lacan 1977b: 54], and seeks to replace them with a method of scansion that moves from one all-at-once structure to the next' (Bowie 1991: 179).

The clearest Freudian source for this approach occurs in *The Psychopathology of Everyday Life* (1901). Chapter 4, on 'Screen Memories', begins with the observation that a person's earliest childhood memories seem frequently to have preserved what is indifferent and unimportant, whereas (frequently, though certainly not universally) no trace is found in an adult's memory of impressions dating from that time which are important, impressive and rich in affect.

(*PFL* 5: 83)

If Freud believes that the unconscious preserves traces of all preceding impressions, then what concerns him here is the apparent randomness, the lack of ostensible significance, that characterises the selection of impressions by the conscious memory. He asserts, however, that there is method in the apparent senselessness of these recollections, insofar as they function as 'screens' for other, more significant memories; and moreover that the traces of 'an associative relation' between the screen memories and those they repress can be discovered by analysis (*PFL* 5: 83). The simplest example offered is that of the man who recalls learning the difference between the two middle letters of the alphabet: 'His aunt points out to him that the *m* has a whole piece more than the *n*' (83) – as 'literal' a screen as could be found for the childhood discovery of anatomical difference between boys and girls.[10]

Read through Lacan, Freud describes a function that can once more shortcircuit linear temporality: the screen memory can derive from a time before the content it obscures (he calls this *retroactive* or *retrogressive* memory); alternatively, a later memory can screen an earlier one (in this case the screen has been *pushed ahead* or *displaced forward*); finally, memories contemporaneous with a repressed content can be deployed as screens (*contiguous* or *contemporary* screen memories) (*PFL* 5: 84). Without the authority of a chronological priority that establishes a relationship of simple causation, the association between screen memories and repressed content depends upon its management by the psychoanalytic act. In other words it is the analyst who, by reading the drama of memory, decides which impressions constitute motivation (the repressed content) and which function merely as alibis (the screen).

To think of it this way is to recall that an emphasis on motivation is of course one of the foremost gifts which psychoanalysis bequeaths to the audience of written, filmed or theatrical narrative, but also that this legacy was acquired from theatre in the first place, since the inaugural psychoanalytic question was that of Hamlet's motivation for his delay. However, as the many answers to such a question illustrate – Hamlet throws out multiple rationales for his hesitation, just as Iago proffers numerous reasons for his malignity – theatre constitutes a mode in which motivation itself occurs not as a cause of performance but as its product; not as the origin of action but as a by-product of acting. Purpose is the slave to (performed) memory, not the other way round. Again, it seems, the psychoanalytic engagement with the dynamics of theatre deeply compromises its desire for access to an original motivating memory. On the stage, there is no primal scene: there is only the screen.

Freud's own suspicion of the veracity of the primal scene, and his strongest advocacy of *Nachträglichkeit*, occurs when he observes that in very early recollections the remembrancer sometimes sees herself or himself as a child. This suggests that

> in the so-called earliest childhood memories we possess not the genuine memory-trace but a later revision of it, a revision which may have been subjected to the influences of a variety of later psychical forces. Thus the 'childhood memories' of individuals come in general to acquire the significance of 'screen memories' and in doing so offer a remarkable analogy with the childhood memories that a nation preserves in its store of legends and myths.
>
> (*PFL* 5: 88)

Once again the model of individual memory draws upon images of collective history, from the processes of cultural memorialisation. The comparison between childhood memory and the retroactive compilation of national history is expanded in a later work on memory which again recalls the early modern, the essay on 'Leonardo da Vinci and a Memory of his Childhood' (1910):

> Quite unlike conscious memories from the time of maturity, [childhood memories] are not fixed at the moment of being experienced and afterwards repeated, but are only elicited at a later age when childhood is already past; in the process they are altered and falsified, and are put into the service of later trends, so that generally speaking they cannot be sharply distinguished from phantasies. Their nature is perhaps best

illustrated by a comparison with the way in which the writing of history originated among the peoples of antiquity. As long as a nation was small and weak it gave no thought to the writing of its history . . . Then came another age, an age of reflection: men felt themselves to be rich and powerful, and now felt a need to learn where they had come from and how they had developed. Historical writing, which had begun to keep a continuous record of the present, now also cast a glance back to the past, gathered traditions and legends, interpreted the traces of antiquity that survived in customs and usages, and in this way created a history of the past. It was inevitable that this early history should have been an expression of present beliefs and wishes rather than a true picture of the past; for many things had been dropped from the nation's memory, while others were distorted, and some remains of the past were given a wrong interpretation in order to fit in with contemporary ideas. Moreover, people's motive for writing history was not objective curiosity but a desire to influence their contemporaries, to encourage and inspire them, or to hold a mirror up before them. A man's conscious memory of the events of his maturity is in every way comparable to the first kind of historical writing [which was a chronicle of current events]; while the memories that he has of his childhood correspond, as far as their origins and reliability are concerned, to the history of a nation's earliest days, which was compiled later and for tendentious reasons.

(*PFL* 14: 173–4)

Collective history and individual memory are both tendentious fantasies, inventions motivated by present anxieties. Instead of access to an original buried mnemic artefact, this account describes a process of retroactive construction of the past by the politics of the present, and the desires of the future. We seem to be a long way from archaeology, but we are not far from theatre; certainly not far from Shakespearean theatre, which of course revises and rehearses and performs the history of an emergent English nationalism in precisely the way Freud describes. Moreover, when Freud, Rank and Jones read Shakespeare in detail, they more often than not return to his historiographical and mythical sources, seeking to delve through the author's revisions and thereby mark out the 'layers of repression', the consecutive forgettings and rememberings, that construct the play – the same exercise attempted by Borges's scholar, Hermann Sörgel, in his desire to access Shakespeare's memory.[11]

I am arguing, then, that Freud's reliance on early modern texts for the formulation of his theory creates the kind of investment – outside of linear temporality – by means of which the pre- or non- or anti-modern categories and subjectivities find their way in the twentieth century out of the foreclosed space in which they were confined during preceding centuries. Retroactively reconstructed by Lacan, Freudian theory, tracing the descent of modernity from its zenith, thus steps outside of the tyranny of 'progressive realism' and activates a memory of the early modern and, in that process, helps to constitute in advance the memory of the postmodern.[12]

Shakespeare's memory also exemplifies this kind of deferred or retroactive effect. The myth of his transcendent genius, which has so often been supposed to stand outside of history and location, consigns Shakespeare to a kind of cryogenic refrigeration, in which he awaits his regular reactivation as an agent for restructuration of the cultural field. Perhaps the most striking example of this process has been provided in recent decades by *The Tempest*. How else could it be that a Jacobean court spectacle of this kind could be understood – by readers from Europe to Madagascar, from the Caribbean to Kenya – as anticipating with uncanny accuracy both colonialism *and* postcolonialism?

Prospero's memory

Late in his career, Shakespeare writes a play preoccupied with memory. Jonathan Baldo puts it as follows:

> *The Tempest* is often read as a reminiscence writ large, a backward reflection or recapitulation by a playwright near the end of his career, the arch-Remembrancer behind all the injunctions to remember in the play . . . Its almost unique status as a Shakespearean text with few specific dramatic or narrative antecedents apart from the Strachey letter, Montaigne's 'Of Cannibals', and Medea's incantation from Ovid's *Metamorphoses* makes it dubious as an act of memory. In this respect it is a play of weak remembrance.
>
> (Baldo 1995: 142)

Just as the gift of Shakespeare's memory felt to Hermann Sörgel like being 'offered the ocean' (Borges 1999: 510), in *The Tempest* Shakespeare uses the same association to embody the contradictory capacity to preserve and to efface, a threat to drown consciousness and a promise of its unexpected redelivery. Prospero immediately activates this function of memory during his first, extended (auto)biographical discourse to Miranda. Discovering to his surprise that Miranda retains a vague recollection of her previous life in Milan, of 'Four or five women once that tended me' (1.2.47), Prospero asks his daughter

> *Pros.*   What seest thou else
> In the dark backward and abysm of time?
> If thou remembrest aught ere thou cam'st here,
> How thou cam'st here thou mayst.
> *Mir.*   But that I do not.
>   (1.2.49–53)

The awkward phrase 'backward and abysm of time' illustrates the competing forces at work in Prospero's anxious interrogation: the dual functions of remembrance and forgetting are associated with the sea that currently separates his and Miranda's present existence on the island from their past, but that also once provided the medium for their transition from Milan and will later return them there.

As this account proceeds, it becomes evident that the management of memory has played a critical role in the politics of Prospero's past.[13] His fascination with the 'liberal arts' brought its own form of forgetting: 'The government I cast upon my brother, / And to my state grew stranger, being transported / And rapt in secret studies' (1.2.75–7). Antonio, the brother in question, in turn practised those arts of forgetting characteristic of the Machiavel:

>   Like one
> Who having into truth, by telling of it,
> Made such a sinner of his memory,
> To credit his own lie, he did believe
> He was indeed the duke.
>   (1.2.99–103)

Politics and power are conceived here in terms of the studied performance of memory and forgetting; events and circumstances can be managed, and 'truth' told, according to the ethics of the teller/remembrancer: Antonio constructs a memory that can sin in his stead, telling him a lie that he can innocently accept. Prospero's ensuing narrative – which of course constitutes that of the play itself – requires that his own recollection and organisation of events, in his life and in every other character's, be capable of overwriting all other versions.

Moreover, Antonio no sooner lands on the isle than he attempts to repeat his prior expert manipulation of the politics of memory. His circuitous exhortation of Sebastian to kill Alonso and take the throne of Naples deploys a vocabulary familiar to us already:

> We all were sea-swallow'd, though some cast again,
> And by that destiny, to perform an act
> Whereof what's past is prologue; what to come,
> In yours and my discharge.
>
> (2.1.246–9)

Antonio evokes the history of their engulfment and subsequent disgorgement by the ocean as evidence of memory's manipulability or liability to reversal; switching to the language of theatre, he speaks of 'destiny' as a history dictated in advance, urging Sebastian to perform an 'act' which, envisaged as already complete ('what's past is prologue'), requires only faithfulness to its own anticipated memory. What Antonio does not know, of course, is that this compulsion to repeat occurs as an effect of the memory of the other, that is, of Prospero's recollection of his own usurpation. On this island, agency is all Prospero's: the vulnerability in sleep of the king and courtiers that allows the possibility of this second usurpation occurs at Prospero's behest, and so does their sudden wakefulness at the moment of danger.

Prospero's memory reveals its mastery soon enough. In the next scene that features the shipwrecked nobles, an elaborate spectacle of remembrance is staged for them by Prospero's agent, Ariel:

> *Thunder and lightning. Enter* ARIEL *like a Harpy; claps his wings upon the table; and, with a quaint device, the banquet vanishes.*

> *Ari.* You are three men of sin, whom Destiny, –
>   That hath to instrument this lower world
>   And what is in't, – the never-surfeited sea

> Hath caus'd to belch up you; and on this island,
> Where man doth not inhabit, – you 'mongst men
> Being most unfit to live. I have made you mad;
> And even with such-like valour men hang and drown
> Their proper selves.

> (3.3.53–60)

Destiny – the conjunction between a memory of the past and an anticipation of the future – manifests according to Prospero's demand, of reparation for past wrongs. The terrestrial world and ocean, instruments of a providence under his control, constitute Prospero's ultimate memory machine: we have seen him raise a marine tempest, and later he will speak of summoning and dispersing 'the great globe itself' (4.1.153). Rivalling Freud's mystic writing pad, the ocean demonstrates both 'unlimited receptive capacity' – it is 'never-surfeited' – and the capacity for 'retention of permanent traces' – those unforgotten sins for which the sea 'Hath caus'd to belch up' these three men. The attempted drowning mentioned by Ariel only demonstrates the vanity of a desire to gain oblivion from the past in a sea that will not keep its memories down:

> But remember, –
> For that's my business to you, – that you three
> From Milan did supplant good Prospero:
> Expos'd unto the sea, which hath requit it,
> Him and his innocent child: for which foul deed
> The powers, delaying, not forgetting, have
> Incensed the seas and shores, yea, all the creatures,
> Against your peace.

> (3.3.68–75)

Although it is Ariel who repeats Prospero's memory here, Alonso hears his sins enumerated by the vast mechanism of the sea-tempest:

> Methought the billows spoke, and told me of it;
> The winds did sing it to me; and the thunder,
> That deep and dreadful organ-pipe, pronounc'd
> The name of Prosper: it did bass my trespass.
> Therefor my son i' th' ooze is bedded; and

I'll seek him deeper than e'er plummet sounded,
And with him there lie mudded.

(3.3.96–102)

The notion of the 'world' or the 'sea' as an instrument of a providential memory-bank was common enough in the Renaissance,
so that Shakespeare can evoke the image 'of the whole harmony
of nature enforcing upon Alonso the consciousness of his guilt;
the thunder supplies a pedal bass, and seems to name Prospero'
(Kermode 1954: 92, n. 99). The theatre, of course – Ariel's
performance, but also Shakespeare's Globe – presents itself as
the lens of this macrocosmic retrospectoscope. Alonso responds
to these unwelcome memories with a desire to throw himself
back to the bottom of the sea, not to seek oblivion, but rather to
discover and honour memory – that of his son whom he supposes
lost 'deeper than e'er plummet sounded'. Having been repeatedly
reminded that the sea, like memory, always throws up what seems
to be lost in its furthest depths, the audience hearing this phrase
will read it as an anticipation of Ferdinand's return to his father
– as indeed it proves to be. How then will the same words be
interpreted when they are later repeated by Prospero himself, in
renouncing his magic and vowing to drown his book 'deeper than
did ever plummet sound' (5.1.56)? Presumably, we must expect
the return of that book, and what it stands for.

Prospero makes this promise at the end of his most necromantic
speech, the one recalling the incantation of the sorceress Medea
from Ovid's *Metamorphoses*. Prospero's debt to memories of prior
and feminine magical power – and his desire to forget that debt
– will be returned to later. For the moment, we can notice that
Ariel's turn as an avenging Harpy also evokes memories of classical
sources. The figure of the winged tempest-goddess in Greek
mythology embodied the revenge of the gods upon those who
showed disrespect for the proper functioning of memory, either
by forgetting past crimes, or by anticipating the future. The sooth-
sayer Phineus was condemned to everlasting hunger via the agency
of the Harpies, who would swoop down to devour or defecate
on everything he tried to eat. Orestes, who killed his mother
Clytemnestra to avenge her murder of his father Agamemnon
upon his return from the Trojan war, was famously harried for his
crime for many years by the Furies, who were themselves a kind of
subspecies of Harpy.

The image of memory as a vengeful minister of this kind, soiling future promise with the return of past wrongs, is taken by Shakespeare from Virgil but softened by its association in *The Tempest* with the genre of comedy. But memory regains its voracity in Freud's recollection of the classics:

> An entire dimension of Freud's work redramatizes the myth of the Furies: the past is visited upon the individual in a series of violent incursions, and his future, if he has one, can be envisaged only as a prolongation of these and a continuing helpless desire to lift their curse.
>
> (Bowie 1991: 182)

Shakespeare's memory, at least in *The Tempest*, proves at the same time more optimistic and more conservative than Freud's. Prospero – the arch-remembrancer whose name implies hope for the future – restores a memory both proper and prosperous. Returning to all the characters their full recollections, he restructures the past into a pattern that repeats both the prior order of things and the changes that have occurred: regaining his dukedom, he anticipates bequeathing it to his daughter, whose marriage to Ferdinand, Prince of Naples repeats in a new form the memory of Antonio's conspiratorial association with Alonso. In the play's final scene tempestuous memory returns as calm full tide of reason:

> The charm dissolves apace;
> And as the morning steals upon the night,
> Melting the darkness, so their rising senses
> Begin to chase the ignorant fumes that mantle
> Their clearer reason . . . Their understanding
> Begins to swell; and the approaching tide
> Will shortly fill the reasonable shore,
> That now lies foul and muddy.
>
> (5.1.64–82)

No doubt the play's dramatisation of negotiations between competing but always specifically European political memories would constitute its most manifest significance to Shakespeare's contemporaries. In a production at Whitehall or the Blackfriars Theatre, the state-of-the-art engineering feats of the disappearing

banquet, and the courtly artifices of the masque, would make
these scenes climactic, reinforcing the audience's reading of the
play as a conventional meditation on harmonious monarchy
versus disruptive usurpation. In the public playhouse the clown-
ing scenes would come into their own: the drunken emulation
by Trinculo and Stephano of the treacheries contemplated by
Sebastian and Antonio would offer a more carnivalesque version
of the same political narrative. In each of these contexts, the
restructuring of the past into the calm, ordered and reasonable
form of a future polity based on the judicious management of
memory, the ability to recall knowledge as well as to renounce it,
would epitomise the most politically acceptable face of a theatre
indebted, as Shakespeare's was, to the benevolence of the state.

If striking compatibilities are evident between the Shakespearean notion of memory as theatrical management and the
Freudian account of retroactive construction, these are not, as
I have argued, primarily the products of a critical vocabulary
unconscious of its own debt to psychoanalytic categories; nor
are they proof of Shakespeare's genius in identifying a universal
human nature that transcends the ages.[14] Rather, they demonstrate
that psychoanalysis, as a founding contributor to that critique
of humanist reason which will come to dominate twentieth-century
Western thought, reaches back beyond modern Enlightenment
consciousness to reactivate a memory with its own agency beyond
the ken of the ego.[15] In this sense *The Tempest* performs a scenario
that is 'early modern' in the most active sense of that phrase;
like many of Shakespeare's plays, it rehearses a struggle for the
emergence of a humanist subjectivity whose agency depends upon
its capacity to gain autonomy by overwriting the 'memory of
the other' with its own rational, knowledge-based and enlightened
narrative of progress. Hence the triumph of Prospero anticipates
'the dawn of the historical era of the ego', Lacan's description of
the cultural dominance that would accrue to reason and science,
and to the bourgeois rational individual.[16]

Nevertheless, there remain recollections of other pasts, and
anticipations of other futures, that the play overwrites but cannot
erase. Reading for the politics of memory, it becomes desirable to
identify aspects of a pre-egocentric culture repressed by the historical dominance of reason, which will return by paths other than
the psychoanalytic one. In the twentieth century, the evening of
the ego's era, other memories became visible, jostling for position

on Prospero's island. Recent readers tend to remember *The Tempest* not for its rehearsal of intra-European politics, nor as a hymn of praise to humanism, but rather for its simultaneous recollection and anticipation of colonial exchanges between European and other cultures. Of course, the latter reading should be understood as intrinsically bound to the former: the colonial enterprise functions as the repressed memory of the ego's era, the political unconscious of that process by which European consciousness promoted itself to pre-eminence above any other form of subjectivity.[17]

Forgetting Caliban

Completing the recollection of his own and Miranda's past, Prospero sends his daughter into oblivion and summons Ariel. Again, this exchange begins with a struggle for agency over memory. The servant tries to assert his version of the past, daring to remind the master of a contract made: 'Let me remember thee what you hast promis'd . . . Remember I have done thee worthy service . . . : thou did promise / To bate me a full year' (1.2.243–50). Prospero counters with a more authoritative memory, of Ariel's past imprisonment, and a threat of its return: 'Dost thou forget / From what a torment I did free thee? . . . Hast thou forgot / The foul witch Sycorax? . . . Where was she born? speak; tell me' (1.2.250–60). Prospero manages the dialogue in such a way that Ariel must re-learn, re-memorise, his past according to a catechism of his past sufferings and debts: 'I must / Once in a month recount what thou hast been, / Which thou forget'st' (1.2.261–3). This coercive version of events is reinforced with an even more direct form of repetition: the threatened re-enactment of the punishment previously attributed by Sycorax: just as she confined Ariel 'in a cloven pine' a dozen years, Prospero will imprison him in an oak for the same amount of time unless he accede, not just to his commands, but to his version of history (1.2.272–96).

If Prospero's tenure over the island is supposed to be in contrast to the 'earthy and abhorr'd commands' of Sycorax, this moment uncannily repeats her treatment of Ariel – just as his last incantation will repeat the words of that other ghostly witch, Medea. Nor are these the only prior and disavowed narratives upon which

Prospero's mastery depends: the memory of the other most necessary for him to overwrite manifests in his exchanges with Caliban. Here, Prospero's discursive management meets with a far stronger resistance than that of either Miranda or Ariel. As Sycorax's son, Caliban proves a troubling reminder of a potency prior to Prospero's command and yet uncomfortably akin to it.

It has been noted that Shakespeare gives Caliban the only rhetoric in the play to rival Prospero's; this poetic power is closely associated with the vividness of his memories of a prior knowledge of the island, reflected most famously in the rhapsody that begins with the lines 'the isle is full of noises, / Sounds and sweet airs, that give delight, and hurt not' (3.2.133ff.), but also in the promises he makes to Stephano and Trinculo, to show them 'the best springs', and to gather for them berries, crab-apples, pig-nuts, jays' eggs, marmosets, filberts and scamels (2.2.160–72).[18] Where Prospero's recollections of life on the island take the form of abstract metaphysical contests of power, Caliban's memory is sensual, attentive to the habitat and its flora and fauna, and efficient in catering for his appetites and needs. In Caliban, then, Prospero encounters the only memory that rivals his own and will not be either subsumed or rhetorically overruled. At the climax of the play his sudden recollection of Caliban's claims interrupt his concentration upon the production of an elaborate fantasy of sexual cultivation and political order in the form of the masque:

PROSPERO *starts suddenly, and speaks . . .*

Pros. [*aside*] I had forgot that foul conspiracy
    Of the beast Caliban and his confederates
    Against my life: the minute of their plot
    Is almost come.
                                    (4.1.139–42)

The anxiety with which Prospero attempts unsuccessfully to repress this memory of the other is further exemplified by Ariel's comment that 'I thought to have told thee of it; but I fear'd / Lest I might anger thee' (4.1.168–9).

Caliban's alternative memory of the island's politics is lucidly stated at the very outset of his exchanges with Prospero:

> *Cal.*   This island's mine, by Sycorax my mother,
>   Which thou tak'st from me. When thou cam'st first,
>   Thou strok'st me and made much of me; wouldst give
>   me
>   Water with berries in't; and teach me how
>   To name the bigger light, and how the less,
>   That burn by day and night.
>
>   (1.2.333–8)

Of course, the authority of this alternative memory would have been cancelled out, for Shakespeare's audience, by their recognition of two contemporary cultural narratives. First, they would immediately hear in Caliban's lines an echo of that version of sacred history which they would take as primal, that is, the opening chapter of Genesis in which 'God then made two great lights: the greater light to rule the day, and the less light to rule the night' (1.16); thus Prospero's arrival on the island repeats God's creation of order, meaning and history out of the 'formless chaos' that preceded him. This perception in turn would recall a second current belief, that early colonial notion of the non-European's (and especially the Native American's) lack of culture, language and therefore memory (Greenblatt 1990: 16–39; Baldo 1995; Walch 1996), which Miranda's speech to Caliban a little later will make explicit:

>   when thou didst not, savage,
> Know thine own meaning, but wouldst gabble like
> A thing most brutish, I endow'd thy purposes
> With words that made them known.
>
>   (1.2.357–60)

Such echoes identify the operation of an early colonial politics of cultural memory, which provides justification for Europe's imposition of its own knowledge and values upon the New World. When Shakespeare has Caliban repeat three times in a single speech to his conspirators his desire for Prospero's books – 'Remember / First to possess his books; for without them / He's but a sot, as I am, nor hath not / One spirit to command: they all do hate him / As rootedly as I. Burn but his books' (3.2.89–93) – the value that Europe puts on its own technologies of knowledge and memory is represented by means of an envy of them attributed to the non-European other, a rhetoric recalling Lacan's notion that 'man's desire is the desire of the Other' (Lacan 1979: 38, 115).

This same desire receives a vivid recapitulation in *Prospero's Books*, Peter Greenaway's film of the play, which borrows its representations of Prospero, Ariel, Miranda and other characters, as well as its sets, from a disparate collection of Renaissance paintings, engravings and architectures (Greenaway 1991). The film thus embeds the action in a late modernist celebration of, and identification with, Renaissance knowledge, interrupting the narrative periodically with a kind of cinematic palimpsest which opens up, within the scenic frame, the pages of twenty-four magic books.[19] Images and words come to life, moving off the paper, or opening up scenes into which the action moves. As the books appear they are described by an elderly male voice – belonging, we later find out, not to John Gielgud, who in the role of Prospero speaks almost every line in the film, but to the actor playing Gonzalo, that 'lord of weak remembrance' (2.1.227) whose lines constantly evoke memory, albeit in forms his companions do not want to recognise. Bestiaries, cosmographies, atlases, travellers' tales, utopias, games and mythologies: the volumes encapsulate memories of the play's sources, and at the same time recall its fascination with memory itself, as in the case of the book of mirrors, some of which 'simply reflect the reader, some reflect the reader as he was three minutes previously, some reflect the reader as he will be in a year's time' (Greenaway 1991: 17). At the end of the film, when Prospero hurls all his books into the water, we see Caliban diving for them and retrieving two: the first-folio *Complete Works* of Shakespeare, and the folio version of *The Tempest* itself. The film, which seems utterly unconscious of the many postcolonial readings of the play, thereby repeats the Renaissance fantasy about the envious desire of the non-European for European culture, but at the same time unintentionally provides an image of the process by which the history of decolonisation has turned *The Tempest* over to Caliban, allowing its rereading from the perspective of the colonised subject.

Certainly, rather than a flattering envy of the culture of the coloniser, it is this anticipated moment of hybridity, at which Caliban takes European knowledge and uses it against his oppressors, that twentieth-century audiences – at least those in the decolonising world – have found most powerful:

> *Cal.* You taught me language; and my profit on't
>   Is, I know how to curse. The red plague rid you
>   For learning me your language!
>
> (1.2.365–7)

And for these readers, Caliban's alternative memories do retain a positive content that cannot be simply or unambiguously overwritten by Prospero's version of events:

> *Cal.* For I am all the subjects that you have,
>   Which first was mine own King: and here you sty me
>   In this hard rock, whiles you do keep from me
>   The rest o' th' island.
> *Pros.*   Thou most lying slave,
>   Whom stripes may move, not kindness! I have us'd thee,
>   Filth as thou art, with human care; and lodg'd thee
>   In mine own cell, till thou didst seek to violate
>   The honour of my child.
>
> (1.2.343–50)

Prospero attempts to dismiss his slave's memory of events as a lie, but his own corrective account agrees with Caliban's: initially there were good relations between the two, until the attempted rape of Miranda – an allegation that Caliban not only admits, but relishes:

> *Cal.* O ho, O ho! would't had been done!
>   Thou didst prevent me; I had peopled else
>   This isle with Calibans.
>
> (1.2.351–3)

As many recent critics have remarked, Caliban's admission demonstrates an intention to use Miranda's body as the source of a race of inheritors bearing his own name, thus regenerating his rights over the island. Meanwhile, Prospero deploys the narrative of Miranda's near-violation – which she herself rehearses in her own address to Caliban (1.2.353–64) – to overwrite Caliban's claim to prior sovereignty; but then once Ferdinand comes on the scene, Prospero administers his daughter's sexuality – and with it her inheritance of his own titles in Milan – with the same imperious assurance that characterises his rule over the island: 'Then, as my gift, and thine own acquisition / Worthily purchas'd, take my daughter' (4.1.13–14).[20] Taken together, these exchanges demonstrate a similarity between Caliban and Prospero in their attitude to Miranda, both perpetuating that territorialisation of the feminine body which Louis Montrose has called 'the work of gender' in colonial discourse, according to which the acquisition of a feminised terrain could be represented in terms of legitimate 'ravishment'.[21]

In another register these struggles by Caliban and Prospero for sexual possession of Miranda, conceived as the rivalry between adopted son and tyrannous father, provide the focus for the standard psychoanalytic reading of the play. The conversation between these three figures therefore provides the fulcrum for two approaches to *The Tempest* which, despite their apparent disparity in method and intention, have proven surprisingly symmetrical: the postcolonial and the psychoanalytic. The question posed by this conjunction – what historical and epistemological relations exist between such disparate perspectives? – allows a further investigation of the role of Shakespeare's memory in the development of both psychoanalytic and postcolonial theory, and in the troubled but sustained relationship between the two.

Remembering colonialism

A jealous father obstructing his daughter's suitor, and struggling to subdue a rapacious adopted son: no wonder *The Tempest* has been popular among psychoanalytic theorists since Otto Rank first described this version of the incest theme in literature.[22] Norman Holland surveys the first generation of critics who expanded and emulated Rank's account: all agree that Prospero's treatment of Miranda constitutes 'a working out in later life of the relationship of child to mother' (Holland 1964: 274), although they differ somewhat in distributing the main roles of the psychic drama among the key players: Prospero usually plays the ego, Ariel the superego (thanks to his role as conscience to the Neapolitans) and Caliban of course the id (269–74).

The 1980 volume *Representing Shakespeare: New Psychoanalytic Essays* demonstrated both the longevity and the senescence of a Freudian literalism. Thus, according to one account, Prospero castrates Ferdinand's threatening sexuality and represses the maternal principle, but his final renunciation of power represents

Shakespeare's successful sublimation of his own paternal anxieties (Sundelson 1980: 51). Here, as elsewhere in the same volume, the anachronism and universalism of psychoanalytic reading is very evident: the modern Western nuclear family is taken as the norm, and masculinity as the model for self-identity, using Eriksonian developmental models applied without regard for historical differences, non-hetero sexualities, or non-Oedipal relationships. Despite their claim to be 'new psychoanalytic essays' these readings demonstrate that in 1980, before the main impact of new historicism and cultural materialism on Anglo-American criticism, there remained a paucity of ways available for psychoanalytic reading to move beyond the Freudian literalism of a prior generation.

More suggestive deployments of psychoanalytic theory in the reading of *The Tempest* can be found, however, in two articles by Stephen Orgel (1984) and Meredith Anne Skura (1989). Although neither piece escapes the problems that beset any attempt to marry historicist and Freudian critical methods, both are acutely aware of the issues involved, and demonstrate vividly some of the intriguing conjunctions between the postcolonial and the psychoanalytic approaches to the play. Each article divides in two, along a line that represents the critic's attempt to bring historicist contextualisations of the play into conversation with psychoanalytically based quasi-biography.

Skura begins with several pages of analysis, familiar enough by now, of the influence upon *The Tempest* of contemporary 'colonialist discourse', which following Jameson she describes as the 'political unconscious' of the text. The fulcrum of her reading is provided by Caliban's interruption of the masque, at which point this latent content, erupting into the manifest, suddenly appears more psychological than political. Changing key, Skura goes on to survey a range of Shakespearean figures who, like Caliban, embody 'forbidden desires and appetites': gluttony, sexual greed, primitive vengefulness, narcissistic grandiosity (Skura 1989: 63–4). Shakespeare repeatedly associates these qualities with 'infantilised' characters who stand in opposition to the maturity of 'adult' correlatives: Shylock and Antonio, Falstaff and Prince Hal, Lucio and Duke Vincentio. This dramatisation of psychical development, associated by Skura with the playwright's own biography, then becomes superimposed over the play's political context:

To one on the threshold of retirement from the Old World the New World is an appropriate stage on which to enact this last resurgence of the infantile self . . . for Shakespeare the desire for . . . utopias – the golden worlds and fountains of youth – has roots in personal history as well as in 'history' . . . Caliban's utopia of sweet voices and clouds dropping riches (3.2.137–43) draws most directly on the infantile substratum that colored Columbus's report when he returned from his third voyage convinced 'that the newly discovered hemisphere was shaped like a woman's breast, and that the Earthly Paradise was located at a high point corresponding to the nipple'.

(Skura 1989: 67–8)

Skura attempts to establish a dialectic between the colonial and the psychoanalytic origins of the play, but her account of Shakespeare's expressing his nostalgia for childhood by means of imagery of the New World borrowed from Columbus, who in turn gets it from his own 'infantile substratum', establishes a priority of influence: the colonial memory functions as a screen for the real primal scene, the resurgent infantile self – which returns us to Freud.

Stephen Orgel moves in the opposite direction, *from* psychoanalysis *to* political history. He begins with the suggestion that the absence, rhetorically and literally, of Prospero's wife from the play

constitutes a space that is filled by Prospero's creation of surrogates and a ghostly family: the witch Sycorax and her monster child, Caliban (himself, as becomes apparent, a surrogate for the other wicked child, the usurping younger brother), the good child/wife Miranda, the obedient Ariel, the violently libidinized adolescent Ferdinand . . .

Described in this way, the play has an obvious psychoanalytic shape . . . It is almost irresistible to look at the play as a case history.

(Orgel 1984: 2)

He then indulges in a fairly conventional exercise in psychobiography: Shakespeare's youthful marriage to an older woman, from whom he mostly lived apart; the birth of his two daughters and one son; the death of his father in 1601 ('the year of *Hamlet*'), and of his mother in 1608 ('the year of *Coriolanus*'); the existence of a younger brother Edmund who follows him into acting, and whose name might very well evoke for the playwright sibling rivalry (the year of *King Lear*, presumably); the death of his son Hamnet in 1596.

However, Orgel wants to recognise the limits of such an approach: 'The psychoanalytic and biographical questions raised by *The Tempest* are irresistible, but they can supply at best partial clues to its nature . . . Cultural concerns, political and social issues, speak through *The Tempest*' (Orgel 1984: 7). The figure enabling Orgel's move from the psychoanalytic to the political is Prospero's image of exile as rebirth, which also encodes his incorporation of the missing mother:

> When I have deck'd the sea with drops full salt,
> Under my burthen groan'd, which rais'd in me
> An undergoing stomach, to bear up
> Against what should ensue.
>
> (1.2.155–8)

'To come to the island is to start life over again – both his own and Miranda's – with himself as sole parent, but also with himself as favorite child' (Orgel 1984: 4). However, in a mirror-reversal of Skura's approach, Orgel ultimately assigns this 'fantasy' structure of *The Tempest* not to Shakespeare's psychobiographical memory, but to his political one: he cites the image of monarchy as marriage to the nation made famous by King James I – 'I am the husband, and the whole island is my lawful wife; I am the head, and it is my body' – and suggests that here, as in *The Tempest*, incorporation of the wife allows James to conceive himself 'as the head of a single-parent family . . . My point here is not that Shakespeare is representing King James as Prospero and/or Caliban, but that these figures embody the predominant modes of conceiving of royal authority in the period' (Orgel 1984: 9).

Both Orgel and Skura attempt to move, in different directions, between the fantasy structures described by psychoanalysis and those of colonialism and nationalism. To me, the question that remains unanswered (and unasked) is why both narratives should fit together at all – or at least why they seem just compatible enough to invite such repeated attempts at their mutual articulation. One answer emerges from an understanding of the relationship between the two fields in terms of *Nachträglichkeit*, deferred or retroactive construction of memory – which, paradoxically, displaces psychoanalysis from its assumed position of priority.

The Tempest demonstrates vividly the extent to which the representational co-ordinates of colonialist discourse are coterminous with those of the individual ego: nor should this surprise us, insofar as the nuclear family, the bourgeois individual, capitalism and colonialism are contemporaneous and demonstrably complicit cultural developments. In their simplest forms both the colonial and the psychoanalytic narratives describe an agency that seeks separation from an environment which nurtures but threatens to suffocate it and reconstitution on new grounds, in its own terms, answerable to its own authority. For psychoanalysis, this mastery can only ever remain an illusion, combining a nostalgic memory of childhood with a childish anticipation of a potency not yet attained, according to the paradigm, for example, of the Lacanian mirror stage. In a similar way colonial ideology articulates the memory of a past golden age of European culture with the anticipation of its future utopian restoration in a new location. Gonzalo's fantasy of colonial 'plantation' of Prospero's island demonstrates this clearly: his anticipation of a state without monarchy, laws or culture, in which a pure state of nature produces endless bounty and peace for its inhabitants, relies upon the reconfigured memory of the classical 'Golden Age' (2.1.139–64).[23] And King James deployed the same rhetoric, anticipating an imperial Great Britain based on an illusion of colonial mastery far in advance of the political realities of the time.[24]

The more specific symmetries between the structures of colonial ideology and psychoanalytic fantasy result, as I have sought to argue, not from the discovery of a prior and universal truth inherent in the human psyche which then shapes the economies of political representation, but rather from the debt owed by the psychoanalytic descriptions of individual psychic memory to those modes of representing authority, autonomy and the administration of power which emerge from the cultural rhetoric of nationalism and colonialism. In the case of *The Tempest* the psychoanalytic interpretation thus easily reactivates *nachträglich*, at a later date, those colonial memories inscribed in the text at its moment of inception.

No wonder that perhaps the most influential postcolonial reading of the play was produced by a psychoanalyst. Octave

Mannoni's *Prospero and Caliban* arises out of his engagement with the colonial politics of French-occupied Madagascar during the 1940s, but these observations are interleaved with others deriving from the Freudian account of familial politics and, of course, still others from Shakespeare's *The Tempest*. Mannoni's thesis, in brief, is that the colonial 'vocation' arises from the European's desire for autonomy expressed via power over space and over other people, which meets, in the colonial situation, an answering desire on the part of the 'primitive' Malagasy to be dependent upon an external authority figure. The conditions of possibility for colonialism, then, are psychological in the first instance (Mannoni 1964: 85).

The 'predispositions' required for colonialism are manifest, Mannoni considers, in the 'independence' of the European character, defined according to a model of advancement towards faith in rational self-confidence and technological skill exemplified by Descartes (Mannoni 1964: 144). By contrast, the 'dependent' attitude of reliance upon an external authority, which predisposes a people to being colonised, is demonstrated by the Malagasy 'cult of the dead' which centres on the belief 'that though the dead may turn to dust they will none the less continue to be the true fathers and alone possess fertility and authority' (53). Mannoni repeats here an association postulated by Freud in various texts (most notably in 'Totem and Taboo') between the primitive attitude to the authority of the ancestors and the child's attitude to its parents. The Malagasy father, he goes on to remark, acts as the family's intermediary for the ancestors, and the mother as intermediary for the father; but in the colonial context she will use the threat of the *vazaha*, the European, 'as a substitute for the father-image' (57). This explains why, according to Mannoni, the first real hostility to colonial rule arose in Madagascar only after the granting of 'greater liberties and fuller guarantees; they could no longer be forced to contribute their labour and they were given protection against arbitrary punishment'. As a result, 'They felt abandoned because they could no longer be sure of authority' (135–6).

To justify his perverse claim that colonialism produced less conflict in Madagascar than did decolonisation, Mannoni repeats a tactic entirely characteristic of both the psychoanalyst and the colonist requiring access to cultural capital and epistemological authority: he reaches for his Shakespeare. The 'best descriptions' of the twin complexes that predispose an individual or a people to the colonial relation, he asserts, can be found

> in the works of some of the great writers who projected them on to imaginary characters placed in situations which, though imaginary, are typically colonial. The material they drew directly from their own unconscious desires. This is proof enough that the complexes exist even before the colonial situation is experienced.
>
> (Mannoni 1964: 98)

By a typically psychoanalytic chiasmus Mannoni offers *The Tempest* as evidence of the pre-existence of those complexes which he will develop out of its structure. In doing so, he activates a notion of Shakespeare's often-cited ability to delineate the universal attributes of the unconscious, forgetting that the play itself actually contains memories of particular colonial experiences.[25]

The Tempest proves its universal authority by vindicating Mannoni's claim that colonialism answers a psychic need in the native populace:

> It is not that Caliban has savage and uneducable instincts or that he is such poor so[il] that even good seed would bring forth bad plants, as Prospero believes. The real reason is given by Caliban himself:
>
> . . . When thou camest first,
> Thou strok'dst me, and mad'st much of me . . .
> . . . and then I lov'd thee
>
> – and then you abandoned me before I had time to become your equal. . . . In other words: you taught me to be dependent, and I was happy; then you betrayed me and plunged me into inferiority.
>
> (Mannoni 1964: 76–7)

Caliban, Mannoni asserts, complains not of exploitation but of desertion by the colonial master, a point proven by Caliban's conspiracy with Trinculo and Stephano, the goal of which is 'not to win freedom, for he could not support freedom, but to have a new master whose "foot-licker" he can become. He is delighted at the prospect. It would be hard to find a better example of the dependence complex in its pure state' (Mannoni 1964: 106–7).

Leaving aside the obvious point that Prospero does not abandon Caliban – rather he keeps him in a relationship of quite intimate servitude – Mannoni's memory of his authorising text is selective, as Rob Nixon has pointed out (Nixon 1987: 566): in quoting Caliban's lines about his initial dependence upon Prospero – which he does twice in thirty pages (Mannoni 1964: 76–7; 106–7) – Mannoni forgets to include the very claim, voiced in the preceding sentence, that Prospero also covers over with his accusations of lying and rape, namely Caliban's assertion of a prior sovereignty alienated without consent: 'This island's mine, by Sycorax my mother / Which thou tak'st from me' (1.2.333–4).

Mannoni's memory of Shakespeare seems more acute when he describes Prospero as his model for the European colonist, whose administration divides the native into two opposing aspects, the obedient colonial subject who can be assimilated and the savage rebel who must be controlled or eliminated: 'on the one hand there are pictures of monstrous and terrifying creatures, and on the other visions of gracious beings bereft of will and purpose – Caliban and the cannibals at one extreme (Caliban is surely a deliberate anagram); Ariel . . . at the other' (Mannoni 1964: 104).[26] Mannoni also notices the way in which Prospero's ostensibly knowledgeable, rational and enlightened persona screens an 'impatient and almost neurotically touchy' father who punctuates his dictation of Miranda's memory with repeated injunctions to 'Obey and be attentive' (105).[27] The ritual humiliation Prospero arranges for his 'son' recalls the anxious administration of native sexuality characteristic of colonial management: 'the argument: you tried to violate Miranda, *therefore* you shall chop wood, belongs to a non-rational mode of thinking . . . it is primarily a justification of hatred on grounds of sexual guilt, and it is at the root of colonial racialism' (105–6). Thus the psychoanalytic account of a disturbing libidinal economy which must be repressed finds its correlative in a colonial narrative of repression of 'savage' energy.

Primitive memories

To suggest that 'sexual guilt' provides the origin of colonial racialism, however, is to ignore the ways in which the psychoanalytic account of a primitive sexual energy inherent in the psyche develops in the first instance out of the sexual politics of European imperial ethnography. In 'Civilisation and Its Discontents', for example, Freud's account of the relationship between culture and sexuality draws precisely upon an analogy with colonialism: 'civilization behaves toward sexuality as a people or a stratum of its population does which has subjected another one to its exploitation' (*PFL* 12: 293–4). And in his essay on 'The Unconscious' Freud insists that 'The content of the *Ucs.* may be compared with an aboriginal population in the mind' (*PFL* 11: 199), as well as comparing fantasies with 'individuals of mixed race who, taken all round, resemble white men, but who betray their coloured descent by some striking feature or other, and on that account are excluded from society and enjoy none of the privileges' (195). As Homi Bhabha remarks, Freud's comparison here highlights the 'partial nature of fantasy, caught *inappropriately*, between the unconscious and the pre-conscious, making problematic, like mimicry, the very notion of "origins"' (Bhabha 1994: 89). Upon investigation, the origins of Freud's fundamental concepts also begin to seem 'problematic', for they too are produced by a kind of epistemological mimicry that structures the relation between 'primitive' cultures and the development of psychoanalytic theory itself.

It is 'Totem and Taboo', of course, that develops most thoroughly the connection between what the subtitle of that study calls 'the psychic lives of savages' and the various repressed components that Freud considers integral to the 'mature' or 'civilised' adult personality: 'we are encouraged to attempt a comparison between the phases in the development of men's view of the universe and the stages of an individual's libidinal development' (*PFL* 13: 148). Thus totemism encodes that ambivalence between desire for and dread of incest which characterises the primal forms of the Oedipal complex (53–70); taboo (especially in relation to the sanctity of animals, ancestors, kings or patriarchs) represents the surrender of the son's attachment to the maternal, and his introjection of paternal dictates in the formation of the superego (120–31; 187–93); 'savage' rituals designed to propitiate demonic powers correspond to the repetitive rites by which compulsive neurotics overenthusiastically assimilate parental disciplines (79–89); and beliefs about magic, witchcraft and the 'omnipotence of thoughts' correspond to those processes of 'secondary revision' by which the conscious mind attempts to order and systematise, and so to exorcise, the chaotic desires and fears of the unconscious (149–58).

At times, though, the effort required for Freud to process the differences between such alien cultural forms becomes evident. He admits, for example, that 'totemistic' prohibitions on sexual relations or intermarriage (in Australian aboriginal cultures, for instance) frequently pertain between individuals with no blood relationship at all, but who nevertheless share membership of the same totem group; meanwhile, he notes that the father who belongs to a different clan may be 'free to commit incest with his daughters' (*PFL* 13: 58, n. 1). A contradiction thus emerges, in Freud's own description of 'primitive cultures', between their 'unusually great horror of incest' (58) and the operation of a definition of 'incest' so radically different from the European notion that the term hardly seems applicable. This conundrum – which Freud processes into his overall argument via his typical appeals to processes of negation and displacement – merely demonstrates one aspect of a fundamental incommensurability between European modes of social organisation and those Freud describes. As Deleuze and Guattari have argued, in the so-called 'primitive' cultures

> the necessary conditions for Oedipus as a 'familial complex', existing in the framework of the familialism suited to psychiatry and psychoanalysis, are obviously not present. Primitive families constitute a praxis, a politics, a strategy of alliances and filiations; formally, they are the driving elements of social reproduction; they have nothing to do with an expressive microcosm; in these families the father, the mother, and the sister always also function as something other than father, mother, or sister. And in addition to the father, the mother, etc., there is the affine, who constitutes the active, concrete reality and makes the relation between families coextensive with the social field.
>
> (Deleuze and Guattari 1977: 166)

Thus, as I described in the preceding chapter, psychoanalysis 'works' in the colonial context not because it has access to universal truths of human nature, but rather because it is precisely its vocation to co-operate with capitalism in order to reproduce in the colonial context those social and economic structures – the nuclear family, the interiorised subject, the democratic ideal – required for the smooth functioning of the imperial enterprise: 'Oedipus is always colonization pursued by other means' (Deleuze and Guattari 1977: 170).

I would argue, moreover, that this relation also works backwards, as it were; that it is possible to trace the ways in which psychoanalysis constructs its categories in the first place according to its own Eurocentric perception of 'primitive' cultural forms. The result is a complex epistemological interchange (the equivalent of the psychoanalytic process of projection followed by introjection) which first maps the perceived neuroses of the nineteenth-century European nuclear family on to kinship structures organised according to principles radically alien to it, and then incorporates those differences back into the European paradigm, in order to take them as evidence of its maturation away from the primitive. 'Totem and Taboo' therefore reads today as a documentation of the ways in which Freud's developing conceptualisation of every key term in his theoretical vocabulary – the unconscious, repetition compulsion, displacement, neurosis, the Oedipus complex – arise out of, and owe an ineradicable debt to, the epistemological work of European colonialism at its apogee. Freud takes all his accounts of 'primitive' cultural practices from a wide range of nineteenth-century colonial locations: he begins his text describing the 'totem' laws of the Australian aboriginals (*PFL* 13: 53–62), goes on to discuss kinship regimes in the New Hebrides, Fiji and Sumatra (62–3), then various regions of Africa (63–9), and so on around the European-dominated globe. In doing so he draws upon and conflates the various armchair ethnographies of non-European peoples that were in turn enabled by, and contributed to, the specific projects of colonialism in multiple locations: such studies as that of 'an Englishman, J. Long', writing about totemism among 'North American Indians' in 1790; James Frazer's four-volume *Totemism and Exogamy* from 1910; Andrew Lang's *The Secret of Totem* from 1905, and so on (55, n. 2).[28]

At the end of 'Totem and Taboo' Freud therefore insists 'that the beginnings of religion, morals, society and art converge in the Oedipus complex' (*PFL* 13: 219). The greater distance any given culture has attained from this 'primitive' origin, however, the more subtle and complex will be those cultural mechanisms that manage both the repression or forgetting of the primal scenario and the threat posed by its possible return to consciousness; this cultural management of course parallels the individual's introjection of the dead father and his return in the form of the superego or conscience, which is the ultimate symptom of the civilised.

And the spectre of this return, finally, returns Freud to Shakespeare. Given the importance of Shakespearean texts in facilitating those epistemological exchanges by which psychoanalysis extends its own borders, it seems inevitable that Freud should choose, as a prime instance of a (presumably moderately developed or 'adolescent', or perhaps a 'mixed race') form of cultural management of the murder of the primal father, Ariel's song from *The Tempest*:

> Full fathom five thy father lies;
>   Of his bones are coral made;
> Those are pearls that were his eyes:
>   Nothing of him that doth fade,
> But doth suffer a sea-change
> Into something rich and strange.
>   (1.2.399–404;
>   cited in *PFL* 13: 217, n. 2)

Although he does not comment further on these lines, the gesture by which Freud summons Shakespeare to authorise the psychoanalytic insight is familiar enough. In the context of my own discussion the choice of text seems both apposite and ironic. A song by Shakespeare's most obedient 'primitive', from a play often taken to represent the relation between a colonising father and his subjected sons, demonstrates both the transfiguration of one 'species' of colonised indigene (into an ethereal essence of obedience, in contrast to the earthbound resistance offered by Caliban), and the aestheticisation of that desire for the death of the father which Freud perceives at the origins of the individual psyche and culture at large. Recalling the pervasive association in *The Tempest* between the ocean and the functions of memory and forgetting, it seems appropriate that Ariel's 'sea-change' represents a process of preservation – 'Nothing of him that doth fade' – that proceeds by the re-presentation or revision by art of primal memory into a more acceptable form: 'Of his bones are coral made; / Those are pearls that were his eyes'.

To return, finally, to Mannoni: like his theoretical forebear, the author of *Prospero and Caliban* deploys the psychoanalytic account of individual fantasy to explain the forces of history (colonial history, in this case); like 'Totem and Taboo', Mannoni's account forgets that this individual fantasy is the product, as much as it is the cause, of those historical developments it describes: the Oedipalised family, the colonial enterprise, the rise of the bourgeoisie. As in Freud, this dialogic relation is most clearly in evidence when Mannoni's text deals with questions of primitivism and savagery. At times he clearly locates the source of racial stereotyping in the unconscious fears of the coloniser:

> We can explore the retinas of our own eyes by looking at a piece of white paper; if we look at a black man we shall perhaps find out something about our own unconscious – not that the white man's image of the black man tells us anything about his own inner self, though it indicates that part of him which he has not been able to accept: it reveals his secret self, not as he is, but rather as he fears he may be. The negro, then, is the white man's fear of himself.
>
> (Mannoni 1964: 200)

But when Mannoni comments earlier that 'The savage . . . is identified in the unconscious with a certain image of the instincts – of the *id*, in analytical terminology' (Mannoni 1964: 21), this formulation seems far less certain about whether the existence of the idea of 'savagery' and its related notions of appetite – most vividly embodied in the figure of the sexually voracious native, or the gluttonous cannibal – derive initially from unconscious fears and are thence projected on to the other; or whether these representations emerge from a colonial racism which will be swallowed whole by psychoanalytic theory and reproduced in the service of its model of the unconscious.

Prospero and Caliban thus emblematises the various layers of memory that his discussion draws upon: most evidently a Freudian memory seems to underlie and produce his entire analysis, while at other times this seems no more than a screen for a series of other formative narratives: the contemporary colonial politics of Madagascar, a broader history of post-Renaissance European nationalism and imperialism, and, of course, Shakespeare's memory. Ultimately, it proves impossible to locate the navel of Mannoni's 'psycolonial' dream – rather, the texts and contexts he recollects overwrite one another in a series of replacements governed by the demands of a particular rhetorical moment.

As this chapter and the one before it have sought to demonstrate, the complex interleaving of Shakespearean and psychoanalytic narratives will not remain confined to the rarefied spaces of the academy, nor to the secluded clinics of the analytic session: both Mannoni and Sachs represent psychoanalytic Shakespeare as an epistemology-in-action, knee-deep in the trenches of twentieth-century colonisation and decolonisation. By the end of that century the conjunction between the Shakespearean text and psychoanalytic theory also makes it, at long last, into the realm of the popular – as the next chapter aims to show.

5

Shakespeare's sex

At the start of the twentieth century an emergent psychoanalysis took *Hamlet* as its paradigmatic text, the cultural high ground upon which Freud, Rank and Jones could build and extend the Oedipal edifice. Elsewhere, Wulf Sachs uncertainly attempted to stake out the same territory in the contact zone of segregationist South Africa. And later Lacan would wheel out the play once more as a Trojan horse in his campaign against French psychoanalysis, a device for smuggling in his surrealist version of structuralism in the guise of a return to Freud.

By the end of the century the elite cultural hegemony previously associated with Shakespeare no longer seemed secure. Instead, in the context of a globalised, postmodern, high-technology and media-saturated image market, popular products formerly thought well below the grade of Shakespearean drama now took over the cultural high ground. If Shakespeare and psychoanalysis were to retain any purchase (and attract any purchasing power) in the quicksand of postmodern culture, it would depend upon their capacity to appeal to a popular market, and, more specifically, to American youth culture. By the start of the 1990s high-cultural players from the British stage (Kenneth Branagh, Ian McKellen, Trevor Nunn, Tom Stoppard) were hard at work on their crossover scripts; the media involved would encompass film, video, jazz and popular music, and digitalised special effects. Unsurprisingly, though, the play most successful in this context did not turn on the existential dilemmas of a thirty-something intellectual agonising about duty to his parents. Rather, it focused on a youth culture defined by its rejection of, or martyrdom to, the oppressive demands of an older generation; it possessed rapidity of pace, violence, partying, drug-taking, suicide and sex; it was, of course, *Romeo and Juliet.*

During the 1990s three films based on the play were released: Baz Luhrmann's MTV-influenced *William Shakespeare's Romeo and Juliet* (1996), Lloyd Kaufman's splatter grunge comedy, *Tromeo and Juliet* (1996), and John Madden's Oscar-winning historical romance, *Shakespeare in Love* (1998). Each focused on the emergence of a sexual and gender identity not only defined in peculiarly modern terms, but heavily indebted to the psychoanalytic narrative of psychic development. In this chapter I want to examine some of the possible ways in which popular culture, psychoanalytic theory and the Shakespearean text meet to maintain or to challenge those notions of sexuality and gender prevalent in the contemporary 'globe theatre' of cinema.

In doing so, however, it will first be necessary to survey psychoanalytic approaches to questions of sexuality and gender as these have influenced the reading of Shakespeare over the last two decades, focusing in particular upon the influence of feminist and queer theory.

Mother(')s matter

For second-wave feminists, Freudian theory was obviously far too patriarchal. In particular, by privileging the development of the male child, and insisting that the establishment of a healthy adult masculine psychology depends upon an Oedipal scenario predicated on rejection of the mother and identification with the father, Freud validated patriarchy and misogyny as the conditions of possibility for both individual maturation and the coherence of the social structure. Lacan, moreover, by translating Freud's family romance into structuralism, merely reproduced this patriarchal arrangement in a more abstract form, according to which the subject – masculine or feminine – comes into being as such only by acceding to a symbolic order of language explicitly affiliated with the paternal position in the family triangle, the *nom-du-père*, the name (or 'no') of the father.

Reacting against these Freudian and Lacanian father-fixations, feminist psychoanalysts such as Nancy Chodorow, revising the object-relations approach of Melanie Klein, sought to revalue the role of the maternal in the psychic development of the child. Chodorow's account considered rejection of the maternal not as the necessary, albeit painful, precondition of the attainment of adult identity, but rather as a non-inevitable cultural flaw, producing a social structure characterised by a sexually pathological relation between women and men. This account concentrates on the girl (very much a minor term in the Freudian and Lacanian scenarios), who gains her sense of femininity in the first instance from identification with her mother, rather than as Freud would have it, primarily from a heterosexual desire for her father; meanwhile, the boy's sense of masculinity depends first upon separation from his mother, and only second upon identification with his father. Thus, for Chodorow, it is the boy, not the girl, who experiences the most poignant sense of lack (or of castration, to speak in Freudian or Lacanian terms); hence the fundamental malformation afflicting masculinity (Kahn 1985: 75–7).

For critics influenced by this version of events, it is only by means of a thoroughgoing revaluation of the place of the maternal – worked out especially, or at least most urgently, in relation to a masculinity conceived as pathologically misogynistic in its origins – that psychoanalysis can hope to contribute to the feminist project. And so Madelon Sprengnether writes of the possibility of a 'beneficial conjunction between feminism and psychoanalysis' which

> must take account of the fact (as Lacanianism and post-structuralism fail to do) that a woman's body is the carnal origin of every human subject without desubjectifying the mother herself (as object relations theory tends to do) . . . [if] separation from the mother represents not a secondary but an originary condition, then there is no necessary link between the figure of the father and culture, or, in Lacan's terms, the phallus and the Symbolic order. No longer an exile from the process of signification, the body of the (m)other may actually provide a new, and material, ground for understanding the play of language and desire.
>
> (Sprengnether 1990: 9–10)

Sprengnether here describes an agenda that feminist object-relations critics from the 1970s to the 1990s brought to their reading of Shakespeare, who until then had been the poet laureate of both Freudian psychoanalysis and patriarchy.

This project is best exemplified by Janet Adelman's *Suffocating Mothers: Fantasies of Maternal Origin in Shakespeare's Plays* (1992). Adelman describes how early modern child-rearing practices kept the male child bound to the maternal for a much longer period than is typical in more recent Western societies, due to a longer period of wet-nursing, a relatively late and sudden weaning from the breast, and the symbolically laden moment of 'breeching', that is, the first transition into masculine clothing, which also occurred at a relatively late age.[1] And since, as Adelman comments,

> Contemporary object-relations psychoanalysis locates differentiation from the mother as a special site of anxiety for the boy-child, who must form his specifically masculine selfhood against the matrix of her overwhelming femaleness; how much more difficult and anxiety-ridden this process must have been if the period of infantile dependency – with its pleasures and dangers – was prolonged, and if the body itself, in all its vulnerability, could later be understood as the inheritance from her contaminating female matter.
>
> (Adelman 1992: 7)

Given the problematic status of the maternal in Freudian and Lacanian readings of *Hamlet*, as I discussed in the first chapters of this volume, it is hardly surprising that Adelman identifies that text as the pivotal moment after which Shakespeare's works begin to reflect an attempt to reincorporate the maternal principle which had been rigorously removed from the preceding plays:

> in the plays before *Hamlet*, masculine identity is constructed in and through the absence of the maternal . . . But the mother occluded in these plays returns with a vengeance in *Hamlet*; and it is the thesis of this book that the plays from *Hamlet* on all follow from her return.
>
> (Adelman 1992: 10)

In each case, therefore, Adelman analyses the play in terms of the masculine relation to the maternal, represented not only by female characters but by imagery of 'matter' – that is, of the simultaneously desirable and disgusting material body supposed by early modern physiology to be the specific legacy of the female parent, and strongly associated with both sexuality and mortality. Thus, in *Hamlet*

> Shakespeare re-understands the orthodox associations of woman with death by fusing the sexual with the maternal body, re-imagining the legacy of death consequent upon the fall as the legacy specifically of the sexualized maternal body . . . The mother's body brings death into the world because her body itself is death: in the traditional alignment of spirit and matter, the mother gives us the stuff – the female matter – of our bodies and thus our mortality.
>
> (Adelman 1992: 27)

Most often, therefore, the maternal will be seen as a 'contamination' of the masculine, and sexuality as a potentially lethal reabsorption into the maternal: 'all sexuality [presumably Adelman means all heterosexuality] . . . is imagined as an adulterating mixture' (Adelman 1992: 28). So, in *King Lear*, 'Lear's confrontation with his daughters . . . repeatedly leads him back to the mother ostensibly occluded in the play: in recognizing his daughters as part of himself he will be led to recognize also an equally terrifying femaleness within himself – a femaleness that he will come to call "mother" (2.4.56)' (104). And so on to *Macbeth* and *Coriolanus*, in which the maternal features as an active and hungry threat of engulfment: 'the cannibalistic witch-mothers Lear finds in Goneril and Regan are resurrected in Lady Macbeth and Volumnia; and fatherless, these sons are terribly subject to their power' (130). Adelman reads the later plays in terms of a rapid alternation between patriarchal triumph and maternal tyranny: between, on one hand, the misogynistic violence typified by Macbeth's attempt at a self-creation (a male parthenogenesis) which nevertheless remains utterly in thrall to a voracious maternal tyranny represented by the agenda of his wife and by the fateful determinations enunciated by the witches (130–61); and, on the other hand, the patriarchal triumph emblematised by Prospero's incorporation of a devalued maternal into the omnipotent figure of Duke, father and teacher (237–8).

In the midst of these violent oscillations between the tyrannical father and the voracious mother, however, Adelman identifies moments when Shakespeare's writing reaches forward, beyond the sexual constraints of his time – and beyond Freud as well – to envisage the idyll of a masculine and feminine relation that encompasses a proper and non-misogynistic relation to the maternal. At least twice, then, between Macbeth and Prospero,

> Shakespeare momentarily imagines a new psychic economy that can undo these bleak alternatives: in the last act of *Antony and Cleopatra*, Cleopatra reigns triumphant on stage; and her triumph turns crucially on her capacity not to destroy but to recreate Antony, remaking him from her own imaginative amplitude. This moment is fragile: if Shakespeare opens up the possibility of escape from the either/or of psychic scarcity in *Antony and Cleopatra*, he immediately forecloses that possibility again in *Coriolanus*. Nonetheless, the psychic economy glimpsed in Cleopatra's monument will eventually lead Shakespeare to *The Winter's Tale*, where trust in maternal amplitude enables Shakespeare's own imaginative bounty.
>
> (Adelman 1992: 165)

Such moments are visible only as brief and ephemeral fantasies, utopian at best: 'fragile pastoral' instants whose 'festive possibility is largely contained by the surrounding texts' (Adelman 1992: 193).

Working in a critical context in which authorial psychobiography has become anathema, Adelman avoids attributing the psychic structures to the author himself: the subject of the plays' psychoanalytic work is never explicitly identified, and can thus be taken to be Shakespeare, the reader or audience member, the masculine subject in early modern culture, or the subject of patriarchy in general. Nevertheless, *Suffocating Mothers* follows the plays in the presumed chronological sequence of their production, articulating complex relationships between them in such a way that, just as they did for Freud, Jones and Rank, each text comes to represent a particular 'session' in a series of therapeutic interventions, by means of which their masculine subject works out his own Oedipal dilemmas, and, in particular, his relationship to the maternal, beginning with the histories, continuing via the tragedies and the problem comedies, to the romances.

The result of this critical coherency is the implied construction of a narrative of developmental progress, which is 'heteronormative' in its psychosexual attitude – that is to say, it describes a path towards conventional heterosexuality, conceived as the only healthy and proper sexual and psychic state. Thus Adelman describes how patriarchal society insists upon 'the need to come to terms with the sexualized maternal body before embarking on the establishment of a new family through marriage' (Adelman 1992: 76). Again, this heteronormativity could be Shakespeare's, the reader's or the culture's in general – alternatively, it could belong to the psychoanalytic model being deployed. Certainly Adelman's reading does not discover, either within the Shakespearean text or in early modern culture generally, any mode of sexuality not in the service of a reproductive heterosexual union.

It is for this reason that feminist object-relations psychoanalytic approaches have been attacked by recent queer critics. Joseph Porter and Jonathan Goldberg, for example, have both accused Adelman of a 'psychosexual prescriptivism' that pathologises any mode of sexuality outside of a conventional heterosexual relation, that dismisses homosexuality, for example, as digressive, immature and incomplete (Porter 1988: 149–50; Goldberg 1994: 219, 226). These allegations focus on work written at the end of the 1970s and in the early 1980s by both Adelman and Coppélia Kahn in their treatment of *Romeo and Juliet*, in which Kahn wrote, for example, that 'As Janet Adelman points out . . . same sex friendships in Shakespeare (as in the typical life cycle) are chronologically and psychologically prior to marriage' (1980a: 104–5). It is important to note that the queer critique of Kahn and Adelman has been answered, in recent years, by both critics' rethinking of the techniques of psychoanalytic reading in relation to questions of homoeroticism and homophobia in Shakespeare's plays;[2] presumably the reason this kind of heteronormative prescriptivism came to the fore during inaugural experiments in psychoanalytic approaches to *Romeo and Juliet* must be that the play seems to concentrate on the moment defined by twentieth-century developmental psychology as the crucial point in the subject's sexual development, that is, adolescence.

Kahn's *Man's Estate: Masculine Identity in Shakespeare* (1981) is explicitly concerned with adolescence. Like Adelman, Kahn disclaims any attempt at a psychobiography directed either at the author or at particular characters:

I am not trying to psychoanalyze individual characters, but to discover dilemmas of masculine selfhood revealed in the design of the works as a whole. 'Hamlet may not have an Oedipus complex, but *Hamlet* does' [citing Crews 1967: 76].

We do not see Hamlet at his mother's breast, or Leontes learning to walk. Yet we can be confident, from the resonance of the poet's imagery and characterization, that he thought of them as human beings, whose adult selves were shaped by the experience of growing up within a family.

(Kahn 1981: 1–2)

Kahn claims to address those 'dilemmas of masculine selfhood' peculiar to Shakespeare's plays; however, citing with approval the attribution of an 'Oedipus complex' to *Hamlet* (the play rather than the character) suggests an assumption about the universal applicability of the psychoanalytic model being deployed (which is in fact not primarily Oedipal, but object-relational, as implied by the reference to 'Hamlet at his mother's breast'). Moreover, while Adelman acknowledges at the outset of her book certain differences between early modern and modern child-rearing, *Man's Estate* tends to take the Shakespearean family as a replica of the twentieth-century Oedipalised nuclear family – an assumption endemic to psychoanalytic reading prior to the advent of studies attentive to the differences between early modern and modern families, by Kahn herself in later works (1986; 1997), as well as by Belsey (1985; 1999). But as long as *Man's Estate* continues to map the psychoanalytic family on to the early modern, it also projects on to Shakespeare a psychoanalytic narrative of sexual development:

The great normative crisis of identity occurs in adolescence; it is then that instinctual and social imperatives for intimacy with the opposite sex, and pressures toward a settled choice of work and way of life, arise to create a crisis, defined by Erikson as 'a necessary turning point, when development must move one way or another'.[3]

(Kahn 1981: 195; citing Erikson 1968: 16)

Adolescence is here defined as a peculiar psychosexual space: a space of crisis, a space of choice. From a sexual point of view, though, it would seem that psychoanalytic theory allows no choice at all, and only a false crisis: for proper and healthy development to take place, the adolescent cannot help but choose to abandon homosexual desire and accede to the 'instinctual and social imperatives for intimacy with the opposite sex'. Upon this choice everything else rests: not only the health and psychic coherence of the individual, but indeed the social structure as a whole, depending as it presumably must upon the adult's 'settled choice of work and way of life', implying marriage and the production of yet another generation of the nuclear family.

It is this space of choice (which is in fact an absence of choice) that Shakespeare's most famous love story portrays:

> *Romeo and Juliet* is about a pair of adolescents trying to grow up. Growing up requires that they separate themselves from their parents by forming an intimate bond that supersedes filial bonds, a bond with a person of the opposite sex. This, broadly, is an essential task of adolescence, in Renaissance England or Italy as in America today.
>
> (Kahn 1981: 83)

Homosexual desire – now as then, here as there – is reduced to a stage through which the adolescent must pass to attain 'normal' heterosexual love. Similarly, in her discussion of *The Tempest*, Kahn describes 'that state of radical identity confusion typical of adolescence, when the differences between the sexes are as fluid as their desires for each other' (Kahn 1980b: 227), and comments that 'Without the strict differentiation of male from female, psychic integrity disappears and chaos impends' (228).

There are, of course, two kinds of differentiation (or lack of it) associated here with adolescence, and psychoanalysis – both in its Freudian or Oedipal, and its feminist object-relations incarnations – tends to blur the distinction between them. The first is to do with the development of an apparently clear gender distinction (either male or female), and the second entails the establishment of an ostensibly discrete sexual orientation (either homosexual or heterosexual). The blindnesses of psychoanalytic criticism – prior to its engagement with 1980s cultural materialism and new historicism – arise from its failure to attend to the extent to which every one of these aspects of the psyche is culturally constructed, and therefore subject to historical change. The notion of (only) two opposed sexes; the strict opposition between homosexual and heterosexual eroticism; the assumption of an inevitable bond between sexual and gender development; and indeed the whole notion of adolescence itself as the time and space in which these pairs and oppositions are resolved: all of these have been shown to be recent conceptions, and all quite alien to the culture in which Shakespeare wrote. It will be necessary to trace these historical differences one at a time.

Shakespeare's adolescence

According to French cultural historian Philippe Ariès, 'People had no idea of what we call adolescence' in the early modern period; something recognisable as the modern notion of adolescence as a discrete developmental phase, or a psychological space with its own characteristics, did not begin to emerge until the eighteenth century. When it appeared, it did so at first in two almost opposing forms. The first comprised a literary model that stressed 'the ambiguity of puberty' and 'the effeminate side of a boy just emerging from childhood', which 'was linked with the transition from child to adult: it expressed a condition during a certain period, the period of falling in love' (Ariès 1965: 29). The second inaugural image of modern adolescence was that of the military conscript, associated with 'manly strength' and demonstrating 'that combination of (provisional) purity, physical strength, naturism, spontaneity and joie de vivre which was to make the adolescent the hero of our twentieth century, the century of adolescence' (30).

The historical development of adolescence thus implies a masculinist subjectivity, which evolves out of childhood, through effeminacy, and into virile adulthood. This early narrative of adolescence will of course be encompassed, at the start of the twentieth century, by the Freudian account of sexual maturation, and extended by post-Freudian developmentalists such as Erikson, whose theory of individuation via a series of psychological crises (which underlies the argument in *Man's Estate*) makes of adolescence the pivotal moment in the formation of identity. As Ariès goes on to argue, psychoanalysis emerges at the beginning of the 'century of adolescence', the twentieth, in which 'our society has passed from a period which was ignorant of adolescence to a period in which adolescence is the favourite age. We now want to come to it early and linger in it as long as possible' (Ariès 1965: 30).

Following Ariès, John Neubauer conducts a detailed cultural history of the development of twentieth-century notions of adolescence. In particular, his study examines what he describes as a 'symbiotic' relationship, characterised by 'mutual affinities and exchanges', between literary culture and the notion of adolescence (Neubauer 1992: 10), and also the role played by psychoanalytic theory in the establishment of dominant theories of adolescence and in its discursive regulation (122–40). The book also describes the establishment in cultural terms of particular 'mythic habitats' affiliated with adolescence. Caught between the garden, as the childhood locus of purity and nature, and the 'stuffy conference room' of adult culture, the adolescent occupies a paradoxical space that embodies both seclusion and banishment, confinement and liberation; a degraded hybrid between pure nature and contaminating urban civilisation. The best instance is the bedroom, where the typical adolescent reads, plays video games and either daydreams a more idealised escape or fantasises a more complete degradation (66–7). At the beginning of the twentieth century psychologists and sociologists debated whether such privacy was advantageous to the growing youth, but the dominant individualism of many Western cultures made it inevitable that contemporary notions of adolescence should stress the psychological necessity for adolescents of a 'time-out room' (to use the contemporary 'good parenting' cliché) (68). Adolescence thus occurs both in and as an authorised space of privacy – physically, socially and psychologically removed from adult commerce – where youth can be allowed room to complete the development of that imaginative 'inner life' which is perceived to be essential to the formation of individual identity, but which is also eventually required to be locked away or regulated in order for the adolescent to enter fully into mature adult life. In this way certain aspects of sexuality – in particular masturbation and homosexuality – will be pathologised as 'secret vices', endemic to the furtive domain of adolescence, originally considered detrimental to the long-term physical and psychological wellbeing of the individual, and later characterised as transient phases which are not unhealthy insofar as they remain confined to the permitted phase of narcissistic non-maturity that is adolescence, and are left behind upon entry into adulthood (152–9).

Turning to *Romeo and Juliet* with this cultural history in mind, it becomes clear how alien to Shakespeare's culture these modern

attributes of adolescence really are.[4] Appropriately it is the Nurse
– surely a contemporary expert in matters developmental – who
most clearly articulates this difference, describing an incident from
Juliet's childhood:

> 'Tis since the earthquake now eleven years,
> And she was wean'd, – I never shall forget it – . . .
> When it did taste the wormwood on the nipple
> Of my dug and felt it bitter, pretty fool, . . .
> And since that time it is eleven years.
> For then she could stand high-lone, nay, by th'rood,
> She could have run and waddled all about;
> For even the day before she broke her brow,
> And then my husband – God be with his soul,
> A was a merry man – took up the child,
> 'Yea', quoth he, 'dost thou fall upon thy face?
> Thou wilt fall backward when thou hast more wit,
> Wilt thou not, Jule?' and by my holidame,
> The pretty wretch left crying and said 'Ay'.
>
> (1.3.23–44)

The Nurse's comically extended story reinforces in the first place
Juliet's youth; earlier we were told she 'hath not seen the change
of fourteen years' (1.2.9), and yet she is clearly considered mature
enough for marriage, a point which has itself often constituted
something of a difficulty for the modern reader whose notion of
adolescence, as Ariès points out, extends for at least another half-
decade or so beyond this age. But more than this, the Nurse's
account of her husband's joke precipitates the toddler from
childhood play directly into adult sexuality: the day before her
weaning from the Nurse's breast, little Jule's forward tumble allows
an adult man to imagine her falling backwards into bed for her
husband, a sexual destiny she immediately subscribes to: her 'Ay'
sounds at the same time like assent and self-identification ('I'),
reinforcing a precocity troubling rather than amusing to the
modern audience. The joke – which elicits only good humour from
its narrator, and presumably Shakespeare's contemporaries –
sounds distasteful to the modern reader precisely because it elides
an intervening space of adolescence, which is by definition separate
both from the sexual innocence of childhood and the sexual
responsibilities of adulthood. In short, the theory of development

to which the Nurse and her husband subscribe has no place of, or for, adolescence – at least not for the female child.

Nor does it contain any place for a range of sexual choices. The sexuality designated by Juliet's falling on her back is of course implicitly reproductive: the joke summarises the heterosexual destiny of the (female) infant: set on a path towards childbearing maturity one day (falling on her back), weaned from the (surrogate) maternal breast via wormwood the next, precisely in order to reproduce the whole narrative from the start. The cyclicity implied by the forwards–backwards 'tumble' becomes part of the joke.

The over-determination of sexual choice, which here produces humour (albeit of a very culturally specific kind), elsewhere in the play produces tragedy. From the outset – from the Prologue, in fact – Romeo and Juliet's choice of each other as love objects is simultaneously the choice of their mutual deaths. Throughout the play this dynamic will be figured as a conflict between the private delights of love and its public function. One of the most insistent rhetorical strategies in the play is that by which each of the two protagonists invokes an image of public architecture and attempts to rededicate it in the service of a private and individualised feeling for the beloved.

Even at their first meeting, the image of the religious shrine and the literary structure of the sonnet in which it is embodied are cultural edifices inherited from the very public realm of courtly love, but appropriated for a passion that attempts to stake out a space of individual choice and private knowledge (1.5.92–105). It is this desire by the lovers – for a place dedicated to a passion and a choice that is solely their own – which anticipates, for the modern reader, the space of adolescence, the essential function of which is to separate youth from the dependence of childhood and the responsibilities of adulthood by the allocation of several years of permitted experimentation, especially in regard to sexual relations. Significantly, though, it is the literary conventionalism of the 'holy shrine' conceit that Juliet emphasises when she comments that Romeo kisses by the book (1.5.109). All the vocabulary deployed by the lovers remains locked into the standard conceits of courtly love: the face of the beloved imagined picked out in stars in the heavens, for example (3.2.20–5), or the pervasive imagery of Cupid. Their most private moments together are utterly conventionalised, as in the scene in which they wake up after their first night of love, and Juliet speaks a familiar aubade according to which the sun is imagined as an alien and inappropriate intruder (3.5.1–36). Elsewhere, the vain struggle between a private love and its public façade will be expressed again in architectural terms, when Juliet describes their love as a 'mansion' of which she does not have possession (3.2.26–8); or of Romeo himself as a 'gorgeous palace' to which once again she cannot claim secure rights of ownership since it may be inhabited by 'deceit' (3.2.84–5). In the following scene Romeo asks Friar Lawrence to tell him 'In what vile part of this anatomy / Doth my name lodge? Tell me that I may sack / The hateful mansion' (3.3.105–7).

It should be clear from these examples that *Romeo and Juliet* figures not the triumph of a privatised love, but its impossibility. The pervasive architectural images remain over-determined by their public function, and thus the rhetoric of the play simply cannot recognise a separate space of adolescence. Halfway through the action, the imagery of a relationship conceived in terms of shrines, palaces and mansions gives way to the architecture of the tomb: 'Methinks I see thee, now thou art so low, / As one dead in the bottom of a tomb,' says Juliet (3.5.55–6), anticipating the final consummation of their relationship 'In that dim monument where Tybalt lies' (3.5.201), and requesting that she be hidden 'nightly in a charnel-house . . . Or bid me go into a new-made grave' (4.1.81–4). Before taking the Friar's drug, which will itself rehearse her death, Juliet vividly imagines waking up in the Capulet vault, 'an ancient receptacle' which, far from being a private and separate space of intimacy, appears crowded with intruders: 'all my buried ancestors', 'bloody Tybalt yet but green in earth', 'night spirits' and skeletons whose presence she imagines jostling her physically so that she awakens amid her 'forefathers' joints', crushed by 'some great kinsman's bone' (4.3.30–58). The grave may be a fine and private place by the time John Donne gets there, but for Juliet there's scarcely any room left among the prior occupants. And so this private love remains a very public affair: far from being alone together on stage at the end of the play, the lovers carry out their final moments, as Juliet has anticipated, in the overpopulated confines of the Capulet monument, accompanied by Tybalt's body, intruded upon by Paris, Friar Lawrence and finally by Montague and Capulet along with everyone else.

Even the play's final gesture is bequeathed to the two feuding fathers, who sublimate their rivalry and repeat it by rewriting their

children's attempted private love in terms of a new and very public
architecture:

> *Mont.*   . . . I will raise her statue in pure gold,
> That whiles Verona by that name is known,
> There shall no figure at such rate be set
> As that of true and faithful Juliet.
> *Cap.*   As rich shall Romeo's by his lady's lie,
> Poor sacrifices of our enmity.
> (5.3.298–303)

Thus the tragedy monumentalises, from beginning to end, the
lovers' inability to appropriate for themselves an individual domain
of love separate from the socio-cultural determinations of their
respective families.[5] In doing so, *Romeo and Juliet* features as an early
document in the contested emergence of the privatised family
during the late sixteenth and seventeenth centuries, demonstrating
in particular the impossibility, at the end of the sixteenth century,
of imagining adolescence as a space of individualised identity
formation – a notion that would not become a generally recognised
cultural feature for another century or two.[6]

Star-crossed lovers, cross-dressed stars

Another aspect of the psychoanalytic account of *Romeo and
Juliet* also demands re-examination, namely that assumption of
a compulsory heterosexuality which has been so thoroughly
critiqued by Goldberg and Porter.

The play opens, it must be noted, with a rather queer genealogy.
In reference to the feuding Montague and Capulet households,
the Chorus announces that

> From forth the fatal loins of these two foes
> A pair of star-cross'd lovers take their life,
> Whose misadventur'd piteous overthrows
> Doth with their death bury their parents' strife.
> (Prologue 5–8)

Anticipating as it does the (fatal) trajectory of the lovers' desire,
from its inception to its death, the Prologue makes it sound like a

working out of the relation between Capulet and Montague. More than this, the 'pair of star-crossed lovers take their life' from 'the fatal loins of these two foes': these lines write both mothers out of the picture, replacing them with the fantasy of an aggressive rivalry between two men which is also a homogenetic marriage. The next lines reinforce this, referring to Capulet and Montague as 'their parents', so that the two lovers sound like siblings, whose love is fatal not because their parents are irremediably opposed, but rather because they are the same.

The first scene then plays out in vivid action and imagery this interlocking of the 'fatal loins' of the Montague and Capulet men; the homoerotically engendered violence (or violently engendered homoerotics) of the fathers is bequeathed to the younger generations and their households: aggressively virile Capulet and Montague retainers front up to each other, their aggression highly sexually charged: 'To move is to stir, and to be valiant is to stand', 'I will push Montague's men from the wall, and thrust his maids to the wall', 'take it in what sense you wilt', 'They must take it in sense that feel it', 'Draw thy tool', ''tis known I am a pretty piece of flesh', 'My naked weapon is out', 'I will back thee' (1.1.8–33). In this way they rehearse the feud in preparation for the entry of Old Capulet: 'What noise is this? Give me my long sword, ho! . . . My sword I say! Old Montague is come, / And flourishes his blade in spite of me' (1.1.73–6). The same homoerotic aggressivity will characterise the language of Romeo, Mercutio and Benvolio versus Tybalt later on.

No wonder, then, that since *Romeo and Juliet* has recently functioned as the focal point for the working out of modern notions of adolescence, it has also become for critics a locus for the working out of those questions about the necessity or desirability of a heteronormative developmentalism; that is, the interrogation by queer theory of the assumptions that heterosexuality constitutes the only normal and healthy sexual location of the mature adult, and that homosexual desire attains validity only as temporary attraction on the route to that more conventional destination.

Initially, critical approaches to non-heterosexuality in Shakespeare's plays tended to focus on the comedies, and in particular on the homoerotic and transgender implications of early modern theatrical transvestism. Stephen Orgel points out that the widespread use of boy actors in female roles constitutes a 'uniquely

English solution', which was tried without success in Spanish theatres in 1599 (Orgel 1989: 7–8). Like many critics, Orgel links the sexual ambiguity of transvestite acting with gender ambiguity, implying that it is the femininity – or more accurately the effeminisation – of the cross-dressed male actor that excites sexual anxiety in these plays. Lisa Jardine, too, argues that 'the *double entendres* of . . . speeches by blushing heroines (played by boys) as they adopt male dress to follow their male lover are both compatible with the heterosexual plot, and evocative of the bisexual image of the "wanton female boy"' (Jardine 1983: 30). And Laura Levine cites antitheatrical pamphleteer Phillip Stubbes, who defines men who wear women's clothes as 'monsters, of both kindes, half women, half men'. According to this attitude, Levine asserts, 'the hermaphroditic actor, the boy with the properties of both sexes, becomes the embodiment of all that is frightening about the self' (Levine 1994: 19). She goes on to cite assertions by other antitheatrical campaigners: Stephen Gosson's concern that watching theatre has an effeminising effect on men in the audience (20), William Prynne's narrative about the warrior who 'degenerates' into a woman (44).[7]

According to Jonathan Goldberg, however, whenever Orgel, Jardine and Levine focus on the antitheatrical concern with cross-dressing, they continue to confuse issues of sexuality in Shakespearean theatre with anxiety about a masculine liability to effeminisation. This, however, is hardly the same thing as homoeroticism, since it resituates the desire of the male spectator – and the male lover within the drama – not in the masculinity of the cross-dressed body but in its putative femininity. For Goldberg, then, all of these critics thereby risk dissolving both homophobia and homoeroticism into fear of and desire for women: the cross-dressed actor is perceived to be both threatening and sexy not because he is a man, but because she/he might be(come) a woman. Moreover, he argues,

> When effeminacy is taken as the transfer point from hetero- to homo-sexuality, Levine and Orgel lose sight of something they both know, that effeminacy was more easily associated with, and was a charge more often made about, men who displayed excessive attention to women than taken as an indication of same-sex attraction.
>
> (Goldberg 1992: 110–11)

Romeo clearly demonstrates this when he remarks, 'O sweet Juliet, / Thy beauty hath made me effeminate / And in my temper soften'd valour's steel' (3.1.115–17). This argument can be reversed, too: if heterosexual desire can have an effeminising effect on the male lover, due to its excessive proximity to and investment in the feminine, then homosexual desire can in contrast reinforce phallic virility, by means of an exaggerated proximity to and investment in a masculinity untainted by the feminine. As Valerie Traub points out,

> To the extent that heterosexual desire in Shakespearean drama is often associated with detumescence (the triumph of Venus over Mars, the pervasive puns on dying), and homoerotic desire is figured as permanently erect, it is the desire of man for man that is coded as the more 'masculine' . . . extreme virility, manifested in Spartan self-denial and military exploits, is not only depicted as consistent with erotic desire for other men; it also is expressed in it, as when Aufidius says to Coriolanus, 'Let me twine / Mine arms about that body, whereagainst / My grained ash an hundred times hath broke', and goes on to compare the joy he feels at seeing Coriolanus as being greater than that which he felt 'when I first my wedded mistress saw / Bestride my threshold'.
>
> (Traub 1992: 134; citing *Coriolanus* 4.5.111–23)

Bruce Smith observes, with respect to the deployment of bridal imagery by Aufidius in relation to his rival, that

> What Shakespeare invites us to see, at least for the space of the metaphor, is a *continuum* of erotic desire that embraces both male and female objects, both arch rival and new bride. The rhetorical focus is on the speaker, on Aufidius as the desiring subject, and not as Freudian psychology would have it on the anatomies of the object-bodies he desires.
>
> (Smith 1991: 55)

For Goldberg, Traub and Smith, influenced as they are by queer theory, understanding desire in Shakespearean drama requires a constant awareness that the categories of 'homosexual' and 'heterosexual', and the opposition between them, are inventions of a later cultural moment than the dramaturgy that produced these plays.

More than this, the notion of sexuality as a defining point for individual identity is also anachronistic, the legacy of the same nineteenth-century medical and psychological discourse from which Freudianism derives:

> in the sixteenth and seventeenth centuries, sexuality was not, as it is for us, the starting place for anyone's self-definition. Just because sexuality has become an obsessive concern in our own culture does not mean that it has always been so . . . No one in Shakespeare's day would have labeled himself a 'Homosexual'. The term itself is a clinical, scientific coinage of the clinical, scientific nineteenth century . . . The structures of knowledge that impinged on what we would now call 'homosexuality' did not ask a man who had sexual relations with another man to think of himself as fundamentally different from his peers. Just the opposite was true. Prevailing ideas asked him to castigate himself for falling into the general depravity to which *all* mankind is subject.
>
> (Smith 1991: 11)

As Alan Bray points out, for an early modern Puritan such as John Rainolds, far from being a distinct category of sexual depravity or perversion, 'homosexuality was a sin to which "men's natural corruption and viciousness is prone"' (Bray 1982: 16). And Susan Zimmerman, citing Rainolds's assertion that the kisses of 'beautiful boyes' will sting men with 'a kinde of poyson, the poyson of incontinencie', remarks that in moving immediately 'from a specific instance of homoeroticism to a general statement on all amatory kissing and embracing, Rainolds did not distinguish between male and female as unholy erotic object(s)' (Zimmerman 1992: 45).

None of which is to say that Shakespeare's society always, or even routinely, embraced non-heterosexuality. Rather, Bruce Smith argues that the attitude towards same-sex desire in early modern England betrays a thoroughgoing contradiction, or rather a disparity between different discursive fields: while 'the arguments of the moralists and the laws of the jurists' of Shakespeare's time (like those of Rainolds) appear to suggest a virulent homophobia, the 'laxity with which these arguments and laws were enforced' indicates 'a society that was at least tolerant of homosexual behaviour if not positively disposed towards it'. As Smith reasonably concludes, 'Surely the truth lies somewhere in between' (Smith 1991: 73), in the third of those possibilities identified by Eve Sedgwick for the management of same-sex desire within a patriarchal society: 'ideological homophobia, ideological homosexuality, or some highly conflicted but intensively structured combination of the two' (Sedgwick 1985: 25).

By combining this re-historicisation of sexual identity with the insights of queer theory, critics such as Goldberg, Smith, Traub and Zimmerman therefore rethink theatrical transvestism in terms very different from those of their critical predecessors. Both the pleasure and the anxiety attaching to the cross-dressed actor derives, in their account, less from the possible effeminisation of the actor, and more from the play of a sexual desire that traverses both the male and the female body without constraint. It is in these terms that queer criticism would reread, for example, the Epilogue of *As You Like It*:

> Having just taken off his disguise as Ganymede, the actor starts out in the person of Rosalind: 'It is not the fashion to see the lady the epilogue . . .' (Epi. 1–2). But he completes the step-by-step stripping away of the disguise by finishing the epilogue in his own person as a body . . . his pose as androgynous flirt invites us to take with us as we leave the theater some of the liminal freedom we allowed ourselves during the play.
>
> (Smith 1991: 155)

Similarly Traub suggests that Rosalind's crossing back and forth between shifting gender and sexual investments 'leads the play into a mode of desire neither heterosexual nor homoerotic, but both heterosexual *and* homoerotic. As much as she displays her desire for Orlando, she also enjoys her position as male object of Phebe's desire and, more importantly, of Orlando's' (Traub 1992: 124). This suggestion introduces yet another possibility to the reading of the cross-dressed actor, who has not previously been thought to embody female–female desire: 'If we focus on the text rather than theatrical practice, the desires circulating through the Phebe/Rosalind/Ganymede relation, or the Olivia/Viola/Cesario interaction, represent woman's desire for woman' (107–8).

In these accounts, then, the sexuality of the Shakespearean stage remains altogether prior to, and unassimilable by, sexual categorisations of the kind with which modern readers will be most familiar. Traub is not arguing that Rosalind or Orlando or Phebe 'is' 'a' 'homosexual'. Rather, at various moments in the play, these characters temporarily inhabit a homoerotic position of desire ... The entire logic of *As You Like It* works against ... categorization, against fixing upon and reifying any one mode of desire.

(Traub 1992: 128–9)

In contrast to these discussions about the self-conscious trans-vestism in Shakespearean comedy, many critics have thought that the seriousness and solemnity required of tragic narrative demanded a more stable relation to both sexual and gender characterisation. Susan Zimmerman describes a 'common critical assumption, often unconscious, ... that Jacobean spectators essentially blocked awareness of transvestism while viewing serious drama' (Zimmerman 1992: 55), but she goes on to argue that the 'democratic eroticism, accessible to all, emanating from the *process* of creating sexual confusions, from the jumblings of overlapping sexual nuances' which characterised early modern English drama cannot be confined to comedy. On the contrary, it is necessary to recall that Shakespeare's audience was very practised at moving rapidly between theatrical modes, and changes in affect, that a modern spectator may find incompatible:

> We can credit Jacobean spectators with a compartmentalized mental programming that shut out transvestite nuances in serious drama; or we can credit them with an ability to sustain dual levels of erotic awareness without rendering serious fictions ridiculous.

(Zimmerman 1992: 55)

Queer theory thus demands the rethinking of transvestism in terms of a homoeroticism that can neither be understood according to modern conceptions of homosexuality and heterosexuality, nor assumed to achieve a stability in the tragic plays upon which psychoanalytic reading has more traditionally focused its attention. Nor, moreover, is it necessary to delimit the 'queerness' of the plays to the question of cross-dressed actors; so that for Goldberg and Smith the primary locus for the working out of homoerotic desire in the plays is not transvestism, but rather the representation of eroticised relationships between male characters and other male characters, or between female characters and other female characters: Antonio and Bassanio in *The Merchant of Venice*; Sebastian and Antonio, Orsino and Cesario in *Twelfth Night*; Orlando and Ganymede, Phebe and Rosalind in *As You Like It*; Achilles and Patroclus in *Troilus and Cressida*; Cassio and Iago in *Othello*; Prospero and Ariel, Sebastian and Antonio in *The Tempest* (Goldberg 1992: 142–3).

And, of course, Romeo and Mercutio. So, as Bruce Smith comments, the 'specific object of Mercutio's sexual and verbal interest . . . is not Juliet's pudenda . . . but Romeo's':

> 'O Romeo, that she were, O that she were / An open-arse, and thou a poperin' pear' (2.1.27–38): Mercutio's lewdest verbal jab, the immediate foil to Romeo's 'But soft, what light through yonder window breaks?' (2.1.44), is an image of anal sex, and it climaxes a whole series of earlier jokes to which Romeo's member supplies the point. 'If love be rough with you', Mercutio has advised, 'be rough with love. / Prick love for pricking, and you beat love down' (1.4.27–28).
>
> (Smith 1991: 63–4)

Jonathan Goldberg, in his wittily entitled '*Romeo and Juliet*'s Open Rs', also traces the homoeroticism that pervades Mercutio's lines and insistently evades modern distinctions between homosexual and heterosexual trajectories of desire. Discussing Mercutio's line in the garden following the Capulet Ball, 'In his mistress' name / I conjure only but to raise up him' (2.1.28–9), Goldberg writes:

> this is how Mercutio voices – through Rosaline – his desire for Romeo . . . [in a later scene] Tybalt charges Mercutio with being Romeo's 'consort' ('Mercutio, thou consortest with Romeo. / *Mer.* Consort?' 3.1.44–45) . . . If Mercutio counsels Romeo to prick love for pricking (1.4.28), it is, it appears, because he fears that his Valentine has received the 'butt-shaft' (2.4.16) of love, that Rosaline, armed like Diana, has hit his mark, that the boy love has come to the depth of his tail and buried his bauble in that hole rather than in his (see 2.4.90–100).
>
> (Goldberg 1994: 230–1)

Goldberg's conflation of queer innuendoes into an extended and increasingly explicit sentence demonstrates vividly the pan-erotic repartee that typifies the first half of the play – especially the scenes involving Mercutio.

But as the multiple forms of queer desire described by recent critics suggest, Mercutio's death need not be the point at which alternative forms of eroticism disappear; for example, there remains Romeo's 'effeminisation' by his passion for Juliet, and also the polymorphous possibilities of passionate scenes between two young male actors playing the eponymous leads. As Goldberg puts it, 'gender and sexuality in *Romeo and Juliet* do not subscribe to the compulsions of modern critics of the play' (Goldberg 1994: 227); similarly, Dympna Callaghan argues that the institution of the play as a founding document in modern normative heterosexuality 'becomes consolidated and intensified with subsequent re-narrations' (Callaghan 1994: 61).

It is only in these modern rewritings, then, that the death of Mercutio becomes the pivot point upon which the play turns from an immature homoeroticism to a properly heterosexual destiny: Mercutio's lethal penetration by Tybalt 'under [Romeo's] arm' (3.1.105) comes to signal the destruction of Romeo's participation in same-sex eroticism, and his turn towards a more definitive, because more doomed, 'true love' with Juliet. There are two reasons why today versions of *Romeo and Juliet* inevitably consign same-sex and other-sex desire to different halves of the play, and represent the latter as an advance upon the former: first, the casting of women actors to play Juliet; and second, the replaying of the psychoanalytic narrative of adolescent sexuality as a movement towards reproductive maturity. It is with the interaction between these two factors that the rest of this chapter will be concerned.

Freud's sexual fables

In the first of his 'Three Essays on the Theory of Sexuality' (1905) – the title of which is 'The Sexual Aberrations' – Freud begins by describing a common perception that the anatomical gender distinction between male and female goes hand in hand, as it were, with heterosexual object choice:

> The popular view of the sexual instinct is beautifully reflected in the poetic fable which tells how the original human beings

were cut up into two halves – man and woman – and how these are always striving to unite again in love. It comes as a great surprise therefore to learn that there are men whose sexual object is a man and not a woman, and women whose sexual object is a woman and not a man.

(*PFL* 7: 46)

This is a distortion of the fable of Aristophanes from Plato's *Symposium*, in which the originally 'whole' beings split in two were not in all cases half-man and half-woman at all; on the contrary, some were male–male and some female–female. The 'surprise' Freud associates with homosexual object choice therefore represents a projection on to the Aristophanic myth of a heteronormativity totally absent from its original form, and clearly the product of a modern intertwining of the development of sexuality with the supposed naturalness of the division into two sexes.[8]

The essay goes on to consider whether homosexual object choice ('inversion', as Freud calls it) should thus be seen to entail a deformation of, or a regression from, a mature and unequivocal masculinity or femininity. However, Freud distrusts this conclusion, at least in regard to male homosexuality: he implies a distinction between female homosexual object choice, which he thinks does compromise gender identity – as the female homosexual becomes 'mannish' – and male homosexuality, which does not (*PFL* 7: 53), presumably because his investment in the maintenance of a discrete and consistent masculinity is higher:

There can be no doubt that a large proportion of male inverts retain the mental quality of masculinity, that they possess relatively few of the secondary characters of the opposite sex and that what they look for in their sexual object are in fact feminine mental traits.

(*PFL* 7: 55)

Homosexuality in this account becomes virtually a digressive and distasteful form of heterosexuality: what homosexuals desire is the feminine after all, albeit clothed in a male body.

But while this insistent heteronormativity might seem to foreshadow those critics who read the early modern investment in the cross-dressed actor as a disguised form of anxiety about or desire for the feminine, some of Freud's conclusions in this essay provide a contradictory viewpoint, and foreshadow a more radical way of rethinking sexuality, which will eventually be taken up by queer theory and criticism. At the end of the essay he suggests that

> Experience of the cases that are considered abnormal has shown us that in them the sexual instinct and the sexual object are merely soldered together – a fact which we have been in danger of overlooking in consequence of the uniformity of the normal picture, where the object appears to form part and parcel of the instinct. We are thus warned to loosen the bond that exists in our thoughts between instinct and object.
>
> (*PFL* 7: 59)

Study of 'abnormal' sexualities ultimately reveals, Freud thinks, that erotic desire and its objects are 'merely soldered together', that is, linked by an artificial bond, a product of the technology of culture, rather than a unity intrinsic to nature. Typically, Freud reads what he discovers from the 'abnormal' back into the 'normal', thereby destabilising it: if 'inverted' sexuality can detach or reattach the bonds between sexual object and drive, perhaps it is only the 'uniformity of the normal picture', that is to say the conventionality of heterosexuality, that accustoms us to thinking of sexual object choice as a defining feature of different types of desire; perhaps there is only one kind of sexual desire after all, or else many more than two. It is precisely by loosening their fixation on the object, and exploring instead the play of desires, or else the multiple possibilities of the desiring subject, that critics such as Smith, Traub and Zimmerman can produce their revisions of the erotic investments of the early modern theatre.

The radical possibilities of this suggestion, if they are glimpsed by Freud, are soon foreclosed by the essays that follow, which spell out a developmental model of the psyche that recuperates alternative erotologies within a wider and more powerful, because normative, heterosexuality. In the third and final of these essays on sexuality, on 'The Transformations of Puberty', Freud follows through the narrative implications of the Oedipal complex – the mother and father of all psychoanalytic developmentalisms – into the realm of adolescence. Just as the working out of Oedipus in childhood requires the renunciation of the relation to the parent of the same sex, and the transfer of desire to the parent of the opposite sex, in puberty and adulthood also

> There can be no doubt that every object-choice whatever is based . . . on these prototypes. A man, especially, looks for someone who can represent his picture of his mother . . . One of the tasks implicit in object-choice is that it should find its way to the opposite sex. This, as we know, is not accomplished without a certain amount of fumbling. Often enough the first impulses after puberty go astray, though without any permanent harm resulting. Dessoir [1894] has justly remarked upon the regularity with which adolescent boys and girls form sentimental friendships with others of their own sex.
>
> (*PFL* 7: 152–3)

This suggestion relates to a long footnote added in 1915 to the earlier essay on 'The Sexual Aberrations', which binds that essay's liberation from determination by object choice back into this theory of sexual maturation that Freud will bequeath to developmental psychology (for example, Erikson):

> Indeed, libidinal attachments to persons of the same sex play no less a part as factors in normal mental life, and a greater part as a motive force for illness, than do similar attachments to the opposite sex . . . psychoanalysis considers that a choice of an object independently of its sex – freedom to range equally over male and female objects – as it is found in childhood, in primitive states of society and early periods of history, is the original basis from which, as a result of restriction in one direction or the other, both the normal and the inverted types develop.
>
> (*PFL* 7: 56–7, n. 1)

Non-heterosexual object choice becomes, in this account, so common as to be within the purview of the normal, but only insofar as it remains associated with illness, with childhood, with primitivism; that is, it constitutes an immature phase which will be superseded in the developmental drive towards heterosexuality. And the critical space within which this process, this putting behind one of childish things, will take place is of course the space of adolescence: 'A person's final sexual attitude is not decided until after puberty' (*PFL* 7: 57, n. 1).

It is this conception of adolescence as a stage – that is, both a phase and a space – within which the crucial turn from homo-primitivism to hetero-maturity is achieved that *Romeo and Juliet* is taken to embody – especially when read, as it most usually is these days, in the classroom, on the screen and on video.

The spaces of true love: *Romeo and Juliet* on screen

At least in the West, and at least since the overt engagement with Freudian theory characteristic of directors like Hitchcock, cinema has proven singularly hospitable to and productive of psychoanalytic narratives, tending to portray triangulated and Oedipalised structures of desire, to invest fetishistically in certain over-determined signifiers (the cigarette, the curtain, the gun), and to effect in its spectators that receptivity to the unconscious experienced in sleep or hypnosis, by means of a sudden darkening of the auditorium, and the projection of dreamlike and luminous images on to the screen.[9]

No wonder, then, that films based on Shakespearean texts have concentrated on contested interior motivation and intersubjective conflict, eschewing for the most part those political, historical and cultural interests that have dominated the last two decades of Shakespearean criticism. Nor, moreover, is it surprising that each of three recent films focusing on *Romeo and Juliet* takes up the readings produced by an engagement between psychoanalysis and Shakespeare. I will end this chapter by attempting to identify some of the ways in which an awareness of the questions raised by cultural politics and history might impact upon the production and reception of the psychoanalytic Shakespeare as he makes his comeback in the realm of the popular. In particular I will examine how each of the three films represents relations between homosexuality and heterosexuality, masculinity and femininity, and the developmental narratives regulating such relations, which have interested feminist and queer critics in their readings of *Romeo and Juliet*.

Closet and public stage

John Madden's *Shakespeare in Love*, written by Marc Norman and
Tom Stoppard, was a box-office hit in 1998 and won the Best
Film Oscar the following year. Without doubt, a major component
in this success was its skill in suturing together a popular taste
for Hollywood romantic comedy with the high-cultural tastes of
those in the audience who saw themselves as Shakespeareans,
amateur or professional. An integral aspect of this movement
between formerly disparate regimes of taste involved the processing
of historical difference – especially in relation to the theatrical
conventions of late sixteenth-century London – into more
palatable, because more familiar, generic forms. Crucially,
the playing of 'serious' or tragic female roles by cross-dressed
male actors – the most alien convention of all – had to be accom-
modated. For this purpose the film deployed a version of
psychoanalytic developmentalism, that propulsion of the subject
inexorably towards heternormativity and away from homoeroticism, with which a late twentieth-century audience would be
most familiar.

As I discussed in my introduction to this volume, the early
scenes of the film follow Will Shakespeare on his visit to an early
modern Freud, the 'priest of the psyche' Dr Moth, and eavesdrop
on his crudely Oedipal castration anxiety. From this comic
psychoanalysis, we are next introduced to the theme of 'true love'
by the entry of Lady Viola de Lesseps, played by Best Actress
Oscar-winner Gwyneth Paltrow. She attends a play in which some
of Shakespeare's lines are badly delivered – 'What light is light,
if Sylvia be not seen? / What joy is joy . . . ?' (*The Two Gentlemen of
Verona* 3.1.174ff.) – and we identify with her realisation, which no
one else attending the performance shares, that Shakespeare's
lines represent the inauguration of an altogether new sensibility,
that of 'modern' or romantic (as distinct from courtly) love. Back
in her bedchamber, she tells her nurse, 'Stage love will never
be true love while the law of the land has our heroines played by
pipsqueak boys in petticoats', and then goes on to aver, 'I will
have love in my life. Not the artful postures of love, but love that
overthrows life: unbiddable, ungovernable . . . love as there has
never been in a play.'

Having established the primitive inadequacy of contemporary
(transvestite) theatrical representation to do justice to this new

mode of passion, the film then goes on to contrast it with the convention of marriages arranged for financial and social reasons: negotiations are occurring between Viola's father, Sir Robert de Lesseps, and the Earl of Wessex, whose Virginia tobacco plantations require the infusion of new money that marriage to Viola will bring: 'But I don't love you!' says Viola to Wessex; 'How your mind jumps about,' he replies with puzzled irritation. Later he comments acerbically to her theatrically weeping mother on the day of the wedding, 'You are not losing a daughter, you are gaining a colony,' while Viola remarks coldly, on entering the room to see her father and husband exchanging cash, 'I see you are open for business, so let's to church.'[10]

In search of a private space of true love, sheltered from the commerce of arranged marriage, Viola turns, of course, to Shakespeare. She auditions for his new play, for the part of Romeo, in disguise as Thomas Kent. While all the other auditioners choose the Helen of Troy speech from Marlowe's *Dr Faustus*, Viola chooses the speech from *The Two Gentlemen of Verona* (spoken by a character named, inevitably, Valentine – which then becomes Romeo's pseudonym at the Capulet Ball) by which she was so affected during her earlier visit to the theatre. As soon as Will hears 'Thomas' speak, we recognise his attraction to that voice speaking his own lines about 'true love' with a novel passion.

Crucially, though, the film never allows this attraction to be homoerotic: Will responds to a female voice more realistic than any other at the Rose, and he doesn't get a glimpse of Viola/Thomas in this scene, in spite of pursuing her/him out of the theatre. To my eyes 'Kent' looks nothing like a man or a boy, but like Gwyneth Paltrow with a boyish wig and fake facial hair. Pursued from the Rose theatre by Will, she is all floppy breeches and lavender hat, and her body language codifies not masculinity, campness, nor effeminacy, but an entirely recognisable (because thoroughly conventionalised) femininity.

Meanwhile, Will falls for Viola, whom he has spotted at her parents' house, and writes her the sonnet beginning, 'Shall I compare thee to a summer's day?' – which, in the context of the sequence, is known to be addressed to a young man. In *Shakespeare in Love* Will gives it to 'Kent' to take to Viola, thus wittily retaining the reference to the sonnet's original addressee while simultaneously redirecting it to a properly heterosexual destination. In a similar way, the potential homoeroticism of the cross-dressed actor is cleverly reinscribed in the service of a homosocial and unequivocal heterosexuality. When we first meet the young man who is to play Juliet, Will strokes his cheek, and says, 'My pretty one, are you ready to fall in love again?', but on hearing the youth reply, grabs his crotch and asks urgently, 'Your voice – did they drop?' 'No, no,' replies the boy hastily. 'A touch of cold only.' During rehearsals, this actor (who remains obviously and unequivocally male, clad in a dress but minus a wig or make-up) plays Juliet, while Romeo is played by 'Thomas Kent' (still recognisably feminine to us, but not to Shakespeare and his fellow actors). As Katherine Duncan-Jones comments, there is not 'even a bat's squeak of bisexuality', much less of homosexuality, in any of these scenes (Duncan-Jones 1999: 18).[11]

The one moment that might be the exception to this rigorous redirection of homoerotic trajectory towards a heterosexual 'true love' occurs before Will has discovered that 'Kent' is Viola, when the two share a boat crossing the Thames, and Will declares in highly poetic terms his love for Viola. There's a brief moment of humour during which 'Kent' bridles with indignation at Will's lascivious references to Viola's 'bosom', a moment that reminds the audience of the 'true' sex of Will's interlocutor, while also demonstrating how sexually oblivious the playwright is to this young man, merely including him in his standard homosocial badinage about female beauty. Recovering from this momentary annoyance, though, 'Thomas' becomes over-whelmed by Shakespeare's lyrical expressions of love for Viola, and suddenly kisses him. However, neither Will nor the audience is given more than an instant to contemplate the possibly disturb-ing homoerotics of this 'male'–male intimacy: releasing a surprised Shakespeare from the embrace, 'Kent' jumps out of the boat and pays the boatman, whose response of 'Thank you, my lady' immediately resolves any homosexual panic (or desire) that may otherwise have begun to afflict our Will. The audience was never liable to experience the slightest homoerotic frisson at this point, for 'Thomas' never seemed like a man in the first place: as the boatman puts it, 'That's Lady Viola de Lesseps. I've known her since she was a girl. Wouldn't fool anyone.' Moreover, within a minute of screen time, Will follows 'Kent' into the house and a love scene follows in which the unbinding of Viola's breasts, completing her rapid transformation from man into woman, features significantly.[12]

Just as Viola's situation will provide the model for Juliet's – an impending marriage arranged by her father, an illicit affair with a socially inappropriate other, supported by her exasperated nurse – two familiar scenes from the play are wittily shown first occurring during Will's 'real life' encounters with Viola, and thence being transliterated into the play. In the first, Will watches from below while Viola emerges on to the balcony, declaiming, 'O Romeo, Romeo, young man of Verona,' because she is captivated by the idea of playing that role in Will's new play. Throughout their ensuing exchanges he, like Romeo in the equivalent scene, is in danger of being apprehended by her family; and they are interrupted by the nurse calling, to which Viola replies, 'Anon.' Immediately after this scene, the film cuts to Will Shakespeare writing furiously, trimming his quill, cracking his knuckles. The other famous moment from the play to which Will's and Viola's romance alludes is the morning-after scene, during which each lover in turn pretends the light of day is something else in order that they may stay in bed with each other. And then an extended montage shows Viola and Shakespeare spending nights in bed together, making love as they exchange lines from the play they are rehearsing during the daytime. The lines move back and forth, some incorporated into the play from the bedroom, some repeated in the bedroom from the play: what the montage achieves is a vivid reinstatement of that psycho-biographical idiom represented by classic Freudian analysis, which leaves us in no doubt about the very direct relation between the author's art and his psychological state:

Will: And wilt thou leave me so unsatisfied?
Viola: That's my line.
Will: It is mine, too.

More than anything else, however, *Shakespeare in Love* at these points completes *Romeo and Juliet*'s failed attempt to imagine a private space of love by re-privatising the conventions of courtly love and finding their origins in the secret biography of Shakespeare's own life.

The bedchamber – Viola's 'closet', as Shakespearean usage would call it – thus supplies that private space of love, conceived in modern terms, which the film smuggles into its late sixteenth-century setting. Of course, this 'true love' has to remain closeted, being strictly out of space and before its time – which provides an opportunity for a further association between cross-dressing and broad 'cocks-in-frocks' humour, when Will emerges from Viola's bedroom disguised as Willemina, her 'country cousin', clad in an unconvincing wimple and veil, in order to accompany her and Wessex to the royal audience at Greenwich. Meanwhile, the same modern amusement at badly performed drag continues to characterise the representation of the rehearsals taking place at the Rose. The implausibility of Viola's own cross-dressing – she is, of course, far too womanly to be a very good man – emerges when she is exposed to the Master of the Revels by the young and malicious John Webster, who cries, 'I saw her bubbies,' and drops a mouse down her back to make her jump out of her disguise, in a clichéd display of femininity outed from the closet. The same transvestiphobia emerges in the climax of the film, the first public performance of the play, during the exchanges between the large and very butch actor playing the nurse and an equally unconvincing Lady Capulet, who provide a fit contrast for the entry of an utterly realistic Juliet, played now 'properly' by Viola herself.

She takes the role because, in a twist anticipated by Will's original joke about this possibility, the voice of Sam, the boy who played Juliet in rehearsal, breaks on the morning of the first performance. Fortunately Viola knows every word of Juliet's lines 'by heart' – because she originally rehearsed with Romeo, because Will has lovingly sent her a script of the play, and because it embodies in the words of her favourite writer the affair she has been having with him. So the play 'comes to life' in the public playhouse: Will himself plays Romeo, acting out his tragic passion for Viola's Juliet, by means of an ingenious reversal that turns back on itself the early modern convention of cross-dressing. By first having a cross-dressed woman playing Romeo, and a cross-dressed man playing Juliet, and then returning both roles to gender-appropriate actors (appropriate, that is, to a modern audience, although thoroughly inappropriate to Shakespeare's), the film re-enacts with remarkable precision the psychoanalytic development from an immature homoerotics to a fully realised heterosexuality. The implicit developmentalism of this narrative is comically under-scored by the fact that the precipitating factor in this final recasting is the sudden onset of puberty and the consequent discovery of the masculine voice by the boy actor who was to have played Juliet originally.

Out of the homoerotic playing conditions of the Elizabethan stage, *Shakespeare in Love* thereby produces a conventional and convincing heterosexual passion, a 'true' love running according to its proper course, untainted by a hint of the perverse. At the same time, by portraying the Elizabethan stage as both drama-turgically and erotically primitive, it produces a celebration of modern realism, accompanied by an altogether modern audience reaction: at the end of the performance, the crowd in the playhouse respond with the silence of utter identification. The epoch of true love and the epoch of realism, it would seem, go hand in hand.

But disaster waits in the wings. The Master of the Revels has soldiers ready to arrest all the players for flouting the royal order prohibiting women to act on the public stage. It requires a deus ex machina in the form of Judi Dench's Elizabeth I, who is suddenly revealed to have been present throughout the performance: 'The Queen of England does not attend exhibitions of public lewdness, so something is out of joint,' she says. The mere fact of her presence means that the play must conform to the royal will: Juliet cannot be a real woman, she must be a man. Examining 'Master Kent' closely, the Queen announces that 'The illusion is remarkable, but I know something about a woman in a man's profession.' The historical figure of Elizabeth (and a submerged reference to her most famous declaration: 'I may be a mere woman, but I have the heart and stomach of a king') and the actual conditions of Elizabethan theatre are being twisted together here to produce a range of contemporary complacencies: a modern and hetero-sexual 'true love' out of an early modern homoerotic artifice; a twentieth-century liberal feminism out of a sixteenth-century patriarchy; and a narrative of individual freedom out of a culture of absolute monarchy, complete filial obedience and strict class hierarchy.

The amount of effort involved in this transaction is considerable, and *Shakespeare in Love* remains conscious enough of its historical context not to imagine that this modern love can survive its Elizabethan setting. Once outside the theatre, back in the real world of sixteenth-century class, economic and gender deter-minants, the monarch reinstates the status quo: she instructs 'Thomas Kent' to return to the playhouse and emerge again as Lady Viola, and go with her husband Wessex to Virginia. Viola sees Shakespeare for one last time, and between them they construct a fantasy plot in which the ship taking her to America is wrecked, so that she fetches up on a lonely shore, assuming male disguise in order to find a place at the court of the local nobleman. The fantasy is again one of true love achieved via mistaken identity, and cross-dressing resolved into true heterosexual union. By this means, the love between them will discover its happy ending. 'But how?' asks Shakespeare. 'I don't know', replies Viola, 'it's a mystery.'

But the film answers Will's despairing question more specifically: the consummation of this narrative will be achieved by a specifically Freudian means, that is, by sublimation. The playwright's frustrated love for Viola will be redirected into a sustained burst of creative activity beginning with the plot they have devised between them, which becomes *Twelfth Night*. The closing shots of the movie show Viola plunging into the sea, and then walking along a deserted shoreline in the opening scene of the new play, while Shakespeare furiously writes, and his voiceover says, 'She will be my heroine for all time, and her name will be Viola.' Shakespeare's texts themselves provide the monument equivalent to those promised by Montague and Capulet at the end of *Romeo and Juliet*. True love, which cannot survive the material conditions governing social and personal relations in Shakespeare's time, becomes sublimated into art, and thence we receive it now as his legacy to the late twentieth-century cinemagoer, who can live it for real. And, of course, Viola's 'actual' destination at the end of the film is that New World which will eventually deliver this inheritance via the narratives of Hollywood.

However, though, the other reason why *Shakespeare in Love* has to work so very hard to contrive the natural – that is, hetero-romance – out of the artifice and potential homoeroticism of the Elizabethan stage is because, by the 1990s, true love stands desperately in need of renovation: films celebrating an entirely traditional version of heterosexual passion are no longer secure in their dominance even of mainstream Hollywood cinema, let alone outside of it. Two other recent versions of *Romeo and Juliet*, both made two years prior to Madden's film, also demonstrate the difficult cultural work being carried out by the popularisation of a psychoanalytic Shakespeare.

Aquarium and swimming pool

Shakespeare in Love was able, in 1998, to appeal to a cinemagoing audience whose experience of *Romeo and Juliet* had been mediated two years earlier by Baz Luhrmann's MTV-influenced film of the play. The promotional flyers subtitled that movie 'the greatest love story the world has ever known', and are sprinkled with some of the catch phrases from the screenplay: 'Two households, both alike in dignity'; 'My only love sprung from my only hate'. The stills shown are only of Claire Danes and Leonardo DiCaprio, who take the eponymous roles, and are highly gender conventionalised: Juliet gazing wistfully up from the balcony, an angel's (or Cupid's?) wings on her back; Romeo dressed in armour as Mars; the two kissing; Romeo wielding a gun.

As the film opens, the aggressive homoeroticism of the play's first scene is hybridised into a white trash/rap/Latino street culture. The scenes featuring Tybalt (John Leguizamo) cast him as a psychotic Chicano gunfighter, all machismo and fancy leathers; Mercutio (Harrold Perrineau) on the other hand is black, dreadlocked and fluctuates between streetwise hip-hop and glam camp. And so Mercutio comes dressed for the Capulet Ball in a silver sequined miniskirt and bra, with high heels, a silver fright wig, lipstick, eyeshadow and a white satin cape. He prances around the young Montagues, producing Romeo's invitation from his crotch, and then offering him a tab of ecstasy, while delivering a substantial portion of the speech about Queen Mab (the 'fairies' midwife') (1.4.53–95). He can turn from camp into sudden vicious violence, directed either at other men or at women, which he does at the line about 'maids . . . on their backs' (1.4.92); then he changes just as quickly from anger to sorrow, as he delivers the speech beginning 'I talk of dreams' to Romeo, revealing a palpable air of melancholy which is not yet accounted for (1.4.96–103). After the ball we see Mercutio vying with the Nurse for Romeo's attention by firing his gun, making clear that his relation to Romeo is extraordinarily possessive.

His is the central performance of the ball, exemplifying its campy excess with a lypsynching performance of 'Young Hearts Run Free' by Kym Mazelle, a disco hit from the 1970s (of the kind that a number of 1990s films by Australian directors like Baz Luhrmann have revived as queer anthems). It's not clear whether this vision belongs to the real world of the film, or to Romeo's drug-induced hallucination: if the latter is the case, it certainly implies a mutuality in the homoerotic relation between the two friends.[13] But even so, the scenes that follow make it clear that Romeo is ready to farewell the homoerotic diversions of his youth – hence, perhaps, Mercutio's combination of anger and sorrow. Romeo's ecstatic trip starts to disintegrate: his head swims, and Mercutio's performance dissolves into a wider phantasmagoria. Then we see from underwater as Romeo dips his face into a basin to regain his 'normal' perception; at this point, away from the orgiastic excesses of the ball, he meets Juliet. He turns, that is, from the polymorphously perverse opportunities offered by masquerade, transvestism and drugs to normative heterosexuality.

Romeo's face-washing, which repeats exactly the first shot of Juliet earlier in the film, anticipates the way in which this relationship will be associated repeatedly with imagery of water. And so the lovers first catch sight of each other through a huge aquarium, in which Romeo's reflected face melds with the face of Juliet seen through the glass: the image captures the fantasy of exclusive mutuality that they desire from each other. As a cinematic version of Lacanian mirror stage narcissism – Danes and DiCaprio look very alike as they gaze in fascination at each other – this implies a mode of subjectivity prior to gender differentiation.[14] Lacan, moreover, famously deploys the metaphor of the toilet doors labelled 'men' and 'women' to describe the way in which the subject arrives at one of only two opposed sex-and-gender destinations, the product of a binary linguistic and cultural structure (Lacan 1977b: 151–2).[15] Luhrmann's film blurs this parable about what Lacan calls 'the laws of urinary segregation' (151): as Richard Burt comments, 'the shots of Romeo and Juliet meeting outside the ballroom by the huge saltwater fishtank separating the men's and women's rooms are themselves distorted. Less a wall than a membrane seems to separate the sexes' (Burt 1998: 275, n. 3). Romeo and Juliet thus first meet in an imaginary realm apparently prior to gender differentiation, and therefore to the full maturity of a heterosexual relation. And for some time the film continues this representation of their relationship according to a pre-Oedipal amniotic (or perhaps oceanic) fluidity: the balcony scene turns into a tumble into the swimming pool, in which they remain immersed while conducting their courtship. It will be Mercutio's death, again, that allows the lovers to 'mature' into a normative hetero relationship, and permits also the corresponding accession to more conventional gendered behaviours and appearances. Immediately prior to Mercutio's death Romeo seems childlike or emasculated when faced by the bullying Tybalt; immediately after his friend is killed in his place, he becomes an incarnation of active, driving, gun-toting fury.

Nevertheless, various settings continue to associate Romeo and Juliet's relationship with otherworldliness, with a divorce from the parental corruption that taints the rest of their society. The (impossibly) private spaces of the play's imagery – the mansions and palaces with which both lovers associate their relationship – are anticipated in the film by the aquarium and the swimming pool, and are then consummated (as in *Shakespeare in Love*) in the seclusion of the bed itself, where Danes and DiCaprio frolic under the sheets as though once more submerged underwater.

As dictated by the tropology of the play, however, each of these private and idyllic spaces prefigures in turn the fateful architecture of the tomb. However, Luhrmann's film achieves with the Capulet monument what Shakespeare's play could not, by reserving it as an unviolated space, dedicated solely to the lovers' relationship, uninterrupted by anyone else. Luhrmann compressed the death scene, and removes from the tomb not only Tybalt's body but all the other Capulet dead whom Juliet envisages crowding in upon her; nor do Friar Lawrence and Paris ever enter it. Thus the absolute privacy of the final scene is guaranteed: Juliet wakes just as Romeo takes the poison, and sees him dying; he sees her awake, and they kiss; he cannot speak except to say, 'with a kiss I die' (5.3.120); she shoots herself and falls across him, her blood over his body. A montage follows, including the aquarium scene, the underwater kiss in the pool, the ring they have exchanged, the game under the sheets on the morning after the night before: image after image of the absolute exclusivity of their love. Next the camera shows them lying together in the tomb, surrounded by candles, and then cuts to outside as their covered bodies are taken away. The Prince speaks some lines of condemnation, but Montague and Capulet are both silent: no promise of a monument to the lovers, only punishment for the families. Luhrmann seems to presume that the adolescents who constitute his target audience would prefer to fantasise the trauma caused by their own deaths, rather than to imagine their own tragedies subsumed by an ongoing parental agenda.

PC and TV

The same appeal to an adolescent culture defined by its absolute rejection of an overriding family politics provides a far more blatant motivation for a film released in the same year as Luhrmann's:

Lloyd Kaufman's *Tromeo and Juliet*. This film first defines its intended audience – a kind of independent republic of adolescence – by means of its immediate and thoroughgoing affront to middle-class and middle-brow (that is, conventional parental) taste: hanged squirrels, messy fatal beatings with a bludgeon shaped like Hitler's head, pornography and monstrosity are anticipated in the first few minutes of the film, which is preceded by an extended trailer for other trash epics by Troma Studios: *Class of Nuke 'Em High, Surf Nazis Must Die, Bloodsucking Freaks, Killer Condom, Fat Guy Goes Nutzoid, Maniac Nurses Find Ecstasy, Nymphoid Barbarian in Dinosaur Hell, Stuff Stephanie in the Incinerator* and *Rabid Grannies*.[16]

Shakespeare, secondary-school fodder that he is, would be associated in this context with that decorous and pretentious high-cultural conformism demanded by an older generation. From the outset, then, an outrageous misappropriation of the Bard will be accompanied by an emphasis on a fantasised escape from parental hypocrisy: Lenny from 'The House of Motorhead' gives the opening Choric speech, an extended (and determinedly non-metrical) Shakespearean parody that concludes with the following couplet:

> Star crossed lovers both ignore your elders' trivial ploy
> They hold no trace of passion's truer joy.

The opening scene anticipates the film's most radical challenge to the parental regulation of the Oedipalised family unit: Sammy Capulet gropes his sister Georgie, insisting that 'everything's in style . . . if we just throw a little incest into the mix, pretty soon the world will be one great big hug'. Tromeo, meanwhile, articulates the opposite fantasy, the 1950s-style conformism associated with a retro generation prior to that of his and Juliet's babyboomer parents: he dreams of 'a house in the suburbs, a barbecue in the backyard, family picnics'. The final scene of the film will combine Sammy's fantasy with Tromeo's.

The homoerotic aggressivity of the Capulet–Montague feud emerges among the younger generation with the assertion by Murray Martini (Mercutio's equivalent) that 'I still get a piece of wood every time I take one of those bastards out'; during a graphically violent struggle with Murray, Sammy Capulet yells at him, 'Turn around Martini; I gotta urge to fuck you in the ass.'

While the feud continues, Juliet and Tromeo are shown in a series of intercut scenes, each confined to their bedrooms, each engaging in a different kind of adolescent escape fantasy. Tromeo selects from a range of interactive Shakespeare-themed porn CDs: *Et Tu Blowjob, The Merchant of Penis, As You Lick It, Much Ado About Humping*. He chooses one, inserts it, and clicks his mouse on the 'True Love' scenario. A naked woman appears: 'Hello! You are handsome. I *really* love you . . . Would you like to get married . . . Then I could show you my breasts. I will suckle our many happy children.' 'I love you too,' pants Tromeo in reply.

Meanwhile, Capulet Senior assaults his wife on the balcony outside, and Juliet is in her bedroom having sex with Ness, the Capulet household cook, who corresponds to the Nurse in Shakespeare's play. Here, however, just as in the case of Tromeo's Shakesporn, the private adolescent fantasy functions as preparation for each lover's real sexual vocation: a properly mutual and heterosexual relationship: 'Sometimes when you touch me I dream about men,' says Juliet to Ness, who replies with one of the film's many soap clichés: 'It's OK to dream.' Thus the lesbian scene functions as a titillating preparation for the 'main event' of heterosex, just as it would tend to in mainstream pornography.

When Tromeo crashes the Capulet party (disguised as a pantomime cow), he discovers Rosaline very obviously occupied with another man. He then encounters Juliet, and they deliver verbatim and in full the sonnet jointly spoken by the lovers at their meeting in Shakespeare's play. As they do so everyone else disappears from the frame: stars twinkle in the background, and the sounds of the party mute, while the camera spins around the two locked in a distinctly non-Shakespearean kiss. Like Luhrmann's film, *Tromeo and Juliet* clearly recognises the necessity of producing at this point a virtual but absolute private space within which the two protagonists' love is played out – although here, of course, the romance remains rather more fleeting and liable to interruption by invective: their solitary idyll is shattered by Tyrone (Tybalt's equivalent) shouting, 'What the fuck?'

That night Juliet has one of her serial nightmares, for which her abusive father punishes her by locking her in what he calls the 'time-out room', a parody of the enlightened parenting practices supposedly associated with the babyboomer generation. As he drags her off, moreover, Old Capulet snarls 'how sharper than a serpent's tooth / It is to have a thankless child'. Throughout the film he is characterised by the self-conscious appropriation of the cultural capital of high art; he often quotes Shakespeare directly to the camera, even providing act, scene and line numbers. The pitch-dark 'time-out room' contains a lighted transparent cell in which he shackles her with the kind of pink plastic handcuffs sold as sex toys in adult shops. We have been prepared for this image several times by hearing Lenny, as the Chorus, predict 'love in the glass box', and its importance is highlighted when Tromeo discovers Juliet's imprisonment: entering the darkened room and gazing at the lighted cube in which she is framed, he says, 'What light from yonder Plexiglas breaks? / It is a right-angled cosmos, and Juliet is its sun.'

This 'right-angled' plastic cell, the space of adolescent imprisonment, now becomes available for reappropriation by the lovers as the fantasy space of adolescent escape. Tromeo and Juliet sit in the glass box speaking clichés from Sunday night weepies or daytime talk shows about misunderstood adolescence:

> *Tromeo:* If you're told a curved line is straight your whole life, you start to believe it.
> *Juliet:* Maybe we're more afraid of the risk of something new than staying with something we hate that's familiar.

Then they have sex in the glass box, which now encapsulates the privacy of the bedroom as well as the fantasy space of the cinema screen, the TV or the PC monitor. And behind them the stars reappear from their first meeting. Once again, the film offers a representation parallel to the idealisation of DiCaprio and Danes in their swimming pool, their aquarium or under their billowing sheets. The monumentalisation of romanticised love thus takes place within – takes the place of – that space of confinement and punishment constructed by parental authority.

But where Baz Luhrmann's film permits this privatised triumph and celebrates it (albeit in the mode of high tragedy), Kaufman's film mockingly hollows it out. From first attempting to inhabit and transform the carceral architecture of the parental prohibition, Tromeo and Juliet ultimately find they have no choice but to escape and invert it. In the climactic scene where Old Capulet seizes Juliet threatening to 'fuck and kill you at the same time' as punishment for the failure of her arranged marriage to London

Arbuckle, Tromeo and Juliet fight with him, assaulting him in turn with a series of items from the paraphernalia typical of the female adolescent's bedroom: Juliet's curling iron, her hairclips, her blow-dryer and a pack of 'Troma Lites' tampons. Eventually Juliet knocks her father unconscious with the PC monitor, which she crashes right over his head so that his face appears in the screen. But he recovers and, seizing a gun, forces them into the 'time-out room', still wearing the monitor on his head. As he crouches in the Plexiglas box arranging the handcuffs, preparing to lock them both up, Juliet plugs the monitor into a socket. Entombed in his own Plexiglas cell, helmeted with and electrocuted by the PC monitor, Capulet's corpse finally embodies the film's fantasy of turning inside-out each of those virtual spaces of adolescent escape and resistance to parental power.

Once he has been confined to this virtual tomb for good, Tromeo and Juliet appear to be free to pursue their 'true love' fantasy beyond parental and Oedipal prohibitions. As they prepare to leave together on their motorbike, though, Juliet's mother and Tromeo's father, Monty Que, reveal that they used to be married, but that Ingrid had an affair with Capulet which produced a child, Tromeo himself. They are therefore full brother and sister, so, as their mother points out, 'That's why you can't be together.' TV soap opera narrative appears to have its revenge, by producing a repressed incest taboo to thwart true love for ever. But this is a Troma film after all:

Juliet: [*to Tromeo*] Well?
Tromeo: [*to Juliet*] Well?
Juliet: Sweet are the uses of adversity,
          Which like the toad, ugly and venomous,
          Wears yet a precious jewel on his head.
Tromeo: Let thy eye negotiate for itself, and trust no agent.
Juliet: Fuck it! We've come this far!

Fortified by their Shakespearean exchange, they ride off together, leaving behind a horrified Ingrid and Monty, and a smiling Benny (Benvolio). The Epilogue shows them playing out their degraded adolescent fantasies in a transformed 'outside world': they become the stereotyped parents of the 1950s American dream – the house in the suburbs, the barbecue in the backyard

– with three bouncy (albeit monstrous) babies. Lenny's voice speaks the final Choric lines:

> So this is the dawn of the twenty-first age
> Where love ever rules and all is insane;
> And all of our hearts free to let all base things go
> As taught by Juliet and her Tromeo.

The subversive body, which for Shakespeare's audience might have been the sexually indeterminate one (that of the woman or the androgynous actor), becomes in *Tromeo and Juliet* the monstrous corporeality of the sexually active adolescent. Earlier in the film, Capulet says to Juliet: 'Are there any lines that can't be crossed for you generation of freaks?' Later Juliet answers him by metamorphosing, by means of drugs supplied by Rastafarian apothecary Fu Chang, into a bovine–human hybrid: 'It's just acne,' she tells London, the meat tycoon, when he recoils from her in horror on their wedding day; 'Tell me your love for me goes beneath the hide'. Juliet's freakish transformation doesn't just cross the line between animal and human: she reveals she has a long bull's penis as well: 'Surprise! You always said you loved *The Crying Game.*' At the end of the film, although by then she has regained her normal form, Juliet's marriage to her brother Tromeo produces twin daughters, each with an extra vestigial half-face on the side of her head.

Whatever fantastic, hybrid and self-ironic possibilities for liberation this conclusion may encode, it also, like both of the other recent versions of the Romeo and Juliet narrative I have discussed, insists on the necessity of leaving behind the possibility of a permanent and full non-heterosexuality. Throughout *Tromeo and Juliet* homosexuality is assigned the same elegiac and self-deprecating role represented in Baz Luhrmann's version by Mercutio. During the crucial scene of 'love in the glass box', for example, Tromeo and Juliet's romantic fantasy is not as private as it seems: at one moment the camera cuts from the star-backlit lovers to Ness, previously Juliet's sexual partner, watching from a darkened corner of the room, a position excluded from their fantasy. Moreover, it was Ness who helped Tromeo find the time-out room in the first place, telling him, 'I know how you feel about her; I feel that way too.' Lesbian desire can be permitted to inhabit the film as long as it remains a willing martyr to the properly heterosexual narrative outcome. A comparable function is allocated to Tromeo's best friend and the film's version of Mercutio, Murray Martini. To begin with he typifies the homoerotic aggressivity of the part: his long litany of abuse directed at Tyrone (Tybalt) includes the terms 'assfuck', 'hermaphrodite' and 'the one that suits you best . . . bitch'. When Tyrone tries to hit Tromeo with his Hitler-headed club he embeds it instead in the forehead of Murray, whose final request as he dies surprises everyone: he asks his friend for a kiss, and dies smiling when Tromeo, with evident tenderness, grants this wish. The spaces available for male–male homoeroticism here replicate those of Luhrmann's film: a homoerotic aggressivity (between Murray/Mercutio and Tyrone/Tybalt) and a mourned-for but inevitably forsaken desire (between Murray/Mercutio and Tromeo/Romeo). And the limitations of Troma Studios' experiments with sexuality are evident in the minor role of Benny, Tromeo's cousin, who comments at this point in disgust, 'Fuck – Murray was a fag!', but who stands smiling with approval by Tromeo and Juliet's horrified parents as the incestuous lovers ride off together at the end of the film.

So despite an apparent intention to cross all available boundaries, the only permanent disruption to the sexual structure inherited from the parental generation will be the breaking of the incest taboo. In this way *Tromeo and Juliet* leaves intact a mutant, ironised but still Oedipalised family, while gesturing elegiacally, as Luhrmann's film does, towards a homosexuality that might be temporarily experimented with by women (Juliet and Ness) but must be kissed goodbye by men (Tromeo and Murray). The film thereby acknowledges the place of a homosexuality that it must exclude, presuming it still too threatening for the target audience of American teenagers; all it can do is parody the parental nuclear heterosexuality against which adolescence seeks to define itself, but which provides the only option in the end.

The question remains why, in spite of the state-of-the-art generic and cinematic virtuosity of these recent filmmakers, they cannot help but reproduce – sometimes ironically, sometimes naively – narratives persistently organised around three fundamental premises: that sexuality is the fundamental ground for the development of a mature subjectivity; that a period of necessarily separate adolescent sexual experimentation constitutes a crucial phase in this process of maturation; and that nuclear heterosexuality remains the only appropriate outcome of the entire transaction.

Perhaps it is clear by now that one reason why even the most irreverent cinematic 'readers' of the play find it difficult to break free from these assumptions is because they are legitimated and perpetuated by an intimate marriage between Shakespearean cultural capital and a psychoanalytic paradigm disseminated, popularised and glamourised in the Western imagination via (among other things) cinema itself.

The challenge, then, would be to escape such normalising narrative imperatives by attempting to take the Shakespeare out of psychoanalysis, and the psychoanalysis out of Shakespeare – a task which, of course, can only begin with a recognition of how they have become so intimately engaged in the first place, and have remained so in the popular and critical mind. I am suggesting, in other words, that maybe those who do not understand the history of Shakespeare in psychoanalysis are condemned to repeat it. Ultimately, of course, it is yet to be seen whether a thoroughgoing disentangling of two such culturally privileged narratives can be achieved, in theory and practice – and whether, if such a dismantling were achieved, anything of value could be found in what remained.

Conclusion

At the end of yet another book on Shakespeare, and on psycho-analysis, perhaps one question seems more urgent than any other: given the suspicion with which I have often treated both terms in my title throughout this study, why keep dealing with them?

Certainly I have tried to suggest that the predominant way of thinking about the relationship between psychoanalysis and Shakespeare for most of the twentieth century – the attempt to explore how psychoanalysis can help us to read Shakespeare – is no longer the crucial one. Since Shakespearean texts have shaped both psychoanalytic and literary critical hermeneutics from the outset, and since psychoanalytic categories are now so thoroughly disseminated within, and are so constitutive of, our current reading practices, the results of any such enquiry could only be as accurate as they were tautological: psychoanalysis 'works' in reading Shakespeare precisely to the extent that it was shaped by doing so.

To my mind, however, 'Shakespeare' and 'psychoanalysis' still need to be read together, because the relationship between them remains in force in the academy as well as in the Academy – that is, in the university as well as in Hollywood. While elite forms of cultural capital were vital for the institutional investments involved in the establishment of both literary critical and psychoanalytic authority, the recent wave of Shakespearean cinema demonstrates that popular culture is vigorously reclaiming, and reinvesting in, both the Shakespearean text and, I have argued, its specifically psychoanalytic reading. This return of the Freudian Bard – of 'Shakespeareanalysis', as I am tempted to call it – requires the introduction of those other perspectives from which both the Shakespearean and the psychoanalytic text can be seen as cultural objects, rather than as speaking subjects who dictate all that can be said about them: the perspectives, that is, of feminist, post-colonial, queer, new historicist and cultural materialist projects of various kinds. As I have suggested, these approaches coalesce, broadly speaking, into two projects already in progress and no doubt susceptible to further development.

The one adumbrated in the second half of this volume involves tracing the ways in which early modern categories, via the Shake-spearean text, shape the development of psychoanalytic thought: the work of gender and sexual difference in the inauguration of a humanist subject, and the recovery of performative models of memory and of the ego by the post-humanist critique of that subject; the association between corporealised notions of individual and collective identity in pre-modern and postmodern represen-tations of the self; the impact upon psychoanalysis of such cultural developments as the early modern nuclear family, the Renaissance visual regime, colonial primitivism, religious or secular notions of conscience and humanist rationality.

The other dimension of continuing critical work on the psychoanalysis–Shakespeare connection, as discussed in my first three chapters, is the examination of the role played by readings of Shakespearean texts in the institutional and epistemological development of psychoanalysis from the start of the twentieth century onwards. It is no accident that both literary criticism and Freudianism establish their discursive and cultural capital at the same time, in the same places, and so often by such similar means. The foundational relation between *Hamlet* and the Oedipus complex is only the first and most overt example of a complicity that repeats itself in the work of Rank, Jones, Lacan, Sachs and Mannoni. In each case there is much to be learned by both literary criticism and psychoanalysis in an intensive reading of the local politics specific to each of these readings of Shakespeare.

Other instances will continue to manifest themselves, no doubt. I would like to close this volume with one more manifestation of the uncanny durability of Shakespeareanalysis, its ability to return in the most unexpected locations, to take on the most unpredictable of guises. In this final scenario Shakespeare and psychoanalysis take turns at playing two mutually dependent roles integral to a growing number of movies and TV shows: the police psychologist and the sexual psychopath.

Perhaps no figure better embodies a postmodern psychopathology than the stalker: from the famous case involving Madonna in 1995 to that of Princess Diana in 1997, supposedly pursued to her death by 'stalkerazzi' on motorbikes in Paris, the stalker has cast a longer and longer shadow over media culture, and performed the ambiguous cultural function of mediating the everyday politics and violence of rape into the dark mystique of a sexual obsessiveness endured by stars, whether in films or in their so-called real lives. Thus, while the stalker has become a psycho-accessory crucial for any celebrity worthy of the name, the proliferation of anti-stalking legislation in many American states has the democratising effect of making available to everyone those sexual persecutions formerly reserved for the famous. In this respect the glamorisation of the stalker also, unfortunately, perpetuates the myth of sexual violence as a pathology peculiar to the stranger and the outsider, rather than as a possibility endemic to relationships between ordinary couples and within ordinary families.

A recent inaugural anthology of academic psychological perspectives on the topic opens by remarking that 'Stalking is an old behaviour, but a new crime'; however, 'Public fascination and dramatic portrayal of stalking have far outstripped our scientific understanding of this behaviour – until now.' Between these two introductory assertions, and reinforcing them both – the denial of stalking as a contemporary cultural product and the statement of a need for a properly scientific analysis – comes a reference to Shakespeare, who 'captured certain aspects of [stalking] in the obsessive and murderous thoughts of Othello' (Meloy 1998: xix). Later in the volume, this hint will be taken up in detail in a chapter entitled 'The Archetypes and the Psychodynamics of Stalking' by Glen Skoler, a clinical and forensic psychologist working in Washington, DC.

Skoler argues that 'modern psychoanalytic theories', by which he means psychodynamic therapies developed in the 1970s and 1980s, are having (as he believes they should) an increasing influence upon forensic psychology, as practised within the legal, juridical and correctional institutions of the United States. The only barrier to a further merging of psychoanalytic theory and forensic practice is the forbidding 'sophistication and complexity' of such theories for those engaged in their application: 'This is the reason why, in training presentations, I began using archetypes in Western culture, as expressed in literature, drama, films, and the media, to render modern psychodynamic constructs of stalkers more convincing and cogent' (Skoler, in Meloy 1998: 87). In short, Skoler trains staff in the National Security Agency and the Central Intelligence Agency, and he uses psychoanalytic theory presented through Shakespeare to do so.

Since, as he argues in reference to Bloom, 'Shakespeare *is* the center of the Western canon of literature', his sonnets serve 'to introduce a complete outline of the psychodynamics of violent stalkers': the narrative that unfolds through the sequence reveals a psychopathological 'erotomania' (Skoler, in Meloy 1998: 88) arising from an 'oedipal' love triangle between Shakespeare, the fair friend and the dark lady. At this point, Skoler needs to add in a parenthesis the assertion that 'Most critics' dismiss the 'implication of homosexuality' between the poet and the young man addressed in the earlier sonnets (89); as my discussion of 'Shakespeare's sex' in Chapter 5 might suggest, this airy refusal to consider any kind of sexual attachment other than heterosexual represents at once a misreading of the sonnets and the sexual culture from which they derive, and a symptom of heteronormative prescriptivism.

The rest of the argument, despite its claim to engage with recent theory, repeats other classically psychoanalytic gestures: Shakespeare attempts to 'sublimate' the triangulation of this desire, but he cannot help producing a 'mother/whore splitting fantasy first described by Freud' (Skoler, in Meloy 1998: 90); ultimately the poet, 'in the face of obvious sexual rejection and inadequacy, adopts the psychological role not of the "oedipal victor" but of the "oedipal loser"'. All of these strategies, Skoler avers, are 'frequently seen in the psychosexual histories of actual stalkers' (91) – a point proven by a now conventional comparison: 'There are not many instances in the canon of Western literature when one can segue from the writings of William Shakespeare to the writings of O. J. Simpson without missing a psychological beat, but the stalker's conviction of being victimized and controlled by the object of his love obsession is universal' (92).

Shakespeare and psychoanalysis, in this case, continue actively to collaborate in the formation and dissemination of current psychological categories, and moreover in the training of those agents whose task it is to police them. This exchange is possible because of the familiar ascription to both the Shakespearean and the psychoanalytic text of a psychological authority transcending historical and cultural difference. This has one slightly peculiar result: although he points out that the purpose of reading the sonnets in this way 'is not to portray Shakespeare as a "stalker", but to make use of his profound artistic ability to consciously articulate the human unconscious', Skoler implies that it might be just as well that the Bard is not available for interrogation by his own trainees:

> Shakespeare's references to going 'mad' and of being 'past reason', his threats of slander and angry warnings that he not be 'pressed' too far, his venomous and vicious name calling, and his explicitly obscene begging to literally place his erect penis into the vagina he contemptuously portrays as a promiscuous, one-woman venereal plague would certainly appear to meet modern American stalking criteria.
>
> (Skoler, in Meloy 1998: 94–5)

Lock him up and throw away the key: Shakespeare's forensic profile reveals a man better avoided, but at the same time impossible to avoid.

While the relationship between early modern and contemporary modes of masculine aggression and misogyny certainly requires plenty of examination, I would suggest that such a project is badly served by the kind of psychological universalism and inattention either to literary convention or to the possibilities of historical and cultural difference demonstrated by Skoler's account. And although anxiety about the CIA's use of Freudian Shakespeare in its policing and prosecution of contemporary sexual subjectivities might seem paranoid (although it is apparently not, in Washington, DC at least), Skoler's article does serve to illustrate an investment by the legal, juridical and correctional establishment in an entirely traditional psychoanalytic account of sexual relations – which is equally evident in other chapters of the same anthology (see, for example, Meloy 1998: vii, xix; also articles in Meloy 1998 by Meloy:

2–27; Kienlen: 52–69; Lloyd-Goldstein: 195–213; and Lipson and Mills: 258–74). This account has always been, as I have tried to show, reinforced and shaped by the assiduous reading of Shakespeare, alongside a normative or Oedipalised heterosexuality and in conjunction with certain modes of institutional coercion. All of these investments, it seems to me, keep Shakespeare in psycho-analysis; all make it difficult for various cultural forms to extract themselves from either Shakespeare or psychoanalysis. Skoler's description of his training practice therefore represents an especially vivid instance of the way in which Shakespeare, construed as analyst and as patient at once, continues to provide a means by which psychoanalysis grows and develops in its many incarnations: as therapeutic practice, philosophical paradigm, instrument of cultural imperialism, feminist theory, literary critical tool, cinematic apparatus, popular cultural myth.

I am reminded again of the difficulty of getting away from psycho-Shakespeare in flipping the celebrity gossip pages of a recent New Zealand edition of the *Woman's Day* magazine. It seems that even the 'real life' of Neve Campbell, star of the stalker-slasher *Scream* trilogy – which trades on the postmodern and comedic possibilities of having both the masked stalkers and their stalkees constantly referring to the generic conventions of horror cinema – has begun to resemble a combination of Wes Craven plot, Shakespearean fiction and forensic psychology case study:

> Neve Campbell has at last joined the big time by getting her very own stalker . . . Neve's wacko fan thinks he's the incarnation of William Shakespeare, and has been bombarding the *Scream* star with creepy sonnets and poems dedicated to his Juliet (her *Party of Five* character is called Julia) . . . Cops believe this is the first case of iambic pentameter being used in a threatening manner.
>
> (Pitchers 2000: 39)

Not the first case, perhaps, but a striking repetition of a very old crime.

Shakespeare the psychoanalyst opened this volume; who better to close it than Shakespeare the psychopath? Neither incarnation can be easily escaped. They're both just behind you, over your shoulder. Don't look now.

Notes

Introducing . . .

1 In relation to literary studies John Guillory understands cultural capital in terms of 'access to the means of literary production and consumption'; in fact, Bourdieu tends to use the phrase 'symbolic capital', which Guillory defines as 'a kind of knowledge-capital whose possession can be displayed upon request and which thereby entitles its possessor to the cultural and material rewards of the well-educated person' (Guillory 1993: ix).

2 My title borrows the ambiguity discussed by Lupton and Reinhard (1993: 5–7), as well as echoing the subtitle of their book *After Oedipus: Shakespeare in Psychoanalysis*.

1 In Vienna

1 For accounts of these critical approaches and cultural phenomena see, for example, Holderness (1988), Taylor (1989: 231–411) and Hawkes (1992).

2 Benjamin describes 'aura' as the mystified status that attaches to an object considered unique, original and worthy of veneration (Benjamin 1970: 225–6). In the twentieth century the increased technological capacity for reproduction liquidates aura because it destroys the authenticity that attaches to the unique and original: 'that which withers in the age of mechanical reproduction is the aura of the work of art'. Film, in particular, is destructive of aura, because of its reproducibility: 'the film . . . is inconceivable without its destructive, cathartic aspect, that is, the liquidation of the traditional value of the cultural heritage'. Benjamin attributes aura not only to

works of art or to nature, but also to such embodiments of 'cultural heritage' as Shakespeare: 'In 1927 Abel Gance exclaimed enthusiastically: "Shakespeare, Rembrandt, Beethoven will make films ..." Presumably without intending it, he issued an invitation to a far-reaching liquidation' (223–4). As Linda Charnes has suggested, Shakespeare's auratic notoriety has in fact survived twentieth-century cultural technologies, albeit in a disseminated, rather than a liquidated, form (Charnes 1993). For a detailed clarification of the notion of aura see Weber (1996: 76–107).

3 Gary Taylor identifies the 'discovery of *Hamlet*' as the pre-eminent Shakespearean tragedy with its production in the early 1660s, 'adapted by Davenant, acted by Betterton, celebrated by Pepys, criticized by Dryden' (Taylor 1989: 39–40).

4 A brief account of the critical history of this 'problem' is given in the introduction to the Arden edition by Harold Jenkins (Jenkins 1982: 136–40).

5 Bradley's dismissive footnote on the question of incest would strike Freud as a masterpiece of denial: 'This aspect of the matter leaves *us* comparatively unaffected, but Shakespeare evidently means it to be of importance' (Bradley 1992: 98, n. 19).

6 See, for example, the final chapter of Marjorie Garber's *Shakespeare's Ghost Writers* (Garber 1987: 124–9).

7 Marjorie Garber illustrates the kind of analysis to which Freud's own 'childhood memories' might be subject by relating Freud's development of the Oedipal theory to his abandonment of the seduction theory, which

> came dangerously close to an accusation of the father, as is pointed out in the famous letter to Fliess of September, 1897. Jeffrey Mas[s]on, [in his] controversial book, *The Assault on Truth: Freud's Suppression of the Seduction Theory* [1985] ... notes that the original English edition of the letters (itself provocatively entitled *The Origins of Psychoanalysis*) omitted the reference to Freud's own father, by using an ellipsis: 'in every case ... blame was laid on perverse acts by the father'. The three dots appear in the letter in place of the phrase Masson translates as 'the father, not excluding my own'.
>
> (Garber 1987: 167)

Thus Freud replaces this near accusation against his own father, according to Masson and Garber, with the theory of Oedipal fantasy.

8 Ernest Jones echoes this anxiety that the conclusions reached by psychoanalytic investigations 'have their general validity vitiated by their origins in a study of the "abnormal". This quite logical objection, however, lost its force when it was discovered that the neurotic symptoms that had given rise to the suffering proceed from primordial difficulties and conflicts inherent in every mind' (Jones 1949: 15). Rank finds it necessary to make a similar disclaimer: 'We would have no occasion or procedure for research on the psychic creations of normals had not both been provided for us by the psychic creations

of the demented, which exceed what is normal in sharpness and clarity'
(Rank 1992: 40).

9   The relation between science and art remains a highly ambivalent one
for Freud: in 'Totem and Taboo', for instance, he associates scientific
thought with the attainment of psychological 'maturity' at both the
cultural and individual levels, while 'art' represents the vestigial survival
within European civilisation of 'primitive' thoughts, desires and fears
(*PFL* 13: 148–9). As such, the cultural relation between science and
art parallels the psychic relation between super-ego and id; it is for this
reason that Freud insists on trying to articulate a relation between
the two fields, and on deriving the authority of psychoanalysis from
this conjunction.

10   Freud also proclaimed his conversion to the Oxfordian theory of
Thomas Looney in a footnote to the *Autobiographical Study* (Freud 1966,
vol. XX: 63–4); in his 1930 'Address in the Goethe House' (vol. XXI:
211); and, according to Jones (1957: 461), in 'the last essay he wrote,
in the final year of his life' (Freud 1966, vol. XXIII). In a letter to J. S.
H. Branson on 25 March 1934 Freud asserts at length a corre-
spondence between de Vere's relationship with his three daughters,
and the psychoanalytic reading of *King Lear* (Jones 1957: 487–8). Jones
considers that Freud's fascination with the Shakespearean authorship controversy arises from his motivating conviction that 'things
are not what they seem', creating an 'inner connection' between those
two themes which Freud confessed 'always perplexed him to dis-
traction': the authorship of the Shakespearean canon and the question
of telepathy (459–62). Royle describes the Freudian desire to use the
plays to get inside the head of 'Shakespeare' as itself a kind of
telepathic fantasy (Royle 1991; 1995); for Schoenbaum, on the other
hand, the arguments of the anti-Stratfordians appealed to Freud
because their methods, like his, resembled 'a game of detection'
(Schoenbaum 1970; cited in Royle 1995: 87).

11   Both Royle (1995) and Lukacher (1994) conduct 'deconstructive'
psychoanalytic readings that re-sign the text with the *name*
Shakespeare, finding it in various encrypted versions throughout
(particularly) *Hamlet*; Lukacher argues that the Stratfordian biography
is also reinstalled by this process (Lukacher 1994: 126–61; Royle 1995:
85–123).

12   Challenges to the search for an authorial voice, presence or intention
have been advanced by formalism, new criticism, reception theory,
structuralism, discourse analysis and deconstruction. For a brief
and lucid summary of these developments see the chapter on 'Author'
by Donald Pease, in Lentricchia and McLaughlin (1995: 105–17).

13   See Tennenhouse (1986), Stallybrass and White (1986) and Morris
(1994).

14   Examples of each of these readings can be found by the following
critics respectively: (a) Ridley (1958), (b) Greenblatt (1980),
(c) Parker (1985) and (d) Newman (1987) and Orkin (1987).

15   According to Freud, the essential artistry of the literary work lies
in this technique of masking the presentation of repressed material

by means of 'insignificant' or purely aesthetic forms: the author thus

> bribes us by the purely formal – that is, aesthetic – yield of pleasure which he offers us in the presentation of his phantasies. We give the name *incentive bonus* or *fore-pleasure* to a yield of pleasure such as this, which is offered to us so as to make possible the release of still greater pleasure arising from deeper psychical sources.
>
> (*PFL* 14: 141)

16 Elizabeth Freund's essay on '"Ariachne's Broken Woof": The Rhetoric of Citation in *Troilus and Cressida*' (1985), Patricia Parker's on 'Shakespeare's Rhetoric: "Dilation" and "Delation" in *Othello*' (1985), and the latter's work in *Shakespeare from the Margins* (1996) are examples of approaches that constitute entire rereadings of their respective plays on the basis of a sustained 'deconstructive' focus on apparently insignificant details – one or two words, in fact, that occur either singly or rarely – which are taken to betray contradictory tendencies within the text.

17 As Sarah Kofman puts it in *Freud and Fiction*, her deconstructive analysis of the relation between Freudian theory and literature: 'If on the one hand Freud recognizes the uncertainty of the scientific process and asserts the identity – or near identity – of science and fiction, on the other he accords high status to the author of fiction whom he takes to be a witness to the analytic truth' (Kofman 1991: 5).

18 These commonalities have allowed many exchanges between literary criticism and psychoanalytic theory: thus the division of rhetoric along the axes of metaphor and metonymy by Roman Jakobson, a member of the Russian formalist group, was taken up and modified by Lacan in his structuralist reconceptualisation of the Freudian dream mechanism (Lacan 1977b: 159–71; Roudinesco 1990: 306). For a clear and extended explication of the relationship between psychoanalytic and linguistic or literary figures, see Silverman (1983) or Payne (1993: 74–85).

19 One instance is the phrase 'thou owest Nature a death', which Freud misquotes from *1 Henry IV* (5.1.126). This phrase suits him in two slightly different but related ways. In a letter to Fliess, where he mentions the supposed replacement of 'the old religion' by 'the religion of science', it suits Freud's purpose to substitute the word 'Nature' for the word 'God', which Prince Hal uses to Falstaff in the play (Freud 1985: 343–4). Elsewhere, the phrase is repeated insofar as the notion of death as a debt, obligation or imperative obviously fits with – or influences – his development of the notion of the 'death drive' (*PFL* 4: 294–6 and n. 1; *PFL* 12: 77 and n. 1).

20 Freud also repeats the key phrase from *Julius Caesar* in his case history of the 'Rat Man', again in the context of an individual's contradictory attitude towards a superior (*PFL* 9: 60–1).

21 Freud identifies at this point a childhood memory that even more closely ties the figure of Brutus to the affect of simultaneous admiration and aggressivity which the dream embodies: when at the age of

fourteen he 'acted in the scene between Brutus and Caesar from Schiller', the other role was played by 'a nephew who was a year my senior', a childhood friend for whom he felt love and hostility in equal quantities – a relationship that not only 'had a determining influence on all my subsequent relations with contemporaries' but also on his theories of sibling rivalry, and on the competition between the disciplines of psychoanalysis and science themselves (*PFL* 4: 552–3).

22 A Lacanian reading of this dream, moreover, might also focus on the fact that Freud's hostility in the dream is exercised by means of a lethal gaze. The field of vision, or what he calls the 'scopic drive', is fundamental to Lacanian theory from 'The Mirror Stage' to *The Four Fundamental Concepts*. For recent approaches to Shakespeare influenced by the Lacanian discussion of the gaze, see Goldberg (1988), Pye (1990), Freedman (1991) and Armstrong (2000).

23 Lacan explicitly asserts that 'the unconscious is structured like a language' in more than one place (for example, Lacan 1977b: 234; 1979: 20), but the notion also underlies his theoretical discussions elsewhere, for example, in 'The Agency of the Letter in the Unconscious' (Lacan 1977b: 146–78).

24 For an especially irritable survey of these psychoanalytic vices, see Vickers (1993: 272–324).

25 Jones refers here to two sources I have not been able to track down: one is an essay by Vining called 'The Mystery of Hamlet' (1881), the other is by Harris, 'The Man Shakespeare and his Tragic Life-story' (1909).

2 In Paris

1 The totalising tendency of Jungian-influenced 'archetype' reading can be seen in the work of Joseph Campbell on mythology (1949), in Northrop Frye's *Anatomy of Criticism* (1957) or in Robert Graves's *The White Goddess* (1966).

2 Although Aronson does also conduct an analysis from the point of view of Ophelia herself, discussing the process of her individuation in relation to her father (Aronson 1972: 175–80), it is nevertheless the masculine process of individuation – that of Hamlet himself – which Aronson privileges and universalises as 'a personalized history of the evolution of human consciousness' (236).

3 For expansions on these definitions see Laplanche and Pontalis (1988).

4 As Roudinesco points out, Lacan owes this formulation to grammarian Édouard Pichon (Roudinesco 1990: 301). For further analysis of Lacan's successive translations of the Freudian aphorism, see Fink (1990: 108–11).

5 For introductory accounts of Saussurian linguistics see, for example, Hawkes (1977: 19–28), Belsey (1980: 37–47) and Eagleton (1983: 96–7).

6 For explanations or developments of Lacan's seminars on *Hamlet*, see Ragland-Sullivan (1988), Lee (1990: 108–22) and Armstrong (2000: 6–29).

7 Mladen Dolar describes Lacan's definition of the uncanny in the field of vision as arising from 'that mirror image in which the object *a* is included . . . Lacan uses the gaze as the best presentation of that missing object; . . . imagine that one could see one's mirror image close its eyes: that would make the object as gaze appear in the mirror' (Dolar 1991: 13).

8 During the heyday of poststructuralist readings of Shakespeare, critics influenced by Lacan challenged the notion of Hamlet's 'interiority' as the imposition on to the play of a modern or post-Enlightenment notion of the self, which their own postmodern analyses could strip away: thus Terry Eagleton argues that Hamlet 'has no "essence" of being whatsoever, no inner sanctum to be safeguarded: he is pure deferral and diffusion, a hollow void which offers nothing determinate to be known . . . Hamlet's jealous sense of unique selfhood is no more than the negation of anything in particular' (Eagleton 1986: 72); Jonathan Goldberg comments that 'The depth of his interiority is his foldedness within a text that enfolds him and which cannot be unfolded' (Goldberg 1986: 99). See also the comments by Belsey, Fineman, Barker, Neill, and Freedman cited in the preceding chapter of this volume.

9 The OED defines a sense of 'character' as the meeting between these alternatives – 'the face or features as betokening moral qualities; personal appearance' – and offers two Shakespearean examples of this usage (*Twelfth Night* 1.2.51; *Coriolanus* 5.4.28).

10 For a discussion of the effects of the misdirected letters in *King Lear*, see Armstrong (2000: 30–7).

11 For a discussion of Lacan's debt to surrealism see Macey (1988).

12 For a discussion of this narrative which focuses on the signature of the letter, see Royle (1995: 101–2).

13 Diana Harris points out the way in which Kenneth Branagh's 1997 film of the play highlights both the narcissistic aspect of Hamlet's relation to Ophelia, and its disruption by an intruding Other gaze, by showing Hamlet gazing, during his scene with her, into a one-way mirror, behind which his parents are hiding and watching (Harris 2000: 149–53).

14 Freud writes that when the melancholic

> describes himself as petty, egoistic, dishonest, lacking in indepen-
> dence, one whose sole aim has been to hide the weaknesses of his
> own nature . . . there can be no doubt that if anyone holds and
> expresses to others an opinion of himself such as this (an opinion
> which Hamlet held both of himself and of everyone else), he is ill,
> whether he is speaking the truth or whether he is being more or
> less unfair to himself.
>
> (*PFL* 11: 255)

A footnote attached to the parenthesis quotes from the play itself: 'Use every man after his desert, and who shall scape whipping?' (*PFL* 11: 255, n. 1; 2.2.524–5).

15 A number of critics have analysed, from different perspectives, the triangulated relation between Hamlet, Gertrude and the two kings, including René Girard (1991: 271–89), Joel Fineman (1980) and Janet Adelman, who suggests that, faced with the threat to both representation and subjectivity posed by the maternal body, Hamlet can only regain a purified image of his mother by separating her from her vilified sexuality (Adelman 1992: 11–37).

16 My reading here coincides with that of Lupton and Reinhard (1993), for whom Freud's discussion of *Hamlet* functions as a kind of mourning which disguises the loss of the maternal relation, covering it over with the Oedipal relation to the father; Lacan, returning to the Freudian *Hamlet*, uncovers this repressed material. Lupton and Reinhard also note that imagery of water links Ophelia with Gertrude: the former's death is narrated by the latter, and where Ophelia drowns, her garments 'heavy with their drink', Gertrude dies poisoned by 'the drink, the drink' (Lupton and Reinhard 1993: 82; citing 4.7.180, 5.2.315–16).

17 For a discussion of the play's obsessive concern with 'funeral proprieties', see Neill (1997: 300–4).

18 Slavoj Zizek comments that 'Lacan conceives this difference between the two deaths as the difference between real (biological) death and its symbolisation, the "settling of accounts", the accomplishment of symbolic destiny' (Zizek 1989: 135).

19 This reading of Lacan will influence Rose's reading of psychoanalytic approaches to *Hamlet* too, according to which the play 'constantly unleashes an anxiety which returns to the question of femininity' (Rose 1986: 138–9).

20 Lupton and Reinhard conflate the relation between the maternal and Lacan's (to my mind rather different) approach to the 'real' in *The Ethics of Psychoanalysis* (Lupton and Reinhard 1993: 126).

21 Moreover, as Easthope points out, Lacan actually 'attacks psychoanalysts who believe they have "access to a reality transcending aspects of history" . . . Instead he stresses that the concepts and theoretical framework of psychoanalysis are relative to the modern period and the modern ego' (Easthope 1999: 152; the phrase of Lacan's cited here by Easthope is a retranslation of what he considers the misleading English version given by Alan Sheridan in Lacan 1977b: 120).

3 In Johannesburg

1 I owe my use of the term 'contact zone' to Mary Louise Pratt, who uses it 'to refer to the space of colonial encounters, the space in which peoples geographically and historically separated come into contact with each other and establish ongoing relations, usually involving

conditions of coercion, radical inequality, and intractable conflict' (Pratt 1992: 6).

2 For an assessment of the cultural capital that accrued to Shakespeare in mid-century South Africa, see Johnson (1996: 74–146).

3 It is clear from Sachs's repetition of this same line in his introductory book on psychoanalysis that this mutuality in the mother–son relation is integral to his perception of the Oedipal structure (Sachs 1934: 202).

4 For Bhabha, colonial mimicry functions as an ambivalence similar to that constituted by power in Foucauldian theory: a tensile dialectic between domination and resistance, with each term (re)producing the other. Mimicry constitutes both the product of colonial desire (to make the colonised replicate colonial culture), and a frustration of that desire (because the colonised cannot ever be the same as the coloniser) (Bhabha 1994: 86).

5 Deleuze and Guattari are here citing Victor Turner (1964) 'Magic, Faith and Healing' in *An Ndembu Doctor in Practice* (New York: Collier Macmillan): no page reference given.

4 Shakespeare's memory

1 I am indebted to Michael Neill for first drawing my attention to this story.

2 Moreover, Greenblatt forgets that the same figure with which he describes his personal desire as a historicist reader also opens Michel de Certeau's *The Writing of History* – a work that draws out many of the implications of Freudian psychoanalysis for the writing and reading of historical texts; de Certeau in turn is quoting Michelet: 'Studious and charitable, tender as I am for the dead of the world' (cited in de Certeau 1988: 1). (My attention was first drawn to this hidden connection by Catherine Belsey.) According to de Certeau, further-more, the other influences of psychoanalysis upon recent forms of historiography would include an interest in 'The persistence and lingering action of the *irrational*, the violence at work inside scientificity and theory itself'; 'A dynamics of *nature* (drives, affects, the libido) conjoined with language – in opposition to the ideologies of history which privilege the relations among people and reduce nature to a passive terrain permanently open to social or scientific conquest'; and 'The relevance of pleasure (orgasmic, festive, etc.) which was repressed by the incredibly ascetic ethic of progress' (de Certeau 1986: 16). These concerns – which are clearly in evidence in the work of Greenblatt and other new historicists and cultural materialists on pleasure and subversion (Dollimore, in Dollimore and Sinfield 1985: 2–17, 72–87), carnival (Tennenhouse 1986: 17–71; Stallybrass and White 1986) and the alterity of the natural (Greenblatt 1990: 31–3) – 'are not necessarily the signs of a psychoanalytic affiliation, but they do signal a Freudian debt and Freudian tasks' (de Certeau 1986: 16).

3 See Skura (1995) for a response to Greenblatt's essay; but while for Skura, although 'The analyst may differ from the historian in assuming

what produces a historical text or how to read it, . . . history itself is not the problem' (Skura 1995: 104–5), to my mind the disparities and conjunctions between historicist and psychoanalytical 'assumptions' about what produces a text are *precisely* the problem.

4 For one example of Freud's application of Darwinian evolutionary theory to cultural developments, see 'Totem and Taboo' (*PFL* 13: 185–6).

5 Michel de Certeau asserts that Freud 'invalidates the break between individual psychology and collective psychology' (de Certeau 1986: 5), but this seems too sweeping a suggestion to be accepted unconditionally. Antony Easthope considers the question more carefully when he writes that

> It would be pointless to argue it is only the case either that external social structures become internalised subjectively or that human society is an expression of the needs and desires of the human subject. Both effects occur reciprocally and without a point of origin in a simultaneity which is not that of identity.
>
> (Easthope 1995: 355)

It is precisely the reciprocality of the relation between individual and social memories and desires that interests me here.

6 Pompeii was rediscovered in 1748, and sporadically excavated over the next two centuries. During the eighteenth and nineteenth centuries it became popular, along with other famous archaeological sites in Egypt, Greece, Italy and throughout the classical world, as a destination for the growing tourist trade. The emergence of tourism among the European leisured classes enabled a comparison between their own 'civilisation' and those of earlier periods: see, for example, Chaney (1998).

7 I owe the notion of public theatre as the 'memory bank' of Shakespeare's society to Terence Hawkes (1973: 125).

8 See Jonas Barish's essay on 'Remembering and Forgetting in Shakespeare' for a detailed discussion of the suggestion that, in Shakespearean theatre, 'meaningful, purposive activity' constitutes the most powerful manifestation of memory (Barish 1996: 218–20); as the Player King puts it, 'Purpose is but the slave to memory' (3.2.183).

9 Jonathan Baldo describes in detail the relationship between colonialist assumptions about European superiority and the supposed 'forgetfulness' – due to lack of writing technology – of the New World native (Baldo 1995).

10 Or perhaps, more accurately, the letters *m* and *n* stand for the difference between *m*asculine and *n*euter, since the Freudian account sees the girl as nothing other than a boy minus his 'whole piece more'.

11 For instances of 'source criticism' in Freud, see his discussions of *Macbeth* (*PFL* 14: 305–7), *The Merchant of Venice* and *King Lear* (235–47). Similar approaches can be found in Rank (1992: 165–88) and Jones (1949: 127–57).

12 'Progressive realism' is Wilson Harris's term for the association

between the Cartesian rationality of European colonialism and the dominant modes of Enlightenment narrative (Harris 1992: 71–2).

13 See Paul Brown's description of Prospero's strategy as a 'remembrance of things past soon revealed as a mnemonic of power' (Brown 1985: 59–60).

14 Critics writing about Shakespeare's notions of memory often demonstrate both of these latter attitudes, however. Barbara Hardy, for example, writes that 'Shakespeare creates a psychopathology of everyday (and everynight) life which not only contributes to his mimesis . . . but invents, collects, observes, compares, analyses – and in short, studies – the workings of the conscious and unconscious mind' (Hardy 1989: 105). Jonas Barish compares Caius Martius's memory lapse in *Coriolanus* with the analysis of 'tendentious forget-fulness motivated by repression' in Freud's *Psychopathology of Everyday Life* (Barish 1996: 215). Even Paul Brown's cultural materialist read-ing of *The Tempest* cannot resist an excursion into what he calls the 'metaphor' of Freudian dreamwork, although he attaches a garbled footnote insisting that 'My use of Feudian [sic] terms does not mean that I endorse its [sic] ahistorical, Europocentric and sexist models of psychical development' (Brown 1985: 66–7, 71 n. 35).

15 It has, of course, been convincingly argued that the notion of 'Enlightenment' or the 'Age of Reason' as an era consistently and monolithically characterised by a rational and knowledge-based humanist ego is itself a falsity too often perpetuated by the critics of modernity. Recent work in Pacific cultural history, for example, has demonstrated how disparate, and how irrational, were many of the ventures of seventeenth-century European epistemology – especially those of the colonial enterprise, which forced 'men of reason' into encounters that could not be assimilated into the tabular archives of the scientific 'order of things': see, for example, the introduction to *Voyages and Beaches* (Calder, Lamb and Orr 1999: 1–24), and David Mackay's essay from the same volume (100–13). While I am persuaded of this, I suggest that it is precisely the illusory nature of the Enlightenment ego (especially in that form constructed by the official ideology of objective, empirical science) that is both inherited by Freud, who often imitates its voice, and yet ultimately challenged by the psychoanalytic project.

16 See Teresa Brennan for a discussion of Lacan's identification of the sixteenth century as the 'dawn of the historical era of the ego' (Brennan 1993: 39–40; Lacan 1977b: 71).

17 There are many recent accounts of the complicity between early colonialism, memory and *The Tempest*: Michael Neill describes how memories of early colonial activity indelibly mark Prospero's redirection of the past, insofar as the play deploys New World imagery to rediscover the Old World (Neill 1983: 46–7); Malcolm Evans describes the relation between Europe and the Americas as an 'ideological mirror . . . which could reflect contradictory images – of the civilization of the European face and also of its barbarism' (Evans 1986: 48); Jonathan Baldo concentrates on the way in which *The*

Tempest appropriates and manipulates the notion of forgetfulness, commonly associated with New World natives, for its own ends (Baldo 1995).

18 Citing these lines, Greenblatt argues that the 'rich, irreducible concreteness of the verse compels us to acknowledge the independence and integrity of Caliban's construction of reality' (Greenblatt 1990: 31).

19 I owe to a conversation with Sarah Beaven the suggestion that Greenaway's film is not postmodernist but 'late modernist'. Insofar as it fails altogether to engage productively with popular culture, and also constitutes a wholesale celebration of the redemptive power of art (both Shakespearean and cinematic), *Prospero's Books* typifies two aspects of a full-blown modernism that is belated in time – not even the kind of self-ironising modernism that has advanced epistemologically or formally beyond high modernism.

20 Paul Brown relates this strategy to other colonialist descriptions of the rapacity of the colonised (Brown 1985: 62–3); for feminist analyses of this moment see Ania Loomba (1989: 148–56) and Jyotsna Singh (1996).

21 Montrose gives the example of Raleigh's description of Guiana as 'a countrey that hath yet her maydenhead', and the image by Jan van der Straet of the discovery of a naked female America by the lubricious gaze of Vespucci: the accompanying Latin tag roughly translates as 'Amerigo discovers America: roused by him, she is always aroused' (my translation; see Montrose 1991: 3–7, 12). There are many examples that demonstrate an acceptance by Shakespeare of the notion of 'legitimate rape': see King John's use of the trope of rape as military invasion (*King John* 2.1.206–34); and Henry V's use of the same rhetoric before the gates of Harfleur (*Henry V* 3.3.84–126) – not to mention the latter's forced marriage to Katherine at the end of that play.

22 Holland attributes to Rank a direct discussion of *The Tempest* in these terms (Holland 1964: 269), but I can find no explicit reference to the play in the English translation of the chapter from Rank to which he refers (Rank 1992: 300–37).

23 Gonzalo's utopian vision also borrows its rhetoric from Montaigne's essay 'Of Cannibals' which projects the Golden Age on to Native American culture in order to critique European corruption. The passage thus occurs as a series of overwritings or screens without a bottom layer or original source.

24 See Goldberg (1983) on Jacobean imperial rhetoric, and Helgerson (1992: 164–5) for a discussion of the 'proleptic' nature of British colonialist rhetoric.

25 Most obviously, the opening tempest scene and other phrases in the play echo accounts of colonial activity by the Virginia Company, especially William Strachey's account of a hurricane in the Bermudas (Kermode 1954, Appendix A: 135–41). Skura gives a very full survey of the vast critical literature on this aspect of the play's sources up to the end of the 1980s (Skura 1989: 42–3, n. 1); key contributions over the last decade include Loomba (1989), Vaughan and Vaughan

(1991), Baldo (1995), Hayes (1995), Gurr (1996), Salingar (1996), Singh (1996) and Walch (1996).

26 Mannoni's sometime pupil Aimé Césaire famously rewrites the play as *Une Tempête*, dramatising this image of Ariel and Caliban according to the coloniser's division of colonised subjects according to the duality obedient/disobedient. For Peter Hulme, this tactic has its origins in early European ethnographies of the Caribbean, starting with that of Columbus, which divided the indigenous peoples of the region into a placid, docile, settled, farming population (the Arawak), and a savage, warlike, nomadic and cannibalistic population (from whose name, Carib, the word cannibal may in fact derive) (Hulme 1986: 44–87). Rod Edmond claims that the same duality is repeated by eighteenth- and nineteenth-century European voyagers in the Pacific, for example, in Darwin's division Tahitian and Maori (Edmond 1997: 32).

27 Césaire describes Prospero as 'the complete totalitarian . . . the man of cold reason, the man of methodical conquest – in other words, a portrait of the "enlightened" European', in contrast to Caliban, whose link with the natural allows him to participate in the world rather than simply exploiting it (Césaire, cited in Belhassen 1972: 176). Gananath Obeyesekere suggests that what he describes as the 'Prospero myth' – the narrative of the rational civiliser illuminating the benighted primitive – plays a constitutive role in colonial activity in the Pacific during the Enlightenment, as exemplified by what he calls the 'apotheosis' of James Cook (Obeyesekere 1992: 10–12).

28 For the specific colonial contexts out of which Frazer's sources came see, for example, Fraser (1990: 80–6).

5 Shakespeare's sex

1 According to Philippe Ariès, from the sixteenth century until the eighteenth 'it became impossible to distinguish a little boy from a little girl before the age of four or five' (Ariès 1965: 58). Lawrence Stone describes breeching as a 'critically important *rite de passage*, when [boys] shifted out of the long frocks of their childhood into the breeches and sword-carrying of the adult world' (Stone 1977: 409).

2 I am thinking of Kahn's discussion of the homosocial structure that pertains between Antony and Caesar (Kahn 1997: 112–37), and of Adelman's suggestive reading of the connections between the discourses of anti-Semitism, anti-Catholicism and sodomy in *The Merchant of Venice* (Adelman 2000).

3 Erikson himself associates homoeroticism in adolescence with what he calls 'regressive trends' such as bisexuality, gender ambivalence and identity confusion in general (Erikson 1968: 185–7).

4 Oddly, given the general thrust of his argument, Neubauer does explicitly assert at one point that 'Although Shakespeare did not use the term and he described the age differently, he knew of an

adolescent period in life,' and gives as examples not only 'Romeo and Juliet's passionate "mid-adolescence"' but (stretching the customary age demarcations somewhat) Hamlet and Prince Hal (Neubauer 1992: 76). My argument here represents a fundamental disagreement with this suggestion, which underestimates the cultural difference between early modern and contemporary social psychology.

5 As Jonathan Goldberg puts it,

> The marriage of their corpses in eternal monuments of 'pure gold' attempts to perform what marriage normally aims at in comedy: to provide the bedrock of the social order. Or, to speak somewhat more exactly, the heterosexual order . . . Indeed, what makes their love so valuable is that it serves as a nexus for the social and can be mystified as outside the social.
>
> (Goldberg 1994: 219)

Valerie Traub argues similarly that

> the two lovers attempt to forge an erotic alliance beyond the physical and ideological constraints of the feuding houses of Capulet and Montague. To the extent that their erotic love is given expression in spheres untouched by the feud – the balcony, the bedroom, the abbey, the tomb – they succeed. But the tragedy of the play is precisely the futility of such a desire: each space of transcendent love is ultimately shown to be contained within, and even invaded by, the dominant ideology and effects of masculine violence.
>
> (Traub 1992: 2)

See also Dympna Callaghan's suggestion that '*Romeo and Juliet* was written at the historical moment when the ideologies and institutions of desire – romantic love and the family, which are now for us completely naturalized – were being negotiated.' Callaghan's essay goes on to 'examine the role of *Romeo and Juliet* in the cultural construction of desire' (1994: 59). My argument seeks to clarify some of the relations between the play, psychoanalysis and history, which I think Callaghan's essay elides; in particular, I think her reading of the Nurse's story about Juliet's weaning as a 'palimpsest' that represents 'female sensuality, maternity, and eroticism' (86) misses precisely the cultural historical questions about adolescence and heteronormativity that interest me here.

6 For the cultural history of the development of the nuclear family in relation to early modern English drama, see Catherine Belsey's account of *Arden of Faversham* in *The Subject of Tragedy* (Belsey 1985: 129–48), and also her most recent book, *Shakespeare and the Loss of Eden: The Construction of Family Values in Early Modern Culture* (1999).

7 Early modern anxieties about the blurring of gender distinctions need to be considered in the light of two contemporary discourses on gender. The first relates to that distinction which Bakhtin observes between the 'classical' body on one hand (self-contained, impervious

to either penetration from the outside or leakage from within, and increasingly associated with masculinity) and, on the other, the 'grotesque' body (open to the environment via its permeable boundaries and overactive orifices, and thus dangerously feminised) (see Stallybrass 1986 and Traub 1992). The second involves the Galenic 'one-sex' model, according to which male and female bodies, and in particular their genitals, are mirror images of each other; those of the male are simply an extended, externalised and more developed version of structures that remain inverted, internal and imperfect in the female – and thus maleness and femaleness are simply different stages in the development from a single sex (Greenblatt 1988: 80–1; Laquer 1990: 25–8). In both cases sex therefore comprises a difference in degree rather than in kind, creating the possibility that there is either only one sex or else many more than two. Moreover, sexual identity, which is taken as foundational to the modern subject, proves to be far more labile and subject to cultural and social determinants than class, for example (Greenblatt 1988: 76; Laquer 1990: 61–2) – hence the proliferation of contemporary anxieties about so-called 'effeminisation'. For further discussion of these matters, see Paster (1993) and Kahn (1997).

8 See Zimmerman on Freud's utilisation of the Aristophanic myth (Zimmerman 1992: 41, 57, n. 5); see Laquer for an account of Freud's replacement of a 'one-sex' or Galenic model of sexuality by a 'two-sex' model (Laquer 1990: 233–43).

9 In particular, Hollywood cinema over many decades has proven highly compatible with Lacanian-influenced psychoanalytic theorists, from the work of Christian Metz on identification in the cinema (Metz [trans. 1982]), to the critics associated with the journal *Screen* (Mulvey 1975; MacCabe 1976; Heath 1976; Rose 1986), to the many works by Slavoj Zizek on the function of the Lacanian 'real' in relation to film, especially the work of Hitchcock (Zizek 1991).

10 For accounts of the early modern emergence of 'companionate' marriage, rather than marriage choices determined primarily by economic or social considerations, see Belsey (1985; 1999).

11 Neither does Ben Affleck's Mercutio display the slightest hint of homoeroticism in his relation to Romeo. Nor does Marlowe during his appearances; oddly, the well-known homosexuality of the actor playing Marlowe seems to be effaced from the film altogether, since on my copy of the videotape at least Rupert Everett's and Marlowe's names are nowhere to be seen on the credits.

12 Unlike a Shakespeare plot, *Shakespeare in Love* does not trust its audience or characters with unresolved misunderstandings for any length of time at all: later in the film Viola mistakenly thinks Will has been killed, but is relieved of her grief by his re-entry within two minutes of screen time; similarly, she feels anger at the revelation of his having a secret wife for about three minutes all told. The rigidity of the plot suggests some difficult ideological work being undertaken that cannot afford space for alternative possibilities.

13 As Richard Burt points out,

Unlike in Franco Zeffirelli's version, in which Juliet appears at the
ball from behind Rosaline, here Rosaline is absent and Mercutio
is in her position. Mercutio is the first person Romeo sees at the
ball. When Romeo looks in the mirror after washing up in the men's
room, is he seeing himself reflected in Mercutio? Romeo's
hallucination could be said to feminize Mercutio in that it strips
him of his gun (worn in the fireworks scene but not at the ball; he
has left it at the hat check). Perhaps it is Juliet's very boyishness that
attracts Romeo to her. Wearing a white angel costume that makes
her so flat-chested as to appear prepubescent, Juliet (Claire Danes)
appears in the ball as Mercutio's apposite rather than opposite
number. She is, after all, the daughter of a transvestite, at least in
Romeo's hallucination.

(Burt 1998: 274–5, n. 3)

14 I'm grateful to Diana Harris, whose analysis of this mirrored narcissism
I am borrowing here (Harris 2000: 213–15), along with her
observations about the film's fetishisation of water (Harris 2000:
249–51).

15 Lacan accompanies his diagram of the toilet doors with a story about
a little brother and sister in a train pulling into a station who argue
over whether they have arrived at 'Ladies' or at 'Gentlemen'. Lacan's
toilets demonstrate his revision of the Saussurian priority of the
signified over the signifier; in the Lacanian account the signifier
(that is, the categories and constructions of culture, in this case those
relating to gender) produces and determines the signified (the
meanings and referents assigned to the signifier, in this case, anatomical sexual difference): 'I use this example . . . to show how in
fact the signifier enters the signified' (Lacan 1977b: 151). Thus
conceptualisations of gender even shape understandings of so-called
'biological' sex.

16 By the late 1990s the array of bad tastes displayed by *Tromeo and Juliet*
already looked rather stale. As Richard Burt points out, 'Both
Luhrmann and Kaufman reveal less about youth culture than they do
about the way middle-aged directors perceive it' (Burt 1998: 231).
Speaking as a cinemagoer more easily shocked than many, even
I found little in Kaufman's film objectionable, with the exception of
its emphasis on the display of cruelty to animals as a form of machismo.
For a reading of *Tromeo and Juliet* that attends to associations between
the animal and gender politics of the film, as well as finding many
points of contact with my own, see Kidnie (2000).

Bibliography

Adelman, Janet (1985) 'Male Bonding in Shakespeare's Comedies', in Peter Erickson and Coppélia Kahn (eds) *Shakespeare's Rough Magic: Renaissance Essays in Honor of C. L. Barber*, Newark: University of Delaware Press, 73–103.

—— (1992) *Suffocating Mothers: Fantasies of Maternal Origin in Shakespeare's Plays*, Hamlet *to* The Tempest, London and New York: Routledge.

—— (2000) 'Incising Difference in *The Merchant of Venice*: Shakespeare and the Inquisition', paper delivered at Dislocating Shakespeare: The Sixth Biennial Conference of the Australian and New Zealand Shakespeare Association, University of Auckland, Aotearoa New Zealand, 10 July.

Adler, Alfred (1938) *Social Interest*, London: Faber & Faber.

Ariès, Philippe (1965) *Centuries of Childhood: A Social History of Family Life*, trans. Robert Baldick, New York: Vintage.

Armstrong, Philip (2000) *Shakespeare's Visual Regime: Tragedy, Psychoanalysis and the Gaze*, London: Palgrave.

Aronson, Alex (1972) *Symbol and Psyche in Shakespeare*, Bloomington and London: Indiana University Press.

—— (1995) *Shakespeare and the Ocular Proof*, New York: Vantage.

Baldo, Jonathan (1995) 'Exporting Oblivion in *The Tempest*', *Modern Language Quarterly* 56.2 (June): 111–14.

Barish, Jonas (1996) 'Remembering and Forgetting in Shakespeare', in R. B. Parker and S. P. Zitner (eds) *Elizabethan Theater: Essays in*

Honor of S. Schoenbaum, Newark: University of Delaware Press, 214–21.

Barker, Francis (1984) *The Tremulous Private Body: Essays on Subjection*, London: Methuen.

Belhassen, S. (1972) 'Aimé Césaire's *A Tempest*', in Lee Baxandall (ed.) *Radical Perspectives in the Arts*, Hardmondsworth: Penguin, 175–7.

Belsey, Catherine (1980) *Critical Practice*, London and New York: Routledge.

—— (1985) *The Subject of Tragedy: Identity and Difference in Renaissance Drama*, New York: Methuen.

—— (1994) *Desire: Love Stories in Western Culture*, Oxford: Blackwell.

—— (1999) *Shakespeare and the Loss of Eden: The Construction of Family Values in Early Modern Culture*, London: Macmillan.

Benjamin, Walter (1970) *Illuminations*, ed. Hannah Arendt, London: Cape.

Berger, Harry (1970) 'Miraculous Harp: A Reading of Shakespeare's *The Tempest*', *Shakespeare Studies* 5: 253–83.

Bertoldi, Andreas (1998) 'Shakespeare, Psychoanalysis, and the Colonial Encounter: The Case of Wulf Sachs's *Black Hamlet*', in Ania Loomba and Martin Orkin (eds) *Post-colonial Shakespeares*, London and New York: Routledge, 235–58.

Bhabha, Homi (1994) *The Location of Culture*, London and New York: Routledge.

Bloom, Harold (1999) *Shakespeare: The Invention of the Human*, London: Fourth Estate.

Bristol, Michael D. (1996) *Big-Time Shakespeare*, London and New York: Routledge.

Borges, Jorge Luis (1998) 'Shakespeare's Memory', in *Collected Fictions*, trans. Andrew Hurley, London and New York: Allen Lane, Penguin, 508–15.

Bourdieu, Pierre (1984) *Distinction: A Social Critique of the Judgement of Taste*, trans. Richard Nice, Cambridge, Mass.: Harvard University Press.

Bowie, Malcom (1991) *Lacan*, London: Fontana.

Bradley, A. C. (1955) *Oxford Lectures on Poetry*, London: Macmillan.

—— (1992 [1904]) *Shakespearean Tragedy: Lectures on Hamlet, Othello, King Lear, Macbeth*, ed. John Russell Brown, New York: St Martin's Press.

Bray, Alan (1982) *Homosexuality in Renaissance England*, London: Gay Men's Press.

Brennan, Teresa (ed.) (1989) *Between Feminism and Psychoanalysis*, London: Routledge.

—— (1993) *History after Lacan*, London and New York: Routledge.

Brown, Paul (1985) '"This Thing of Darkness I Acknowledge Mine": *The Tempest* and the Discourse of Colonialism', in Jonathan Dollimore and Alan Sinfield (eds) *Political Shakespeare: New Essays in Cultural Materialism*, Manchester: Manchester University Press, 48–71.

Burt, Richard (1998) *Unspeakable ShaXXXpeares: Queer Theory and American Kiddie Culture*, New York: St Martin's Press.

Calder, Alex, Jonathan Lamb and Bridget Orr (eds) (1999) *Voyages and Beaches: Pacific Encounters, 1769–1840*, Honolulu: University of Hawai'i Press.

Callaghan, Dympna (1994) 'The Ideology of Romantic Love: The Case of *Romeo and Juliet*', in Dympna Callaghan, Lorraine Helms and Jyotsna Singh (eds) *The Weyward Sisters: Shakespeare and Feminist Politics*, Oxford: Blackwell, 59–101.

Caxton, W. (1928) *The Prologues and Epilogues*, ed. W. J. B. Crotch, London: Early English Texts Society.

Certeau, Michel de (1986) *Heterologies: Discourse on the Other*, trans. Brian Massumi, Minneapolis: University of Minnesota Press.

—— (1988) *The Writing of History*, trans. Tom Conley, New York: Columbia University Press.

Chaney, Edward (1998) *The Evolution of the Grand Tour*, London: Frank Cass.

Charnes, Linda (1993) *Notorious Identity: Materializing the Subject in Shakespeare*, Cambridge, Mass.: Harvard University Press.

Crews, Frederick (1967) 'Literature and Psychology', in James Thorpe (ed.) *Relations of Literary Study: Essays in Interdisciplinary Contributions*, New York: Modern Language Association, 73–87.

Culler, Jonathan (1982) *On Deconstruction: Theory and Criticism after Structuralism*, Ithaca, NY: Cornell University Press.

Deleuze, Gilles and Felix Guattari (1977) *Anti-Oedipus: Capitalism and Schizophrenia*, trans. Robert Hurley, Mark Seem and Helen R. Lane, New York: Viking.

Derrida, Jacques (1972) *Writing and Difference*, trans. Alan Bass, London: Routledge and Kegan Paul.

—— (1987) *The Post Card: From Socrates to Freud and Beyond*, trans. Alan Bass, Chicago: University of Chicago Press.

Dolar, Mladen (1991) '"I Shall Be with You on Your Wedding-night": Lacan and the Uncanny', *October* 58 (Fall): 5–23.

Dollimore, Jonathan (1989) *Radical Tragedy: Religion, Ideology and Power in the Drama of Shakespeare and his Contemporaries*, 2nd edn, New York: Harvester Wheatsheaf.

Dollimore, Jonathan and Alan Sinfield (eds) (1985) *Political Shakespeare*, Manchester: Manchester University Press.

Dubow, Saul (1996) 'Introduction: Part One', in Wulf Sachs, *Black Hamlet*, Baltimore: Johns Hopkins University Press, 1–37.

Duncan-Jones, Katherine (1999) 'Why, Then, O Brawling Love!', *Times Literary Supplement*, 5 February: 18.

Eagleton, Terry (1983) *Literary Theory: An Introduction*, Oxford: Basil Blackwell.

Easthope, Antony (1995) 'History and Psychoanalysis', *Textual Practice* 9.2 (Summer): 349–63.

—— (1999) *The Unconscious*, London and New York: Routledge.

Edmond, Rod (1997) *Representing the South Pacific: Colonial Discourse from Cook to Gauguin*, Cambridge: Cambridge University Press.

Erikson, Erik (1968) *Identity: Youth and Crisis*, London: Faber & Faber.

Erlich, Avi (1977) *Hamlet's Absent Father*, Princeton, NJ: Princeton University Press.

Evans, Malcolm (1986) *Signifying Nothing: Truth's True Contents in Shakespeare's Text*, Brighton: Harvester.

Felman, Shoshana (1977) 'To Open the Question', in Shoshana Felman (ed.) *Literature and Psychoanalysis: The Question of Reading: Otherwise, Yale French Studies* 55/56, 5–10.

—— (1987) *Jacques Lacan and the Adventure of Insight: Psychoanalysis in Contemporary Culture*, Cambridge, Mass.: Harvard University Press.

Fineman, Joel (1980) 'Fratricide and Cuckoldry: Shakespeare's Doubles', in Murray Schwartz and Coppélia Kahn (eds) *Representing Shakespeare: New Psychoanalytic Essays*, Baltimore: Johns Hopkins University Press, 86–91.

—— (1986) *Shakespeare's Perjured Eye: The Invention of Poetic Subjectivity in the Sonnets*, Berkeley: University of California Press.

—— (1991) *The Subjectivity Effect in Western Literary Tradition: Essays Toward the Release of Shakespeare's Will*, Cambridge, Mass., and London: MIT Press.

Fink, Bruce (1990) 'Alienation and Separation: Logical Moments of Lacan's Dialectic of Desire', *Newsletter of the Freudian Field* 4 (Fall): 78–119.

Finucci, Valeria and Regina Schwartz (eds) (1994) *Desire in the Renaissance: Psychoanalysis and Literature*, Princeton, NJ: Princeton University Press.

Fraser, Robert (1990) *The Making of* The Golden Bough, New York: St Martin's Press.

Freedman, Barbara (1991) *Staging the Gaze: Postmodernism, Psychoanalysis and Shakespearian Comedy*, Ithaca, NY: Cornell University Press.

Freud, Sigmund (1966) *The Standard Edition of the Complete Psychological Works of Sigmund Freud*, ed. and trans. James Strachey *et al.*, London: Hogarth.

—— (1973–85) *The Penguin Freud Library*, trans. James Strachey, gen. eds Angela Richards and Albert Dickson, London and New York: Penguin:

PFL 2 (1973) *New Introductory Lectures on Psychoanalysis*

PFL 4 (1976) *The Interpretation of Dreams*

PFL 5 (1976) *The Psychopathology of Everyday Life*

PFL 7 (1977) *On Sexuality*

PFL 9 (1979) *Case Histories II*

PFL 10 (1979) *On Psychopathology*

PFL 11 (1984) *On Metapsychology*

PFL 12 (1985) *Civilization, Society and Religion*

PFL 13 (1985) *The Origins of Religion*

PFL 14 (1985) *Art and Literature*

—— (1985) *The Complete Letters of Sigmund Freud to Wilhelm Fliess 1887–1904*, ed. and trans. Jeffrey Moussaieff Masson, Cambridge, Mass.: Harvard University Press.

Freund, Elizabeth (1985) '"Ariachne's Broken Woof": The Rhetoric of Citation in *Troilus and Cressida*', in Patricia Parker and Geoffrey Hartman (eds) *Shakespeare and the Question of Theory*, New York and London: Methuen, 19–36.

Frye, Northrop (1957) *The Anatomy of Criticism: Four Essays*, Princeton, NJ: Princeton University Press.

Garber, Marjorie (1987) *Shakespeare's Ghost Writers: Literature as Uncanny Causality*, New York: Methuen.

Girard, René (1991) *A Theater of Envy*, Oxford and New York: Oxford University Press.

Goldberg, Jonathan (1983) *James I and the Politics of Literature: Jonson, Shakespeare, Donne, and Their Contemporaries*, Baltimore: Johns Hopkins University Press.

—— (1986) *Voice Terminal Echo: Postmodernism and English Renaissance Texts*, New York: Methuen.

—— (1988) 'Perspectives: Dover Cliff and the Conditions of Representation', *Shakespeare and Deconstruction*, ed. G. Douglas Atkins and David M. Bergeron, New York: Peter Lang, 245–65.

—— (1992) *Sodometries: Renaissance Texts, Modern Sexualities*, Stanford: Stanford University Press.

—— (1994) '*Romeo and Juliet*'s Open Rs', in Jonathan Goldberg (ed.) *Queering the Renaissance*, Durham, NC, and London: Duke University Press, 218–35.

Graves, Robert (1966) *The White Goddess: A Historical Grammar of Poetic Myth*, New York: Noonday Press.

Greenaway, Peter (1991) *Prospero's Books: A Film of Shakespeare's* The Tempest, New York: Four Walls Eight Windows.

Greenblatt, Stephen (1980) *Renaissance Self-fashioning: From More to Shakespeare*, Chicago: University of Chicago.

—— (1988) *Shakespearean Negotiations: The Circulation of Social Energy in Renaissance England*, Berkeley: University of California Press.

—— (1990) *Learning to Curse: Essays in Early Modern Culture*, New York: Routledge.

Guillory, John (1993) *Cultural Capital: The Problem of Literary Canon Formation*, Chicago and London: University of Chicago Press.

Gurr, Andrew (1996) 'Industrious Ariel, Idle Caliban', *Travel and Drama in Shakespeare's Time*, ed. Jean-Pierre Maquerlot and Michèle Williams, Cambridge: Cambridge University Press, 193–208.

Hardy, Barbara (1989) 'Shakespeare's Narrative: Acts of Memory', *Essays in Criticism* 39.2 (April): 93–115.

Harris, Diana (2000) 'A Consideration of the Soundtrack in Screen Adaptations of Shakespeare', unpublished Ph.D. thesis, University of Auckland.

Harris, Wilson (1992) *The Radical Imagination: Lectures and Talks*, ed. Alan Riach and Mark Williams, Liège: Université de Liège.

Hawkes, Terence (1973) *Shakespeare's Talking Animals: Language and Drama in Society*, London: Edward Arnold.

—— (1977) *Structuralism and Semiotics*, London: Methuen.

—— (1992) *Meaning by Shakespeare*, London: Routledge.

Hayes, Tom (1995) 'Cannibalizing the Humanist Subject: A Genealogy of Prospero', *Genealogy and Literature*, ed. Lee Quinby, Minneapolis: University of Minnesota Press, 96–115.

Heath, Stephen (1976) 'Narrative Space', *Screen* 17.3: 68–112.

Hegel, G. W. F. (1977) *Phenomenology of Spirit*, trans. A. V. Miller, Oxford: Clarendon.

Helgerson, Richard (1992) *Forms of Nationhood: The Elizabethan Writing of England*, Chicago and London: University of Chicago Press.

Holderness, Graham (ed.) (1988) *The Shakespeare Myth*, Manchester: Manchester University Press.

Holland, Norman (1964) *Psychoanalysis and Shakespeare*, New York: McGraw-Hill.

Hulme, Peter (1986) *Colonial Encounters: Europe and the Native Caribbean 1492–1797*, London and New York: Methuen.

Hunter, G. K. (ed.) (1972) *King Lear. The New Penguin Shakespeare*, gen. ed. T. J. B. Spencer, London: Penguin.

Irigaray, Luce (1985) *Speculum of the Other Woman*, trans. Gillian C. Gill, Ithaca, NY: Cornell University Press.

Jardine, Lisa (1983) *Still Harping on Daughters: Women and Drama in the Age of Shakespeare*, Brighton: Harvester.

Jenkins, Harold (ed.) (1982) *Hamlet. The Arden Shakespeare*, gen. eds Richard Proudfoot and Anne Thompson, London: Routledge.

Johnson, David (1996) *Shakespeare and South Africa*, Oxford: Clarendon.

Jones, Ernest (1949) *Hamlet and Oedipus*, London: Victor Gollancz.

—— (1951) *Essays in Applied Psycho-analysis*, London: Hogarth.

—— (1957) *Sigmund Freud: Life and Work, Vol. 3: – The Last Phase, 1919–1939*, London: Hogarth.

Kahn, Coppélia (1980a) 'Coming of Age in Verona', in *The Woman's Part*, ed. Carolyn Ruth Swift Lenz, Gayle Greene and Carol Thomas Neely, Urbana: University of Illinois Press, 171–93.

—— (1980b) 'The Providential Tempest and the Shakespearean Family', in Murray Schwartz and Coppélia Kahn (eds) *Representing Shakespeare: New Psychoanalytic Essays*, Baltimore and London: Johns Hopkins University Press, 217–43.

—— (1981) *Man's Estate: Masculine Identity in Shakespeare*, Berkeley: University of California Press.

—— (1985) 'The Hand that Rocks the Cradle: Recent Gender Theories and Their Implications', in Shirley Nelson Garner, Claire Kahane and Madelon Sprengnether (eds) *The (M)Other Tongue: Essays in Feminist Psychoanalytic Interpretation*, Ithaca, NY: Cornell University Press, 72–88.

—— (1986) 'The Absent Mother in *King Lear*', in Margaret Ferguson, Maureen Quilligan and Nancy Vickers (eds) *Rewriting the Renaissance: The Discourses of Sexual Difference in Early Modern Europe*, Chicago: University of Chicago Press, 33–49.

—— (1997) *Roman Shakespeare: Warriors, Wounds, and Women*, London and New York: Routledge.

Kaufman, Lloyd (dir.) (1996) *Tromeo and Juliet*, Troma Studios.

Kermode, Frank (ed.) (1954) *The Tempest. The Arden Shakespeare*, gen. eds Richard Proudfoot and Anne Thompson, London: Methuen.

Kidnie, Margaret Jane (2000) '"The Way the World Is Now": Love in the Troma Zone', in Mark Thornton Burnett and Ramona Wray (eds) *Shakespeare, Film, Fin de Siècle,* London and New York: Routledge, 102–20.

Kofman, Sarah (1985) *The Enigma of Woman: Woman in Freud's Writings,* trans. Catherine Porter, Ithaca, NY: Cornell University Press.

—— (1991) *Freud and Fiction,* trans. Sarah Wykes, Cambridge: Polity.

Kott, Jan (1964) *Shakespeare Our Contemporary,* London: Methuen.

Lacan, Jacques (1972) 'Seminar on "The Purloined Letter"', trans. Jeffrey Mehlman, *Yale French Studies* 48: 38–72.

—— (1977a) 'Desire and the Interpretation of Desire in *Hamlet*', trans. James Hulbert, in Shoshana Felman (ed.) *Literature and Psychoanalysis: The Question of Reading: Otherwise, Yale French Studies* 55/56, 11–52.

—— (1977b) *Écrits: A Selection,* trans. Alan Sheridan, London: Tavistock/Routledge.

—— (1979) *The Four Fundamental Concepts of Psychoanalysis,* trans. Alan Sheridan, London: Penguin.

—— (1981) '*Hamlet,* par Lacan', seminars 1 and 2, *Ornicar?* 24: 1–31.

—— (1982a) '*Hamlet,* par Lacan', seminars 3 and 4, *Ornicar?* 25: 13–36.

—— (1982b) *Feminine Sexuality: Jacques Lacan and the École Freudienne,* ed. and trans. Juliet Mitchell and Jacqueline Rose, London: Macmillan.

—— (1983) '*Hamlet,* par Lacan', seminars 5, 6, and 7, *Ornicar?* 26–27: 7–44.

—— (1988a) *Freud's Papers on Technique 1953–1954,* trans. John Forrester, vol. 1 of *The Seminar of Jacques Lacan,* gen. ed. Jacques-Alain Miller, Cambridge: Cambridge University Press.

—— (1988b) *The Ego in Freud's Theory and in the Technique of Psychoanalysis 1954–1955,* trans. Sylvana Thomaselli, vol. 2 of *The Seminar of Jacques Lacan,* gen. ed. Jacques-Alain Miller, Cambridge: Cambridge University Press.

—— (1992) *The Ethics of Psychoanalysis 1959–1960,* trans. Dennis Porter, vol. 7 of *The Seminar of Jacques Lacan,* gen. ed. Jacques-Alain Miller, London and New York: Routledge.

Laplanche, Jean and Jean-Bertrand Pontalis (1988) *The Language of Psycho-analysis,* trans. Donald Nicholson-Smith, London: Hogarth and Karnac.

Laquer, Thomas (1990) *Making Sex: Body and Gender from the Greeks to Freud,* Cambridge: Harvard University Press.

Lee, Jonathan Scott (1990) *Jacques Lacan*, Amherst: University of Massachusetts Press.

Lentricchia, Frank and Thomas McLaughlin (1995) *Critical Terms of Literary Study*, 2nd edn, Chicago: University of Chicago Press.

Levine, Laura (1994) *Men in Women's Clothing: Anti-theatricality and Effeminization, 1579–1642*, Cambridge: Cambridge University Press.

Loomba, Ania (1989) *Gender, Race, Renaissance Drama*, London: Routledge.

Luhrmann, Baz (dir.) (1996) *William Shakespeare's Romeo + Juliet*, Twentieth Century Fox.

Lukacher, Ned (1994) *Daemonic Figures: Shakespeare and the Question of Conscience*, Ithaca, NY: Cornell University Press.

Lupton, Julia Reinhard and Kenneth Reinhard (1993) *After Oedipus: Shakespeare in Psychoanalysis*, Ithaca, NY, and London: Cornell University Press.

MacCabe, Colin (1976) 'Theory and Film: Principles of Realism and Pleasure', *Screen* 17.3 (Autumn): 68–112.

Macey, David (1988) *Lacan in Contexts*, London and New York: Verso.

Madden, John (dir.) (1998) *Shakespeare in Love*, Miramax.

Mannoni, Octave (1964) *Prospero and Caliban: The Psychology of Colonisation*, trans. Pamela Powesland, New York: Praeger.

Masson, Jeffrey Moussaieff (1985) *The Assault on Truth: Freud's Suppression of the Seduction Theory*, New York: Penguin.

Meloy, J. Reid (ed.) (1998) *The Psychology of Stalking: Clinical and Forensic Perspectives*, San Diego and London: Academic Press.

Metz, Christian (1982) *Psychoanalysis and Cinema: The Imaginary Signifier*, trans. Celia Britton, Annwyl Williams, Ben Brewster and Alfred Guzzetti, London: Macmillan.

Montaigne, Michel de (1958) *Essays*, ed. and trans. J. M. Cohen, Harmondsworth: Penguin.

Montrose, Louis (1991) 'The Work of Gender in the Discourse of Discovery', *Representations* 33 (Winter): 1–41.

Morris, Pam (ed.) (1994) *The Bakhtin Reader*, London: Edward Arnold.

Muller, John (1980) 'Psychosis and Mourning in Lacan's *Hamlet*', *NLH* 12.1: 147–65.

Mulvey, Laura (1975) 'Visual Pleasure and Narrative Cinema', *Screen* 16.3: 6–18.

Neill, Michael (1983) 'Remembrance and Revenge: *Hamlet, Macbeth* and *The Tempest*', in Ian Donaldson (ed.) *Jonson and Shakespeare*, London: Macmillan, 35–56.

—— (1997) *Issues of Death: Mortality and Identity in English Renaissance Tragedy*, Oxford: Clarendon.

Neubauer, John (1992) *The Fin-de-Siècle Culture of Adolescence*, New Haven and London: Yale University Press.

Neumann, Erich (1962) *The Origins and History of Consciousness*, vol. 1., New York: Harper Torchbooks.

Newman, Karen (1987) '"And Wash the Ethiop White": Femininity and the Monstrous in *Othello*', in Jean E. Howard and Marion F. O'Connor (eds) *Shakespeare Reproduced: The Text as History and Ideology*, London and New York: Methuen, 141–62.

Nixon, Rob (1987) 'Caribbean and African Appropriations of *The Tempest*', *Critical Inquiry* 13.3 (Spring): 557–78.

Obeyesekere, Gananath (1992) *The Apotheosis of Captain Cook: European Mythmaking in the Pacific*, Princeton, NJ: Princeton University Press.

Orgel, Stephen (1984) 'Prospero's Wife', *Representations* 8 (Fall): 1–13.

—— (1989) 'Nobody's Perfect', *South Atlantic Quarterly* 88.1 (Winter): 7–29.

Orkin, Martin (1987) '*Othello* and the "Plain Face" of Racism', *Shakespeare Quarterly* 38: 166–88.

Parker, Patricia (1985) 'Shakespeare's Rhetoric: "Dilation" and "Delation" in *Othello*', in Patricia Parker and Geoffrey Hartman (eds) *Shakespeare and the Question of Theory*, New York and London: Methuen, 54–74.

—— (1996) *Shakespeare from the Margins: Language, Culture, Context*, Chicago: University of Chicago Press.

Paster, Gail Kern (1993) *The Body Embarrassed: Drama and the Disciplines of Shame in Early Modern England*, Ithaca, NY: Cornell University Press.

Payne, Michael (1993) *Reading Theory: An Introduction to Lacan, Derrida, and Kristeva*, Oxford: Blackwell.

Pitchers, Bruce (ed.) (2000) 'Entertainment', *Woman's Day*, New Zealand edn (1 May), 38–40.

Porter, Joseph A. (1988) *Shakespeare's Mercutio: His History and Drama*, Chapel Hill: University of North Carolina Press.

Pratt, Mary Louise (1992) *Imperial Eyes: Travel Writing and Transculturation*, London and New York: Routledge.

Pye, Christopher (1990) *The Regal Phantasm: Shakespeare and the Politics of Spectacle*, London and New York: Routledge.

Quinn, David B. and Alison M. Quinn (eds) (1973) *Virginia Voyages from Hakluyt*, London: Oxford University Press.

Ragland-Sullivan, Ellie (1988) '*Hamlet*, Logical Time and the Structure of Obsession', *Newsletter of the Freudian Field* 2 (Fall): 29–45.

Rank, Otto (1992) *The Incest Theme in Literature and Legend: Fundamentals of a Psychology of Literary Creation*, trans. Gregory C. Richter, Baltimore and London: Johns Hopkins University Press.

Ridley, M. R. (ed.) (1958) *Othello. The Arden Shakespeare*, gen. ed. Richard Proudfoot, London: Routledge.

Rose, Jacqueline (1986) *Sexuality in the Field of Vision*, London and New York: Verso.

—— (1996) 'Introduction: Part Two', in Wulf Sachs, *Black Hamlet*, Baltimore: Johns Hopkins University Press, 38–67.

Roth, Michael (1987) *Psychoanalysis as History: Negation and Freedom in Freud*, Ithaca, NY: Cornell University Press.

Roudinesco, Elisabeth (1990) *Jacques Lacan & Co.: A History of Psychoanalysis in France, 1925–1985*, trans. Jeffrey Mehlman, Chicago: University of Chicago Press.

Royle, Nicholas (1991) *Telepathy and Literature: Essays on the Reading Mind*, Oxford and Cambridge, Mass.: Blackwell.

—— (1995) *After Derrida*, Manchester and New York: Manchester University Press.

Sachs, Wulf (1934) *Psychoanalysis: Its Meaning and Practical Applications*, London: Cassel.

—— (1947) *Black Anger*, New York: Grove Press.

—— (1996 [1937]) *Black Hamlet*, ed. Saul Dubow and Jacqueline Rose, Baltimore and London: Johns Hopkins University Press.

Salingar, Leo (1996) 'The New World in *The Tempest*', in Jean-Pierre Maquerlot and Michèle Williams (eds) *Travel and Drama in Shakespeare's Time*, Cambridge: Cambridge University Press, 209–22.

Saussure, Ferdinand de (1966 [1916]) *Course in General Linguistics*, 3rd edn, trans. Wade Baskin, New York: McGraw-Hill.

Schoenbaum, Samuel (1970) *Shakespeare's Lives*, Oxford: Clarendon Press.

Schwartz, Murray and Coppélia Kahn (eds) (1980) *Representing Shakespeare: New Psychoanalytic Essays*, Baltimore and London: Johns Hopkins University Press.

Sedgwick, Eve Kosofsky (1985) *Between Men: English Literature and Male Homosocial Desire*, New York: Columbia University Press.

Showalter, Elaine (1985) 'Representing Ophelia: Women, Madness, and the Responsibilities of Feminist Criticism', in Patricia Parker and Geoffrey Hartman (eds) *Shakespeare and the Question of Theory*, New York and London: Methuen, 77–94.

Sibony, Daniel (1977) '*Hamlet*: A Writing-effect', trans. James Hulbert and Joshua Wilner, in Shoshana Felman (ed.) *Literature and Psychoanalysis: The Question of Reading: Otherwise. Yale French Studies* 55/56, 53–93.

Silverman, Kaja (1983) *The Subject of Semiotics*, Oxford: Oxford University Press.

Sinfield, Alan (1992) *Faultlines: Cultural Materialism and the Politics of Dissident Reading*, Oxford: Clarendon.

Singh, Jyotsna (1996) 'Caliban versus Miranda: Race and Gender Conflicts in Postcolonial Rewritings of *The Tempest*', in Valerie Traub, M. Lindsay Kaplan and Dympna Callaghan (eds) *Feminist Readings of Early Modern Culture: Emerging Subjects*, Cambridge: Cambridge University Press, 191–209.

Skura, Meredith Anne (1989) 'Discourse and the Individual: The Case of Colonialism in *The Tempest*', *Shakespeare Quarterly* 40.1 (Spring): 42–69.

—— (1995) 'Understanding the Living and Talking to the Dead: The Historicity of Psychoanalysis', in Marshall Brown (ed.) *The Uses of Literary History*, Durham, NC, and London: Duke University Press, 93–105.

Smith, Bruce R. (1991) *Homosexual Desire in Shakespeare's England: A Cultural Poetics*, Chicago: University of Chicago Press.

Sprengnether, Madelon (1990) *The Spectral Mother: Freud, Feminism, and Psychoanalysis*, Ithaca, NY: Cornell University Press.

Stallybrass, Peter (1986) 'Patriarchal Territories: The Body Enclosed', in Margaret Ferguson, Maureen Quilligan and Nancy Vickers (eds) *Rewriting the Renaissance*, Chicago: University of Chicago Press, 123–42.

Stallybrass, Peter and Allon White (1986) *The Politics and Poetics of Transgression*, London: Methuen.

Stockholder, Kay (1987) *Dream Works: Lovers and Families in Shakespeare's Plays*, Toronto: Toronto University Press.

Stone, Lawrence (1977) *The Family, Sex and Marriage in England 1500–1800*, New York: Harper & Row.

Sundelson, David (1980) '"So Rare a Wonder'd Father": Prospero's *Tempest*', in Murray Schwartz and Coppélia Kahn (eds) *Representing Shakespeare: New Psychoanalytic Essays*, Baltimore and London: Johns Hopkins University Press, 33–53.

Taylor, Gary (1989) *Reinventing Shakespeare: A Cultural History from the Restoration to the Present*, London: Vintage.

Tennenhouse, Leonard (1986) *Power on Display: The Politics of Shakespeare's Genres*, New York: Methuen.

Traub, Valerie (1992) *Desire and Anxiety: Circulations of Sexuality in Shakespearean Drama*, London: Routledge.

Vaughan, Alden T. and Virginia Mason Vaughan (1991) *Shakespeare's Caliban: A Cultural History*, Cambridge: Cambridge University Press.

Vickers, Brian (1993) *Appropriating Shakespeare: Contemporary Critical Quarrels*, New Haven: Yale University Press.

Walch, Günter (1996) '"What's Past is Prologue": Metatheatrical Memory and Transculturation in *The Tempest*', in Jean-Pierre Maquerlot and Michèle Williams (eds) *Travel and Drama in Shakespeare's Time*, Cambridge: Cambridge University Press, 223–38.

Weber, Samuel (1996) *Mass Mediauras: Form, Technics, Media*, Stanford, Calif.: Stanford University Press.

Yates, Frances (1966) *The Art of Memory*, London: Routledge and Kegan Paul.

Young, Robert (1990) *White Mythologies: Writing History and the West*, London: Routledge.

Zimmerman, Susan (1992) 'Disruptive Desire: Artifice and Indeterminacy in Jacobean Comedy', in Susan Zimmerman (ed.) *Erotic Politics: Desire on the Renaissance Stage*, London: Routledge, 39–63.

Zizek, Slavoj (1989) *The Sublime Object of Ideology*, London: Verso.

—— (1991) *Looking Awry: An Introduction to Jacques Lacan through Popular Culture*, Cambridge, Mass.: MIT Press.

Index

268 Index